GROWN-UP ANGER

GROWN-UP ANGER

DANIEL WOLFF

The Connected
Mysteries of Bob Dylan,
Woody Guthrie, and the
Calumet Massacre
of 1913

HARPER

An Imprint of HarperCollins*Publishers*

HarperCollins books may be purchased for educational, business, or sales promotional use. For information, please email the Special Markets Department at SPsales@harpercollins.com.

FIRST EDITION

DESIGNED BY WILLIAM RUOTO

PHOTO OF BOB DYLAN: BRIAN MOODY / REX / SHUTTERSTOCK
PHOTO OF WOODY GUTHRIE: UNCREDITED / AP / REX / SHUTTERSTOCK

Library of Congress Cataloging-in-Publication Data

Names: Wolff, Daniel J., author.
Title: Grown-up anger : the connected mysteries of Bob Dylan, Woody Guthrie, and the Calumet massacre of 1913 / Daniel Wolff.
Description: First edition. | New York, NY : Harper, 2017. | Includes bibliographical references and index.
Identifiers: LCCN 2017003018 (print) | LCCN 2017008145 (ebook) | ISBN 9780062451699 (hc) | ISBN 9780062451705 (pb) | ISBN 9780062676931 (audio)
| ISBN 9780062451712 (e-book)
Subjects: LCSH: Popular music—Political aspects—United States—History—20th century. | Folk music—Political aspects—United States—History—20th century. | Italian Hall Disaster, Calumet, Mich., 1913. | Dylan, Bob, 1941- | Guthrie, Woody, 1912-1967.
Classification: LCC ML3917.U6 W65 2017 (print) | LCC ML3917.U6 (ebook) | DDC
    782.42164092/2—dc23
LC record available at https://lccn.loc.gov/2017003018

17 18 19 20 21   LSC   10 9 8 7 6 5 4 3 2 1

How do the living live with the dead?

—JOHN BERGER, *HOLD EVERYTHING DEAR*

CONTENTS

GROWN-UP ANGER

ONCE UPON A TIME

was thirteen and angry.

You could start elsewhere.

You could start with geology. Michigan's Upper Peninsula has some of the oldest rocks on the continent: gravel and sand and silt deposited by a billion-year old sea. Mixed in are rich lodes of iron and other minerals. Over time, along a rift that ran through the middle of what we now call North America, the crust of the earth thinned enough to let an upwelling of lava burst through. Between spectacular volcanic eruptions, layers of mixed conglomerate rocks were laid down. As the surface compressed and the resulting pressure drove rock under rock, it produced a huge bowl that would one day be the basin of Lake Superior. The rim of that bowl included a seventy-mile finger of land that pointed toward what is now Canada. Native Americans would call it Keweenaw, which means place of portage. Down the middle of that peninsula, deep veins of copper settled. Northern Michigan is the only place on earth where this pure a copper lode is found this close to the surface.

Or you could start with anthropology. Native Americans were mining Keweenaw's copper at least seven thousand years ago. They used chunks of igneous rock, "hammerstones," to knock the copper loose, then shaped it into hooks, knives, jewelry. Those were traded east all the way to the Atlantic coast and south as far as what's now

Alabama. Explorer Samuel de Champlain met an Algonquin chief in 1610, who "drew out of a sack a piece of copper a foot long. . . . It was very fine and pure." And early Jesuit missionaries discovered boulders of copper along the banks of Lake Superior. Eventually, immigrants poured into the region—Cornish, Russian, Bulgarian, Finnish—hired to work the mines that would make Michigan the source for half the world's copper.

Or you could start with economics. The first transaction, the basic source of wealth, is what we take from the earth: wood, fish, metal. Economists call this harvesting "traditional work:" the beginning of commerce, of exchange, of money itself. In northern Michigan, traditional work met modern industrialization after the Civil War. The railroad network expanded, electrification began, the nation started to see its first large corporations. Copper was a key component in the change. Capital from the victorious Union was invested in the isolated Keweenaw Peninsula, and that, combined with the influx of relatively cheap European labor, helped create the American empire.

But I started with anger. Partly because all these other approaches smack of history, and when I was thirteen, history was dull. It smelled of chalk dust, had the slick feel of textbook pages, spoke in the modulated voice of authority. History happened in a classroom. I didn't (voluntarily) approach the world that way.

I connected, instead, via anger. And through rock & roll. Specifically, through a voice on the radio. More specifically, the voice of Bob Dylan.

The first time that sound cut across my airwaves, the song was "Like a Rolling Stone," and it was as if someone—Dylan— had found a crack in the surface of day-to-day life and pushed up through it, erupting.

"Like a Rolling Stone" was six minutes long, outrageous in a world of two-and-a-half-minute records. It wasn't the opening smack of drums that got my attention. Or the bluesy roll of organ and guitar. And it wasn't the lyrics, though everyone said they were "deep." I could barely hear them—just the slightly chill rush of hip, distorted description and the big chorus that began, "How does it feel?"

No, what made this thirteen-year-old take notice was the sound—especially of Dylan's voice. Strung-out, slurred but piercing, its delayed attack would lag behind the beat, then rush forward, then drop back again: the keening of a tool being sharpened. For all the singer's humor and apparent ease, it was the sound of anger.

It didn't really matter what he was angry about. At thirteen, I recognized the sound and was amazed and delighted: somebody was fighting back. The song amounted to a long, rich, unstoppable rant that kept rising in intensity, as if whatever had pissed him off (or whomever—he kept shouting, ". . . you . . . you!") wouldn't quite die, needed another cut of the blade—and another. The song was one extended build, ratcheting up between each triumphant chorus until six minutes didn't seem long enough. The anger never got resolved; it just blew out through a harmonica before fading into the distance. When the tune finally ended (I couldn't believe a radio station would actually let a song go this long: that was part of the thrill), I only had to wait a little while before it appeared again: a pop hit in regular rotation.

The more I heard "Like a Rolling Stone," the better it got, especially the way the anger didn't seem to need to justify itself. Dylan started pissed. His first words were "Once upon a time"—like a fairy tale—and from that point forward, he was on the hunt. Here was music that declared business as usual a sham. Outrage was the only way to respond to the world, the only way to get out from under the crust of lies to something like the truth.

I was thirteen, and I believed in the truth. As I believed in anger. But that wasn't something you could say out loud. If you did, it led to the inevitable adult question: "What are you angry about? What, exactly, is wrong?" The answer was everything—I was angry about everything—but you couldn't say that. If you did, you got a look that meant, "Oh, yes, you're a child."

I swore I'd never forget that look. Never forget how adults dismiss what kids say, assume they're wrong, treat them like something that isn't finished. "Sure, the present system is messed up," some grown-up would say in a sympathetic voice, "but it's still the best that. . . ." And so on, and so on, till I just wanted to change the channel.

Part of what was great about "Like a Rolling Stone" was it seemed to laugh at all that, brush it aside. Dylan sang as if the whole superstructure—school, government, newspapers—was just so much bullshit. His voice was an outsider's: nobody in power drew out their words like that, pitching them like insinuations, cutting them off abruptly. He had an "unacceptable" nasal voice that amounted to a challenge. Never mind history, never mind practical solutions: those were just more layers added to the ongoing accumulation of half-truths and injustices and deceptions. Hearing Dylan lash out—at what? at everything—was like hearing an alternative national anthem.

In July of 1965, a week after "Like a Rolling Stone" was released, President Lyndon Johnson announced that forty-four additional combat battalions would be sent to Vietnam. "I do not find it easy to send the flower of our youth, our finest young men, into battle, . . ." the president intoned. "I think I know how their mothers weep and how their families sorrow." But send them he did. "We cannot be defeated by force of arms. We will stand in Vietnam."

And the same force, as far as I could tell, would stand at home. The February before Dylan's hit was released, Malcolm X was assassinated. Soon after the record came out, the president signed the Voting Rights Act, which was supposed to be one of the culminating achievements of the modern civil rights movement. But five days later, the Los Angeles neighborhood of Watts exploded in rebellion. Black power challenged nonviolence, calling for militant action, rejecting the idea of assimilation, mocking the country's institutions as "clearly racist." This in an American economy that—pumped by the escalating Vietnam War—was creating the last great lift of a post–World War II golden age.

Dylan's song didn't seem to be about any of this. Not overtly, anyway. In fact, after hearing it a bunch of times, I wasn't sure it was "about" anything. It was sound. And that corrosive, uncompromising sound felt to me like the news. Much more so than anything I read in the paper or saw on TV. Its six-minutes proclaimed, maybe confirmed, that the country was going through its own adolescence—confused, trying to figure out what it wanted to be when it grew up.

The radio was more than Dylan, of course. 1965 saw an almost daily outpouring of great new music, from the Beatles to Motown. When "Like a Rolling Stone" came out, the year had already produced "Eight Days a Week," "Stop in the Name of Love," "You've Lost that Lovin' Feeling," "(I Can't Get No) Satisfaction." Demographics explained part of it. There were lots of us born after the Second World War, coming of age in prosperous, changing times. We helped create the demand for something new, for our own version of the truth. People were beginning to call this upswelling a counterculture—counter to the business culture, the government, schools. To my ears, pop radio signaled that beneath the way things worked, there was an alternative: the way things might work.

I wanted to know more. Bob Dylan turned out to be in his twenties: a pale man with a narrow face, high cheekbones, hooknose, sleepy eyes, all under a lot of curly hair. Pictures of him showed someone keeping a certain distance: an observer, maybe, or someone in on a private joke. He didn't dress like a star, but he didn't look regular, either: vests, motorcycle T-shirts, dark glasses. To hear more of his music involved a little digging in the past, a little (OK) history—but for him, I was willing. Dylan had produced five albums, and I went looking for them.

It was hard to gauge from his records who he was. He seemed to shift from rocker to folk singer, from political agitator to shy Midwesterner. I eventually worked my way back to his first album.

Bob Dylan had come out only three years earlier, but it sounded like a different man singing in a different era. This wasn't speedy, on-the-edge, original rock & roll but old folk songs and obscure blues tunes, sung solo to an acoustic guitar. He wrote only two of the LP's cuts. One was "Talkin' New York," a satire about his arrival in the big city: how he'd rambled in one freezing winter, found a job singing in a Greenwich Village coffeehouse, and then lost the job because he didn't sound like a folksinger but like a "hillbilly." I could tell it was a joke, but I didn't quite get it.

The other original was called "Song to Woody." I latched on to it because it seemed to offer clues to where this guy came from, out of what ground his later, wailing sound had sprung. "Song to Woody" was just his voice and acoustic guitar with the gentle, diminishing melody picked out on the bass strings. In a restrained, careful, almost tender voice, he sang directly to and about Woody Guthrie.

I knew who Guthrie was. He'd written "This Land Is Your Land;" everybody knew that. But I had no idea if he was still alive. Dylan acted like he was: "Hey, hey, Woody Guthrie, I wrote you a song / 'Bout a funny old world that's a-comin' along." A song about the future, then—about what was coming. But it also sounded like a tribute to the past, listing a bunch of Guthrie's friends and traveling companions. The point seemed to be that their era was over and a new one was coming. Except the new one, the future, "looks like it's a-dyin' an' it's hardly been born."

Dylan didn't sound angry. Twenty-one at the time, he sounded wistful: paying homage to some passing of the guard I knew nothing about. His voice had that same cracked, extended, Midwestern accent, which was enough to convince me that "Like a Rolling Stone" had something to do with Woody Guthrie. But I was more interested in this world Dylan claimed was coming. That is, I cared more about the news than history.

And if that coming world was already dying, well, what wasn't? One of the great things about pop music was how it seemed to burst out of nowhere, grab hold, and then disappear. Like all the other consumables around me. Isn't that what the *pop* in pop music meant? A song hit . . . and then disappeared. It got shoved aside by the next hit. It was born and started to die, confirming that nothing was permanent, that it all had to change, that there was this enormous, roiling wealth of sound—of ideas—just below the surface.

People were always going on about my generation—sociologists and so-called spokespeople. I didn't trust them. There was something too easy about their broad conclusions and their categories. To talk about a generation was to lump too many different people together, too many ideas. But my immediate friends and I did have some things in common. For one, we lived in the suburbs, that modern arrangement of split-levels and cul-de-sacs, two cars in a garage, a basketball hoop by the driveway. Our fathers commuted into the city for work. Back when I was born—or so I was told—people had made things: two out of every five US workers were involved in manufacturing. By the time I was a teenager—by the time "Like A Rolling Stone" came out—nearly 90 percent of all new jobs were in the service economy. Not making things but selling them: insurance, stocks, fast food. It felt like there was simultaneously more stuff and less of substance. The era of farming, fishing, mining—traditional work—was fading. In its place: Dylan's funny new world.

I cared about rock & roll because it seemed like the not-so-secret language of that change. And 'cause you could dance to it, of course, and make out to it. While adults went on about politics and property values, the real news was "Help," the Beatles' partly disguised cry of desperation. And the groove of "The In Crowd," with Ramsey Lewis insinuating that there was another, very different scene beyond the suburbs. The news was that Barry McGuire's "Eve of Destruction" was fake: a cheap Dylan imitation sold back to us as the truth. And the news was also the Dave Clark Five's "Catch Us If You Can," which promised that we might escape—and that the world would be shifting under us as we ran.

I remember being told it was kind of cute how much I cared about rock & roll. After all, every generation had its own favorite songs. Music was just a stage you passed through—like anger—and the proof was how quickly the songs disappeared. They weren't texts to study; they were confections: pop! Except as it turned out, the music refused to disappear. Maybe it was just the sheer weight of our generational numbers, but the songs on the radio stayed with us— not only marked certain times but carried certain beliefs and ideas.

I could, for example, use the music to date my high school years, from "Like a Rolling Stone" through the Woodstock festival. Which is to say, from the sound of the truth to the packaging and selling of it. We were supposed to accept that change was inevitable, too, to adjust and fit in. But my anger didn't cool during high school. It changed form, maybe, but it remained. And so, it turns out, did the music.

As "Like a Rolling Stone" hit in 1965, the US was four months into Operation Rolling Thunder, the saturation bombing of North Vietnam. The next year, Dr. Martin Luther King added his voice to the antiwar protest. In 1968, responding to escalating unrest, President Johnson announced he wouldn't run for re-election. Four days later, Dr. King was assassinated. Two months later, Bobby Kennedy was assassinated. By then, more than a hundred cities had exploded into protest and riot. That fall, Richard Nixon was elected president, and in the spring of 1969, he began the secret bombings of Cambodia; that summer was Woodstock. Those were my high school years.

The music on the radio didn't often mention the war, but it was always there. It was the context rock & roll played in, what the sound bounced off. Five thousand US troops died in Vietnam in 1966, eleven thousand the next year. By 1968, a thousand soldiers were dying a month, and by the end of 1969, over forty thousand had been killed. At the same time, the estimate of Vietnamese deaths ranged from one to three million. In those four years, I went from thirteen to eighteen: from being aware of the conflict to being eligible to fight in it.

I was what was then referred to as antiwar. President Johnson said our country was fighting so South Vietnam could "be free of domination from the North," that we were stopping the spread of communism. I didn't care; I couldn't see where communism was much of a threat. At the same time, I was only mildly interested in the antiwar arguments: the talk of America's imperialist aggression, of corporate profiteering and racist oppression. It was all probably true, but mainly, selfishly, I didn't want to get killed.

Vietnam split America in almost cartoon terms: hard hats against longhairs, workers against students. On the radio, it seemed to break down into country music against rock & roll. The year "Like a Rolling Stone" was released, country music was clip-clopping along to Dave Dudley's "Last Day in the Mines," about a miner caught in a cave-in. Merle Haggard yodeled "Sing a Sad Song," and Lefty Frizzell told a story about leaving Saginaw, Michigan, to pan (unsuccessfully) for gold. To me, country music was smoother, often sadder than rock & roll—the sound of dead-end jobs and broken hearts, of facing up to the fact that no new world was actually coming.

To my friends' horror, I liked it. But if I had to pick sides (and it sure felt like I did), mine was with Marvin Gaye's "What's Goin' On," Country Joe and the Fish chanting "I Feel-Like-I'm-Fixin'-to-Die Rag," Jimi Hendrix's version of "The Star Spangled Banner." Those had a sadness, too, but it was mixed with defiance and possibility and a kind of rebellion that country radio seemed to gloss over.

At Woodstock, Jefferson Airplane declared: "One generation got old; one generation got soul./ This generation got no destination to hold." And then launched into their chorus (our chorus?): "Gotta revolution!" It struck me as a little silly: I didn't believe antiwar protests were going to lead to the overthrow of the government. But I loved the sound of it. At least it was angry about the status quo. Country music sounded like it was a duty and an honor to die for your nation; rock & roll offered an alternative—living.

I credited Dylan with helping to create that sound, the sound of opposition. But during my high school years, he seemed to move away from it. After the album with "Like a Rolling Stone" on it, he released a blistering double LP, *Blonde on Blonde*, and toured behind it in the spring of 1966. Then he went silent. There was a rumor he'd been in a motorcycle accident. He released no new music for fifteen months, an eon in the pop music of the day.

When he reemerged in late 1967, the sound was different: quieter, more laid back, more (people were shocked) country. The title song of his new LP, *John Wesley Harding*, was about an outlaw, but he sang it like a farmer. It was almost as if he'd switched sides—or was denying there were sides. If the record commented on politics or the war, it was couched in deep allegory, just about indecipherable.

That fall of 1967, Woody Guthrie died. Dylan's first live appearance in almost two years came at the memorial concert, where he covered Guthrie's songs in rocking, backwoods arrangements. By late 1969, when the United States was openly bombing Cambodia, Dylan was singing about brass beds and country pie.

But even as he changed his sound and look, his earlier music refused to fade away. It was on record, after all, and people in need of a certain kind of inspiration turned back to it. In 1969, the Weathermen, a radical underground cell, took its name from a 1965 Dylan cut, "Subterranean Homesick Blues." The next year, when Bobby Seale was laying out the first Black Panther newspaper, he reported that the LP playing in the background was Dylan's five-year-old *Highway 61 Revisited*. It opens with "Like a Rolling Stone," but the black revolutionaries fixated on a cut called "Ballad of a Thin Man." "We played that record over and over and over," Seale writes. "Huey P. Newton [the party's cofounder] made me recognize the lyrics. . . . Huey would say, 'Listen, listen—man, do you hear what he is saying? . . . old Bobby did society a big favor when he made that particular sound.'"

That particular sound. Gone from pop radio, but not forgotten.

On April 30, 1970, as the resistance (was it revolution?) eddied and foamed, President Nixon announced the invasion of Cambodia. I was in Tucson, Arizona. There was no particular reason for me to be there. I'd graduated high school, been accepted into college, then didn't know whether I wanted to go. I worked, instead, in New

York City for eight months and, with the money I'd saved, hitch-hiked down the East Coast. A month in a transient hotel in Virginia; a Greyhound bus to a little Bible Belt town in Tennessee. It wasn't "hard travelin'" like Dylan said Guthrie had done, but that was part of my inspiration. The truth was out there, on the road. I eventually ended up in Tucson.

I found a room on a quiet residential block not far from the university. My landlord was a young guy whose wife had just left him. He spent a lot of time indoors. So did I. The streets of Tucson were flat, with a white-hot glare I'd never seen before. To be on them midday felt like being pinned under glass. So I stayed in the shade of my rented room and tried to think about the future. I didn't know what I wanted to do. I had a couple of months till my name was put in the lottery that would decide if I'd be drafted for the war.

Through the walls, I could hear my landlord playing the latest Joni Mitchell record. Early in the morning, he'd put the needle down on the first cut. From there, it would go all day and into the night, pausing only long enough to flip the LP over and over again. All I could make out were the folky melodies, her high voice, and an occasional phrase: something about a blue boy and a carousel. There was a song about Woodstock: how we were golden, stardust, half a million strong, and "we got to get ourselves back to the garden." I'd lie on my rented bed and wonder, *What garden?* And why did we have to go backward to get there? And who was this "we"?

On May 1, Tucson woke to the news of Nixon's invasion of Cambodia. I looked out the window and saw people starting to gather on the still bearable streets. The war had gone on for over five years now. I'd done my share of protest marches and understood the drill. It was a kind of staged drama: you walked, and the cops either broke things up (which produced TV images that helped the antiwar effort: how the government arrested its own) or they stood back and let the protest happen (which produced TV images that helped the antiwar effort: how the government couldn't control its own). I didn't think protesting made much difference, finally: our nation's policies seemed unaffected by what we thought. But I joined the marchers. I was eighteen and angry.

Soon the street was full of people, with lines of helmeted police watching us. The same scene was happening all across the country. Three days later, two thousand people would gather at Ohio's Kent State University, and the National Guard would open fire, killing four of them. Ten days later, on the Jackson State campus in Mississippi, police would kill two protestors and wound a dozen more. All told, over four million students would take to the streets that spring, and eight hundred and fifty colleges and universities would be closed down.

Nixon's adviser H. R. Haldeman later said, "[Kent State] marked a turning point, a beginning of [Nixon's] downhill slide toward Watergate." As far as I was concerned, the slide began long before that—before Nixon even—back so far I couldn't actually place it. All I knew was that the notion that my elected officials somehow spoke for me—that this was a functioning representative government—seemed ludicrous. The lesson I'd learned some long time ago was, simply and perfectly: the government lied. It lied in the open, in secret, and continuously. Five years after its release, "Like a Rolling Stone" still represented me better than my representatives. All I could think as I stood on Tucson's now white-hot streets was, *Those fucks. Those fucks.*

When the march started pushing forward, it didn't seem to be headed toward anything in particular. It was just moving to move, stopping traffic as a sign of defiance, protesting the everyday. We walked through the astonishing heat, and then, after a while, I lay down. Even as I did, it struck me as absurd: a person lying down on a street in Tucson. But I couldn't just keep walking forever. So I lay down.

Warm asphalt below, blue sky above, people's feet passing by my head.

Then, a cop came over and asked me to move along. He was unsmiling but polite. He offered me his hand. I took it.

And when my name came up in the lottery that summer, I got a high number: I wouldn't be drafted.

And in the fall, I went to college.

"The four years passed at college were, for his purposes, wasted." That's Henry Adams, writing about Harvard in the 1850s, and it pretty well summed up my experience there. The few professors I met seemed OK; it was the students who got to me. Even as they protested, smoked dope, listened to rock & roll, they gave off this sense of running the world. Or of being in line to run the world. Lots of them were sons and daughters of current leaders. Being inside Harvard made history look seamless—and unchangeable.

I took a lot of classes in the Museum of Comparative Zoology: a big, dark, nineteenth-century building better known as the Agassiz Museum. It felt like the opposite of rock & roll, of anger. Its antique corridors were lined with glass display cases, the cases lined with musty specimens: row after row of dried fish, preserved beetles, the families and subfamilies of small finches. Their faded colors were pinned to sun-bleached mats, and spidery handwriting carefully identified what they were and where they came from. Here was history: dead things made to look alive. It struck me as the pursuit not so much of knowledge as power: proof that the natural world could be collected in one place and preserved. During the years the Pentagon Papers were being leaked, when the Watergate scandal was breaking, when President Nixon was being forced to resign and our country finally withdrew from the war in Southeast Asia, I was in the Agassiz Museum with 10 million mollusk specimens, 6 million insect specimens, 250,000 bird specimens.

Before and after class (and sometimes instead of), I'd go to local record stores. There I'd find amazing treasures: black gospel that revealed where Sam Cooke's soul had sprung from, Chicago blues that had taught the Rolling Stones everything they knew. Here was real history, so exciting I wouldn't have considered calling it that.

One day I sat in my dorm room and listened to a reel-to-reel tape of early blues and folk music. A friend from California had sent it to me like it was the key to some secret code: underground information, source material. The tape had everything from the surreal-sounding white mountain music of "I Wish I Was a Mole in the Ground" to the down-and-dirty of Blind Lemon Jefferson's "Peach Orchard Mama." Bukka White, Leroy Carr, Memphis jug bands, white rural gospel choirs. I realized a lot of what I'd taken to be Dylan, he'd taken from here. It was like hearing where he'd gone to school.

The last song on the tape was by a sixty-nine-year-old black street musician, Reverend Gary Davis. He began by saying in a cracked voice, "This is the truth." Then the verses began to rise and fall over a slow, steady guitar figure, as if the singer had to pause and re-gather his strength with each line. "I will do my last traveling in this land, child, somewhere." He sounded both powerful and broken, and I found myself staring out a window in Cambridge, Massachusetts, with tears in my eyes. It was as absurd, in its way, as lying down on the street in Tucson. But I was moved by something I couldn't name. Except it was beautiful. And that mixed in with it was a good deal of hope.

Among the LPs I was finding were a few reissues of Woody Guthrie records. There was one of him singing traditional tunes with two black bluesmen, Sonny Terry and Brownie McGhee: up-tempo barn-dance numbers with whoops and hollers. And there was an album of children's songs that Guthrie had written, some of which I realized I'd sung as a kid: "Take me riding in the car, car." I splurged on a three-record box set: a folklorist named Alan Lomax interviewing Guthrie for the Library of Congress. The twenty-five-year-old Lomax introduced the twenty-eight-year-old Guthrie as not just a singer and songwriter, not just an interpreter, but the real thing. "He's seen more in those thirty years than most men see before they're seventy. . . . He's gone out in the world. . . . He's lived in hobo jungles. . . ." Guthrie then went on to tell stories about his childhood in Oklahoma, his travels to Texas and California. He sounded modest. And funny in an understated, back-country way. Between stories, he sang.

It was easy to hear what Dylan had learned from Guthrie, but there were big differences, too. Guthrie had none of that flailing, pent-up, rock & roll anger. Lomax pointed out how the songs were largely autobiographical, but in some ways they didn't seem to be about Guthrie. There was a distance to his singing, a calm unruffled surface, and a disarming sense of humor: "As through this world I've hoboed," went one couplet, "I've seen lots of funny men. / Some will rob you with a six-gun, some with a fountain pen." In another, he mentions this "mighty thin stew" that some migrant workers cooked up: "If it had been a little bit thinner, . . . some of our senators could have seen through it."

In 1940, the month before these interviews took place, John Ford's movie *The Grapes of Wrath* came out. Guthrie sang about those Dust Bowl refugees, and the songs had a kind of black-and-white documentary feel: no whining and very little sadness. In a way, the music wasn't emotional—or wasn't emotional like Dylan's, like rock & roll. Instead, there was a quiet pride and a certain patriotism: "This land is your land." What struck me most was Guthrie's optimism. He didn't seem to be attacking history as much as showing how it could mean something different. He was proposing a new and better ending, and he sang like it was just around the corner. Which marked him, more than anything else, as being from another era.

I wanted to hear more, but Woody Guthrie records were hard to find. When I looked in the bins between Grand Funk Railroad and Ritchie Havens, what I found instead were LPs by his son, Arlo Guthrie. Back when I was in high school, Arlo had what was known as an underground hit with a long, funny, rambling song called "Alice's Restaurant Massacree." In a voice somewhere between his father's and Dylan's, Arlo tells about getting a ticket for littering and how, after extended trials and tribulations (the song went on for a deliberately absurd eighteen minutes), the ticket ends up getting him out of the draft. The tongue-in-cheek moral comes at the end when he asks his audience to join in on the catchy ragtime chorus: "You can get anything you want at Alice's restaurant."

If one person sings that chorus, Arlo declares, he might get out of fighting in the war. If three people sing it, "they may think it's an organization." And if fifty people a day sing the chorus, "They may think it's a movement!" I got the joke but wondered who it was on exactly. "Alice's Restaurant Massacree" was a stoner's protest song. It poked fun at the authorities—at the war and the antiwar movement—and at my generation, which seemed to think it could get anything it wanted: all it had to do was ask.

Around my last year in college, Arlo Guthrie put out an album called *Hobo's Lullaby* that included his pop hit, "The City of New Orleans," as well as a cover of a Dylan tune and some originals. It also had a version of one of his father's songs: "1913 Massacre."

That, I thought, is where the son got the title "Alice's Restaurant Massacree." Except his father's song wasn't about a joke *massacree*, with the deliberate misspelling, but the real thing.

To the plain accompaniment of an acoustic guitar and an accordion, the singer tells the story of a bunch of copper miners throwing a Christmas party in Calumet, Michigan: "Singing and dancing is heard everywhere." Then somebody sticks his head in the door and yells "Fire!" It's a false alarm, but the crowd panics. As parents and children run for the exit, men hold the downstairs doors closed. Bodies pile on bodies. "The children that died there were seventy-three."

The song doesn't mention why it happened, only the facts and an odd last line: "See what your greed for money has done."

The tune had this deep, understated sadness, but I didn't understand why this massacre happened. Were the kids killed on purpose? And if it was murder—a mass murder, then—to what end? It had something to do, apparently, with greed and money.

"1913 Massacre," didn't sound like the Woody Guthrie I'd come to know. There was none of his humor or that optimism. It was more like a post mortem, like a description of a lost battle. At the same time, it sounded somehow familiar. Then I realized: Dylan had used the same melody for his "Song to Woody."

That felt like a clue.

The young singer had borrowed from Guthrie's tribute in order to write his own tribute to Guthrie. It was a gesture backward, the beginning of a trail, the start of a story: "Once upon a time."

Over the next few years, I looked for but couldn't find a recording of Woody Guthrie himself singing "1913 Massacre." That particular piece of the past seemed to be out of print. Soon college was over, and adulthood set in. Compared to the years of protest, the nation returned to something like normal. That included the end of its golden age of prosperity. From the early seventies to the early nineties, real wages stagnated, middle-class debt grew, and a growing percentage of US citizens lived in poverty. At the same time, the difference between the salaries of top executives and their workers more than tripled.

Through that last quarter of the twentieth century, rock & roll gradually drifted off pop radio. Dylan still put out LPs: five albums of original material in the seventies, seven in the eighties, seven more in the nineties, and three more as part of a critically acclaimed "comeback" in the first decade of the twenty-first century. I bought and enjoyed most of them, but it wasn't the same. The sound no longer teetered on the edge of change. The howl, the news of the truth, was muted. Had become history.

The revolution didn't happen. Sure, there had been changes—in black rights, women's rights, gay rights. People had marched and sung songs, but no organization had grown out of that, no lasting movement. The basic system had adjusted and remained.

Fifty years after "Like a Rolling Stone," Bob Dylan's story had been worn smooth with retelling. He'd turned into a legend—less a person than a talisman that signified genius, freedom, rebellion. Woody Guthrie, meanwhile, had receded into a dim past: the Johnny Appleseed of American music. And the 1913 massacre—whatever happened there, however those kids died—had all but disappeared.

Is that what happens to anger? Is there no way for it to grow up?

Fifty years after "Like a Rolling Stone," it feels like something's missing. Or hidden. Like this new century was born from a huge struggle it barely knows about. As if forces have long been working underground, and we walk the landscape they've produced like innocents, unaware.

How to go back, to understand? There's a line from Dylan to Guthrie to Calumet: a string of interconnected mysteries. Figure out what happened to those kids in Calumet—what's buried up there—and maybe it helps understand why Guthrie wrote a song about them. Why Dylan used the same melody for his song to Guthrie. And what that has to do with "Like a Rolling Stone" and where we've ended up today. Follow that darkish vein back to find . . . what? The history of anger. Hope. The truth.

TRUE STORIES ABOUT REAL EVENTS

ob Dylan lies. He says so.

"If you told the truth, that was all well and good," he writes in his autobiography, "and if you told the un-truth, well, that's still well and good. Folk songs had taught me that."

For starters, that isn't his given name. He was born Robert Allen Zimmerman, in Duluth, Minnesota, in 1941. When he was six, his family moved seventy-five miles north to the small town of Hibbing, where his mother came from. Her father—Robert's grandfather—had opened a grocery store there in 1913, the year of the Calumet massacre. "Hibbing's a good ol' town," Dylan wrote in a poem. "I ran away from it when I was 10, 12, 13, 15, 15½, 17 an' 18 / I been caught an' brought back all but once."

Funny, but probably not true. After publishing this, Dylan denied it was accurate. Then said it was. Then denied it again.

Around the same time, he wrote: "my youth was spent wildly among the snowy hills an sky blue lakes, willow fields an abandoned open pit mines. contrary t rumors, I am very proud of where I'm from an also of the many blood streams that run in my roots. . . ." His father, Abe Zimmerman, was the son of Ukrainian immigrants. His mother's grandparents were Lithuanian. Through the Depression,

Abe Zimmerman worked for Standard Oil, eventually becoming head of the company-run union: a union set up to keep workers from designing their own. In Hibbing, Abe became a partner in his brothers' electrical appliance store and president of the local B'nai B'rith.

"it was not a rich town /," Dylan would write, "my parents were not rich / it was not a poor town / 'n my parents were not poor / it was a dyin' town / (it was a dyin' town)." Part of that's true. His parents weren't rich—but they were better off than many. And Hibbing, it turns out, wasn't dying; it was changing.

The town sits above the largest iron deposit in the United States. The Mesabi Range was formed three thousand million years ago due west of the copper lode in Michigan. Named for the German immigrant who discovered the iron, Hibbing exists because of the Mesabi; in fact, it had to be moved south in 1919 when the mining undermined Main Street. A town of sixteen thousand when the Zimmermans arrived, it was dwarfed by what Dylan called "the biggest open pit ore mine in the world. . . . You can stand at one end of Hibbing's main drag an' see clear past the city limits on the other end."

The Mesabi produced the iron for World War II's ships and planes and tanks: 188 million tons of it. But when the war ended—as the Zimmermans arrived—Hibbing's ore was all but mined out. Production steadily declined, and as workers elsewhere were getting postwar pay raises, Hibbing entered a "local depression." The "iron depletion," as one of Bobby Zimmerman's classmates recalled, ". . . caused a great deal of unemployment and hardships. . . . It was kind of a bleak time to live. . . ."

Zimmerman would describe Hibbing as a place without any particular troubles or differences. "Where I lived, there aren't any suburbs. There's no poor section and there's no rich section. . . . As far as I knew, where I lived, nobody had anything that anybody else didn't have really."

Or not really.

There were clear distinctions between immigrants and native born, between shopkeepers like Mr. Zimmerman and iron ore miners. According to Dylan's brother, "Bobby always went with the daughters of miners, farmers, and workers in Hibbing. He just found them a lot more interesting." As one of those daughters, Bobby's first serious girlfriend, puts it, "[H]e was from the right side of the tracks, and I was from the wrong side."

In Dylan's version of his past, the Zimmerman part—the store owner and Jewish part—gets less play than the Midwestern, working-class part. "i am only fifteen," he wrote in a poem: "—the only / job around here is mining—but jesus, who wants / to be a miner . . . i refuse to be part of / such a shallow death. . . ."

In fact, he wasn't likely to end up a miner, and this sounds more like one of his heroes: actor and fellow Midwesterner James Dean. *Rebel Without a Cause* came out when Zimmerman was fourteen, and he papered his room with pictures of Dean. "If I had one day when, when I wasn't all confused," Dean's character says, "I didn't have to feel that I was ashamed of everything . . . if I felt I belonged some place, you know?" Listen to a home tape of Zimmerman and a high school friend talking, and the teenagers' drawled, high-pitched hipster lilt sounds a lot like Dean's.

As he was studying Hollywood's version of rebellion, he was tuning his radio to the sounds of Elvis Presley, Buddy Holly, and the man he called his first idol, Hank Williams. Maybe that's how he ran away from home: by identifying with outlaws, the ones who had somehow escaped the "shallow death."

Under the right atmospheric conditions, Zimmerman could pick up a regular rhythm-and-blues program out of Louisiana. "Late at night, I used to listen to Muddy Waters, John Lee Hooker, Jimmy Reed, and Howlin' Wolf blastin' in from Shreveport. . . . I used to stay up till two, three o'clock in the morning. Listened to all those songs, then tried to figure them out." Part of what he and his first serious girlfriend had in common was Chuck Berry's "Maybelline." Both knew it and loved it, and in all-white, far-north Hibbing, that was enough. When a black person passed through Hibbing, the girl-friend recalls, "[Bobby] loved their music so much . . . he'd go and find him, just to meet him and talk to him. . . ."

The summer before he was due to enter high school, in 1955, Emmett Till—a fourteen-year-old black teenager from Chicago—was murdered and thrown into a Mississippi river, allegedly for flirting with a white woman. The outrage that followed marked the start of the modern civil rights movement. Zimmerman was within a couple months of Till's age and would later write a song about the "dreadful tragedy I can still remember well."

He was already trying to express himself through music. As a freshman, he covered Carl Perkins, Lloyd Price, Little Richard. With his curly hair slicked back, he played some basic piano, was cultivating a bluesman's shout, and had picked up enough electric guitar to want to be Scotty Moore, Elvis's guitarist. His high school rock & roll band, loud and in your face, had "a blues sound." When asked about r&b, he could only stutter, "[It's] something you can't quite explain. . . . A chill will go up your spine." The girlfriend and a high school buddy both remember him as basically apolitical—unless you count his love for black music. Under "Ambition" in his high school yearbook, he wrote: "To join the band of Little Richard."

He graduated in the spring of 1959. "I didn't run away from [Hibbing]," he recalled. "I just turned my back on it. It couldn't give me anything." He headed two hundred miles south to the University of Minnesota in Minneapolis. There he discovered something called folk music.

He'd later claim he'd found it in Hibbing a year or so earlier, when he heard a record by Odetta, a black female folksinger with a deep, dramatic voice. "Right then and there, I went out and traded my electric guitar and amplifier for an acoustical guitar, a flat-top Gibson."

Maybe.

But the yearbook quote argues otherwise. And it was in the

university neighborhood called Dinkytown that Zimmerman found a folk community to support and educate him.

In that fall of 1959, folk music was pop music. There, on Top Ten radio—right beside Paul Anka's "Lonely Boy" and Dion and the Belmonts' "A Teenager in Love"—was a song called "Tijuana Jail." The first two were labeled rock & roll, the last was referred to as a folk song.

"Tijuana Jail" was performed by the Kingston Trio, three clean-cut young white men dressed in carefully coordinated collegiate outfits. You could find them on national TV, explaining folk songs to the old vaudevillian, Jack Benny. "I've always wondered," Benny asks, "where do they come from? Who writes the lyrics? Who makes them up?" "Well, Jack," the trio answers, "the lyrics really aren't written in that sense. They're actually true stories about real events." Benny responds with his classic slow take: "Really?"

Well, almost really.

In fact, when the Trio first heard "Tijuana Jail," it was a rock & roll number. They took the recently written lyrics, set them to a traditional tune, and called it folk. The group's earlier, even bigger hit, "Tom Dooley," was closer to the model of "true stories about real events." About an Appalachian murderer who was hanged in 1868, it was first recorded in the twenties, appeared in Alan Lomax's book *Folk Song U.S.A.* in 1947, and by the late fifties was being sung in coffeehouses from New York to San Francisco. The Kingston Trio picked it up and rearranged it to fit their clean-cut style.

Zimmerman lived in a frat house when he got to college, and entering Dinkytown's folk community was a little like that—like joining a vaguely exclusive club with unwritten, half-secret rules. Anything might be a folk song, but only certain stuff was. The Kingston Trio tried to break it down into categories: Traditional Tunes (like "Tom Dooley"), those they called New Words to Old Songs (like "Tijuana Jail"), and Contemporary Folk, meaning brand-new songs that somehow sounded old.

But if you applied those categories to what the radio was playing the year Zimmerman arrived in Minneapolis, you get strange results. For example, a blind, black piano player from Georgia had a hit with an improvised song steeped in the gospel tradition: new material that sounded old. Contemporary Folk, right? Wrong. Instead, people invented a whole a new term for Ray Charles's "What'd I Say": soul music. Next to it on the charts was a song that came out of the New Orleans blues tradition but with cleaned-up lyrics: New Words to Old Tunes. But the last thing the folk world wanted to embrace was the sweaty Elvis Presley singing "One Night with You." Even a nineteenth-century Mexican "folk" song, "La Bamba," sung by a Mexican-American teenager, Richie Valens, was too electrified, too contemporary, to qualify as Traditional Folk.

No, the overriding definition of folk music was that it sounded old. The older the better. Dinkytown was after music from a simpler, purer time, "uncontaminated by mass culture, capitalism, and commercialism." Populist, that is, but not pop. As folk hero Pete Seeger recalled: "We had the utmost contempt for normal commercial music endeavors." Or as Woody Guthrie put it, "A folk song tells a story that really did happen. A pop tune tells a yarn that didn't really take place."

In Dinkytown, even the vehicle of pop music was suspect. "Folksingers, jazz artists and classical musicians made LP's," Dylan later reminisced. ". . . [They] forged identities and tipped the scales, gave more of the big picture. . . . 45s were flimsy and uncrystallized. . . ." You played 45s on a jukebox or a little portable record player and danced to them. That was Dion and the Belmonts. Folk music was somehow more serious, more academic. Sure, there were square dances and hootenannies, but you listened to recorded folk music on a long-playing album, over a hi-fi system, sitting somewhere quiet so you could pay attention. Folk music was studied. It had a history. It *was* history.

The folk scene was rebellious, but rebellious in a specific way. Another of Zimmerman's teen heroes was Jack Kerouac of *On the Road* fame, and the folk and beat scenes overlapped some. They both thought of themselves as being outside the mainstream, breaking away from fifties America. And many of the major folk clubs in Chicago, Los Angeles, San Francisco, New York had been beatnik cafés. Some of Dylan's first New York City gigs would be at the Gaslight, a beat hangout where he remembers the jukebox played mostly jazz: Zoot Sims, Stan Getz. As Dylan saw it, "The Beats tolerated folk music, but they really didn't like it." It was too white, too clean-cut, too old. Both countercultures appreciated black music, especially the blues, but the Beats liked where jazz had taken it: to a cool urban future. Folkies seemed to want to go backward to the jangle of banjo and twelve-string guitar, a sound as outdated as the family farm.

Still, in the fall of 1959, Zimmerman found folk music not out in the country but in a university town. That was partly a result of what Seeger called "cultural guerilla tactics." Back when Bobby Zimmerman was in grade school, Seeger had been blacklisted as a suspected communist. "I couldn't hold a steady job on a single radio or TV station." A lot of his fellow folksingers found themselves in the same position. The solution was to make their "home base," Seeger says, "this one sector of society which refused most courageously to knuckle under to witch hunters: the college students."

The strategy was now starting to pay off. Some three and a half million kids were in college the year Zimmerman entered, up a third from just five years earlier. That summer, the relatively isolated folk scene had emerged and united at the first Newport Folk Festival. Albert Grossman—then owner of a Chicago folk club and soon to be Dylan's manager—chose the headliners. They included Seeger, the blues team of Brownie Terry and Sonny McGhee, Frank Warner (who had brought "Tom Dooley" to Lomax's attention), Reverend Gary Davis, and the Kingston Trio. Joan Baez, an eighteen-year-old daughter of an MIT professor, made her first important public appearance at Newport. "An unspoken feeling was in the air," the festival's producer would remember, "a sense that folk music was approaching a threshold."

When Zimmerman traded in his electric guitar, an international folk revival was in full swing. The Kingston Trio had four of America's top ten LP's—a feat that wouldn't be bettered for half a century. For a music that defined itself as being outside the marketplace, that raised some contradictions, and the question of how to keep the pure sound uncontaminated. By definition, pop music felt "groovy" but didn't mean much—and Top Ten radio wouldn't play songs that tried to "really say it." This, anyway, was how Peter, Paul and Mary looked back on the era in "I Dig Rock and Roll Music"—which must not have been really saying it because it shot to number nine on the charts.

In his autobiography, Dylan says he liked the sound of the Kingston Trio, and maybe he did. But in Dinkytown, he began to learn the rules of the folk fraternity. The music of contemporary folk interpreters like Seeger, Odetta, Dave Van Ronk led him back to an older sound, "out of date," he'd later write, "[with] no proper connection to the actualities, the trends of the time." He says he thought of this almost secret music as "another reality . . . [a] mythical realm."

One of the keys to that realm was the reissuing of a great cache of prewar music: back-porch pickers and juke-joint shouters who had cut records in the twenties and thirties. These kinds of commercial mass-produced recordings were supposed to be the target of folk music's utmost contempt. But that's what the twenty-nine-year-old Harry Smith turned to for his *Anthology of American Folk Music*, released in 1952. Later referred to as the sound of "the old, weird America," Smith's anthology was actually the sound of his parents' generation—Depression-era performers—waxing nostalgic about *their* parents' music. Released to a postwar industrial America, Smith's anthology was mostly songs from the Deep South that appealed to dreams of a time—of a realm?—before the suburbs, before corporate man, before the atomic age.

Soon Bobby Zimmerman was calling himself Bob Dillon, a new name for a new person entering an old myth. He wasn't one of the folk; they were long ago and dead. But to the eighteen-year-old, "Folk music was all I needed to exist." Compared to Hibbing—the appliance store, the B'nai B'rith—the old sound was "so real, so more true to life than life itself. It was life magnified."

He began playing folk clubs in the Minneapolis/Saint Paul area. Round-faced, a little chubby, nearsighted, he sang in a sweet high voice, his Minnesota twang partly hidden. His repertoire included seventeenth-century Scottish ballads like "The Twa Sisters," traditional American tunes like "Columbus Stockade," and the Irish protest music of "Go Down, You Murderers." He also mixed in some older commercial music, like the Bessie Smith blues "Nobody Knows You When You're Down and Out" and a version of country singer Jimmie Rodgers's "Muleskinner Blues." He did up-tempo spirituals like "Sinner Man" and an introspective version of a New Orleans number, "The House of the Rising Sun," as well as the contemporary "Gotta Travel On" sung in a light, sentimental voice. It was fairly standard fare, and the small audiences that heard him remember the kid as, if not special, certainly dedicated and determined to succeed.

Dinkytown was the repository of all kinds of recordings, from imported LPs to old 78s: precious treasure that served as a kind of library or history. As Dylan tells it, that first fall in Minneapolis, he met a red-haired spiritualist named Flo who played him some Woody Guthrie 78s, including "This Land Is Your Land," "Hard Travelin'," and "1913 Massacre." "It was like the record player itself had just picked me up and flung me across the room." One of his friends remembers it differently: "[Dillon] heard Jack Elliott" (real name Elliot Adnopoz, son of a Jewish surgeon, whose 1955 record, *Woody Guthrie Blues*, also included "Hard Travelin'" and "1913 Massacre") ". . . [and] went in two weeks . . . to interpreting Guthrie."

However the connection was made, it seems to have been instantaneous. "Woody Guthrie was the be-all and end-all," Dylan would write. "Woody's songs were about everything at the same time." And it wasn't just the songs. "It was his voice—it was like a stiletto—and his diction. I had never heard anybody sing like that."

The sound, the look, the idea of Guthrie captured Dillon. "When your head gets twisted," he'd write a couple years later, "and your mind grows numb / . . . You say to yourself what am I doin' . . . / You need something special to give you hope / . . . You find Woody Guthrie." He'd heard the truth.

Dillon had already changed his name; now he changed the way he talked and sang, the clothes he wore. Photos show him miming Guthrie down to the way he held a cigarette. "You could listen to his songs," he later wrote, "and actually learn how to live, or how to feel. He was like a guide." And if Guthrie was the guide, his autobiography, *Bound for Glory*, became the teenager's guidebook: it defined what was real and what wasn't.

He says he dropped out of college that spring, "thumbed my way to Galveston," then to California, New Mexico, New Orleans. "I rode freight trains for kicks / An' got beat up for laughs."

Maybe.

In one of his first interviews, Dylan said he was originally from the Southwest—Albuquerque, New Mexico. Later he switched it to Gallup. He claimed to have spent six years traveling with the carnival. When asked about school, he explained, "I skipped a bunch of things." After signing with Columbia Records, he'd tell the publicity department he was actually from Illinois and his father was an electrician. At various times, he claimed to be an orphan, a farmworker, a street hustler. In Greenwich Village, Dylan would become famous for his untruths. "I don't like to be stuck in print" is how he explained it at the time. Later he'd admit that his answers were often "pure hokum—hophead talk."

Another way to say it is that Dylan made himself authentic. He changed who he was to get closer to the truth. Or try to. The sound that eventually came over pop radio—his timed drawl, the rural edge, the off-center sense of humor—was a lot Guthrie. That's how Dylan became an original—through imitation. It's as if he ran from his middle-class, mid-twentieth-century Hibbing and went back to Guthrie's thirties. Or as he put it, "I was making my own depression."

Soon, when he played songs into a Dinkytown friend's reel-to-reel recorder, he was covering Guthrie originals, songs Guthrie had covered, and a few of his own talking blues that sounded like Guthrie. He was steering away from what *Bound for Glory* called "juke-box stuff" and "soap-box music [that's a] little too sissy." All he wanted to play—to be—was the real thing. In early 1961, after a year of "making pretend I was going to class," the nineteen-year-old left college and headed east—to the center of the folk scene and the city where Woody Guthrie lived.

He'd claim he got to New York by hopping freight, just like Woody. Or was it hitchhiking? "Ramblin' outa the Wild West . . . driftin' an learnin' new lessons." In fact, he appears to have gotten a lift out of Chicago from a friend. According to his father, "[W]e made an arrangement that he could have one year to do as he pleased, and if at the end of that year we were not satisfied with his progress, he'd go back to school."

A lot of what he wanted to do was meet Guthrie. He banged on the family's door out in Coney Island, found out that Guthrie was at Greystone Hospital in New Jersey. There he discovered a dying man. Guthrie, not yet fifty, had Huntington's chorea, a degenerative nerve disease. He was so incapacitated that someone had to light his cigarette and place it between his lips.

Forty years later, Dylan remembered the meeting as "sobering and psychologically draining." Still, he stayed, playing Woody Guthrie songs to Woody Guthrie, paying his respects. For Guthrie, it must have been pleasing but strange—to watch a younger, healthy version of himself perform his songs, tell his jokes, mime his gestures. To Dylan, it was a revelation. He sent a postcard home to his Dinkytown friends: "I know Woody . . . I know Woody. I know him and met him and saw him and sang to him. I Know Woody— Goddamn."

Later, he tried to sum up what the meeting meant to him:

> Woody Guthrie was my last idol
> he was the last idol because
> he was the first idol

I'd ever met
face t'face
that taught me
that men are men
shatterin' even himself
as an idol . . .

It was as if he'd finally made his way to the mythical realm, only to discover it wasn't the truth; it was myth.

And it wasn't only his idol that shattered. In the same poem, Dylan writes how he came to New York to find the union halls and meeting places of the "hungry thirties / . . . [But] they're changed / they've been remodeled / . . . where are those forces of yesteryear?"

where is our party?
where all member's held equal
an' vow t'infiltrate that thought
among the people it hopes t'serve
an' sets a respected road
for all those like me
who cry
"I am ragin'ly against absolutely
everything that wants t' force nature
t' be unnatural . . . ?"

Where was the movement Guthrie had talked about? Where was the party that would channel a teenager's rage, set it on a respected road? The answer, Dylan quickly realized, was that it didn't exist anymore. Not as it used to, anyway.

Not long after that first meeting, Dylan wrote "Song to Woody." "I needed to write that song," he said later. "I needed to sing it. So that's why I needed to write it."

He constructs the song as a series of comparisons: the thirties to the just-beginning sixties, Guthrie's life to his own. While the teenager's seen hard times among Hibbing's unemployed miners and done some hitchhiking, the truth is, his manufactured Depression doesn't hold up to Guthrie's real one. "The very last thing I'd like to do," the song ends, "is to say I've been hittin' some hard travelin' too."

It's a tribute, but it's also a farewell—with a sadness that goes beyond even the haunting melody. Listen to the song Dylan felt he needed to sing, and you hear a kid who's come a thousand miles only to discover that what he came for no longer exists. Guthrie's illness accounts for part of that. But it's more.

Dylan would later call "Song to Woody" his first original composition "of any substantial importance." He needed to say good-bye to the idea of being Woody Guthrie—because Guthrie's era was over, because those dreams were shattered, because men are only men. It was a perspective and a type of song he'd keep returning to right through "Like a Rolling Stone." A restless farewell. The sound of someone looking back in order to tell the truth.

A LITTLE BAD LUCK

The teenage Bob Dylan comes to New York to meet his idol, Woody Guthrie, and the idol shatters. That truth no longer exists—if it ever really did. When Guthrie told his life story, he injected enough untruth for him to call *Bound for Glory* an "autobiographical novel."

Dylan's self-invention follows suit. When he calls Hibbing a "good ol' town" where "nobody had anything that anybody else didn't," he's mimicking *Bound for Glory*'s description of Guthrie's birthplace, Okemah, Oklahoma: "[J]ust another one of those little towns, I guess, about a thousand or so people, where everybody knew everybody else. . . ." The idea of Okemah being a typical all-American town let Guthrie be a typical American. "I ain't nothing much but a guy walking along. You can't hardly pick me out in a big crowd, I look so much like everybody else."

In fact, Okemah was a brand-new town carved out of a brand-new state, and if Guthrie looked like everybody else, it was because certain people were kept out. Okemah was founded as a white town, distinct from nearby settlements that were predominantly black or predominantly Native American.

The Oklahoma Territory started as a relocation center for displaced Indians. Humans had lived there for at least eleven thousand years: the Wichita eventually claiming it from the Apache and then losing it to the Comanche and Osage Sioux. When the United States gained control through the Louisiana Purchase of 1803, the white presence was tiny: cowboys passing through with their herds, a few farmers. A quarter century later, President Andrew Jackson's Indian Removal Act drove native tribes out of Mississippi, Alabama, Florida in order to open land for white settlers and the cotton industry. The displaced were marched west on what became known as the Trail of Tears; Oklahoma was the last stop.

The Five Tribes—Choctaws, Chickasaws, Creeks, Seminoles, Cherokees—started over here, adjusting to the new geography, setting up a constitutional government. There were treaties signed promising this would remain a sovereign territory forever: a separate Indian Nation within the United States. But when the Civil War broke out, the Five Tribes mostly sided with the Confederacy. They were, after all, just a couple decades out of the South, had been run off their homelands by the federal (Northern) government, and kept slaves themselves. After the Confederacy lost, the Indian Nation was accused of having declared war on the United States. It was forced to cede the western half of its land. At the time, the Oklahoma Territory contained some fifty thousand Indians, eight thousand freed slaves, and only two thousand whites.

By this point in American history, a pattern had been established. Starting on the eastern coast, settlers "pioneered" native lands, "improved" them by cutting down forests and planting crops, and then, as one historian puts it, proceeded to "mine" the soil till it couldn't produce anymore. When the land was used up, it was time to move west and do it again. That syndrome only gained speed with the Civil War and the development of a national railway system. Starting with the Homestead Act of 1862 (which guaranteed pioneers a free 160 acres of government land), the transformation was astonishing. Between 1870 and 1880, the nation's total of cultivated land grew by 190 million acres, about the size of England and France combined. The next decade, another 303 million were added. And the next decade, another 40 million. As the number of farms jumped from about two million in 1860 to almost six and a half million by 1910, the American frontier disappeared.

The Oklahoma Territory was among the last holdouts. By the late nineteenth century, it was the only area east of the Rockies that hadn't become part of a state. Railroad companies had already laid track across it, buying up local coal fields and importing Czechs, Poles, and Finns to work the mines. Real-estate raiding parties— known as "boomers"—had tried to stake claims on reservation land, but the Indian Nation held on even as the Dawes Acts of 1887 undercut many treaties.

Then in 1895—in America's gilded age, with the railroad barons arguing that they needed more acreage to make more profit— Congress authorized a survey of all tribal land. The Oklahoma hills were carefully mapped out into homestead-size 160-acre parcels. The next year, rolls were prepared documenting who lived where and which land was unoccupied. Two years later came the Curtis Act, giving a parcel to each accredited tribal member but opening the rest to a land rush. It happened on a single day, almost a single hour. At high noon, April 22, 1889, tens of thousands of settlers raced across the border to stake claim to their "free" homesteads.

Guthrie's paternal grandfather, a cowpuncher from Texas, had first tried to get a piece of Oklahoma by passing his family off as part Creek. He traded cattle and raised kids. His son, Charlie, started off as a cowboy too but soon saw that world was dying. He began taking mail-order courses in accounting and law, and when the borders were opened and the land rush hit, the twenty-year-old was positioned to take full advantage. Meanwhile, Woody's mother's family, the Tanners, came down from Kansas.

Charlie Guthrie and Nora Belle Tanner met just after the turn of the century. By then, there were still some fifty thousand Native Americans in Oklahoma, but they'd been joined by thirty-seven thousand blacks—and over three hundred thousand whites. Oklahoma's real estate values had skyrocketed, rising almost 250 percent in a decade. The territory had filled with "grafters," who made their living convincing members of the Five Tribes to sign over their land, or simply grafting their names onto Native American leases.

Charlie Guthrie was a grafter. "Because he was able to speak both Creek and Cherokee," one of Woody's biographers writes, "Charley [sic] became known as especially adept at relieving Indians of their property." Guthrie describes his father as "a man of brimstone and hot fire, . . . always out talking, dancing, drinking and trading with the Indians." In *Bound for Glory*, he has his father say, "I might not stop often enough trying to work and make a lot of money to buy all of you some nice things. Maybe I've got to be so mean trading and trying to make the money, that I don't know how to quit when I come in home. . . ."

Soon the family could afford "all the prettiest and best things in the store." Guthrie says with some pride that his father ended up with thirty farms. His mother, Nora, appreciated the comforts. The educated daughter of a schoolteacher, she liked living in a fine place with hired help to do the housework. She'd ride to town in a carriage pulled by a matched team of horses or stay in the parlor playing old, sad ballads on their new piano. It was a prosperous life—something like what the Zimmermans would have in Hibbing forty years later.

When Oklahoma became a state in 1907, Charlie Guthrie decided to run for District Court clerk. He campaigned as a Democrat, the party of the defeated but not forgotten Confederacy. Their platform, according to the Republicans, could be reduced to "the old familiar howl: Nigger! Nigger!" All around Okemah, free blacks had founded their own towns, drawn to Oklahoma by its strong separatist movement and the chance to start over. They voted Republican, the party of Lincoln and emancipation. In Charlie's district, black voters outnumbered white, so Charlie and the Democrats developed a twofold strategy. First, they featured the old familiar howl—and that extended right through the final count, when they managed to have many black votes disallowed. At the same time, they created a platform to appeal to the dissatisfied and often penniless white tenant farmers.

Oklahoma tenant farming came out of the land rush. In the first year, over 99 percent of its farmers worked their own plots. But soon real estate trading shifted large tracts into the hands of a relative few, see Charlie Guthrie and his thirty farms. By the time Charlie ran for office, over half of the territory's farmers had been reduced to working for big landowners. The new state was duplicating the Old South's system of sharecropping. Democrats crafted a platform that appealed to the small-scale farmers, blaming their troubles on "the parasites in the electric towns"—bankers, railroad owners, the "money power." The combination of attacking big business and "niggers" led to a Democratic sweep of every statewide office.

After his victory, Charlie started construction on a new home. "I wasn't much more than two years old," Woody writes in *Bound for Glory*, "when we built our seven-room house over in the good part of Okemah. . . . I remember a bright yellow outside—a blurred haze of a dark inside. . . ." Then, a month after it was finished, their new house burned to the ground. "[N]obody ever knew how or why, a fire broke out, . . ." Guthrie writes and then goes on to describe the awful flames, the neighbors trying to help, the final picture of "a cement foundation piled full of red-hot ashes and cinders."

Except the fire took place three years before Woody Guthrie was born.

In a later section of his "autobiographical novel," Guthrie—at age five or six—asks his mother if the local gossip is true: had she set the fire on purpose "because she hated the crazier things that [Charlie] was doing to make a lot of money"? As Guthrie tells it, "Mama didn't answer me. She just looked up away from me. She looked a hole through the wall, and then she looked out through my bedroom window up over the hill. . . . I heard everything get quiet."

It's a look and a quiet that will return to haunt the family. As far as Guthrie was concerned, the collapse of his family began here, before he was born. Maybe he put himself at the scene of the fire— wrote it like he was there—to get at this larger truth.

Three years after the fire, Charlie Guthrie ran for a higher office, county assessor. By then, the Democrats had passed a voting act that effectively disenfranchised most of the state's blacks. At the same time, they'd created a state constitution that protected small farmers and limited corporate growth. But the anger at "money power" had found new representation. A coalition of tenant farmers and immigrant mine workers had formed a third party, part of a national movement toward socialism. Between Oklahoma's statehood in 1907 and the start of World War I in 1914, the new party's percentage of the vote would double every election. No state—not even New York, with seven times Oklahoma's population—had more socialist voters.

Their goal was to change the course of history, to "reverse the corporate revolution." According to Eugene Debs, one of the party's leaders, the power of corporations had begun to smack of "tyranny and degradation." The Pullman railroad car company, for example, built "model" towns with company housing, company churches, company libraries; in return, it demanded absolute loyalty. Debs had gotten his political start by leading a boycott against Pullman that eventually led to a nationwide strike. He framed the issue as "right versus wrong, Christianity battling greed, Socialism versus Capitalism."

Charlie Guthrie was on capitalism's side. In his regular newspaper column, he referred to socialists as "Kumrids." He called them amoral, Negro-loving, Antichrists. The spring before the 1912 election, a black mother and her fifteen-year-old son were jailed on charges of killing an Okemah deputy sheriff. A mob broke into their cell, allegedly raped the woman, then lynched her and her son from a nearby bridge. Photographs were taken; Okemah townspeople later sold postcards of the hanging. Rumor had it that Charlie Guthrie was part of the lynch mob and later became an "enthusiastic member" of the Ku Klux Klan.

In his autobiography, Woody Guthrie barely mentions his father's politics, other than to describe him as "one of those ol' hard-hittin', fist-fightin' Democrats." But years later, he'd write a bunch of songs about the Okemah lynching. In one, he has the black mother begging the mob, "You can stretch my neck on that old railroad bridge / But don't kill my baby and my son." She could be pleading with Charlie Guthrie.

Woodrow Wilson Guthrie was born on July 14, 1912, in the midst of his father's campaign for county assessor. Charlie named the Guthries' third child for that year's Democratic nominee for president, and the choice fit the father's politics. Born and raised in the South, Woodrow Wilson was an unreconstructed segregationist. As the leader of Princeton University, he'd deemed it "altogether inadvisable for a colored man to enter." As one of his first acts as president, he would re-segregate the federal civil services. To name his newborn after Wilson was a way for Charlie to identify not only where the boy was from but who he should be, the same way Woody's uncle was named Jefferson Davis Guthrie.

With socialists casting almost a third of the county's votes, Charlie Guthrie lost the 1912 election. Three years later, he ran for and won the post of justice of the peace. Three years after that, he lost a bitter campaign for state legislator. "My dad," Woody remembers, "used to teach me little political speeches and rhymes. And I'd climb up on a hay wagon around at all the political rallies . . . and I'd make my little speeches." For his first public performances—and his introduction to American politics—little Woody entertained fist-fightin', anti-Negro, antisocialist crowds. "It might be," he'd add, decades later, "that I've turned out now where I don't believe the speeches anymore and make speeches just the opposite."

By this time, that look of Nora Guthrie's was happening more often. Woody claims it was because his mother "just worried and worried" about her husband's political fighting. She was, in his words, an "awful scared, nervous kind of woman." Still, the family was doing well, the economy booming with World War I spending and Charlie involved in almost daily land deals. The Guthries had at least two residences: a forty-acre farm and a fine home in town. As Woody would tell Alan Lomax, "I was a little bit different . . . I wasn't in the path that John Steinbeck called the Okies. . . . Because my dad, to start with, was worth about thirty-five, forty thousand. He had everything hunky-dory."

When Woody was seven, his fourteen-year-old sister "either set herself afire," as he put it, "or caught fire accidentally. There's two different stories. . . ." Again it was a fire; again the cause and the truth stay murky.

The family never fully recovered. Charlie Guthrie kept a copy of his daughter's death notice in his wallet the rest of his life. Nora's demons got worse. "She would be all right for a while," Woody writes, "and treat us kids as good as any mother, and all at once it would start in—something bad and awful—something would start coming over her, and it come by slow degrees. Her face would twitch and her lips would snarl and her teeth would show." Or as he put it elsewhere, "She commenced to sing the sadder songs in a loster voice . . . away over yonder in the minor keys."

The next year, the oil boom reached Okemah. Wells had been coming in across the state for two decades, but in Okemah county, Woody wrote, "The oil was a whisper in the dark, a rumor, a gamble." Then in 1920, a gusher hit, and the town's population quintupled. "[You] just wake up one morning and . . . there's fifteen or twenty thousand of them out there in a little town that used to be five or six hundred farming people."

Woody could see both sides of the boom. "Pretty soon the creeks around Okemah was filled with black scum. . . . The grass and the trees and the tangleweed died." On the other hand, "The whole country was alive with men working. . . ." It was a display of capitalism's power: buildings sprang up, music poured out of saloons, families were able to eat. An oil roustabout could earn more in a month than a sharecropper in three years. Eight-year-old Guthrie got a job selling newspapers on the street.

Chasing after the boom, Guthrie wrote, were "oil slickers, oil fakers, oil stakers, and oil takers." They took Charlie Guthrie. "My dad told me that he was the only man in the world that lost a farm a day for thirty days." By the time Woody was eleven, his father was broke. "He went down fighting, but he went right on down. Owed ten times more than he could ever pay . . . He went down and he stayed down."

Soon, Okemah's boom ended too, and Woody was a teenager with an unemployed father who drank too much and a mother who wanted "it all to come back: the house, the lands, good furniture, the part-time maid, and the car to drive around the country." Too broke to raise their youngest children, Guthrie's parents shipped his little brother and sister off to an aunt in Texas. Woody spent more and more time away from home.

The family's final act came in 1927. Again, it was a fire, again Guthrie leaves the story vague. In *Bound for Glory*, he described being at home with his mother when she got "that look. That long-lost, faraway, fiery smoke glare. . . ." Woody ran to get his father, who hurried into the house to find his wife. Next thing, the oil stove exploded. Again Woody isn't actually at the scene, but he offers two explanations: either it was an accident, or his father deliberately set himself on fire. "I always will think that he done it on purpose," Guthrie writes. "Because he lost all his money." The third, unmentioned possibility was that his mother had done it—which is what most people in town thought.

Charlie Guthrie was taken to his sister's in Texas to recuperate. Nora was committed to an insane asylum in Norman, Oklahoma. Woody says he began drifting then, down to Houston and Galveston, earning a little spare change playing harmonica and dancing. Back in Okemah, he became an "alley rat," living alone in a shack on the outskirts of town, taking odd jobs, rarely going to school. He was fifteen.

Dylan's claims of running away from home sound like Guthrie—or Guthrie's image as a drifter, a rambling man. But Woody Guthrie didn't run away from home; home dissolved around him. And he didn't blame hard times for the breakup, or the banks, or capitalism. The next year, a drought begins that will eventually lead to the

Dust Bowl. A couple of years later, the Great Depression strikes. But while Guthrie eventually tied himself to those events, he always saw his family's story as separate, different. "[My father]," he says, "had a little bad luck. My whole family did. . . ."

He eventually went to live with his father a few hundred miles west of Okemah in Pampa, Texas. Charlie Guthrie, a broken man at fifty-one, was running a local whorehouse. Woody describes the country-girl hookers, the pimps, how they shot up morphine in their tiny "stalls . . . , dirty, bed-buggy, slick, slimy. . . ."

He went to high school during the day—a clean-faced kid in button-down shirt and slacks—and worked at the whorehouse at night. Soon, he'd dropped out of school and was taking whatever work he could find: telling fortunes, painting signs, selling moonshine. He got to know his father's customers—"boomchasers" he calls them—workers going from town to town chasing oil, chasing the American dream. Years later, he considers calling his autobiography *The Boomchasers*, the story of people hustling after a payoff that never quite arrives.

In June 1930, Guthrie's mother died in the insane asylum. Woody was about to turn eighteen, a small, thin, strong-jawed young man, his curly hair carefully parted to one side. "I walked the streets [of Pampa] in the drift of the dust and wondered where was I bound for, where was I going, what was I going to do?" He went to the town library and "scratched around in the books. . . . My head was mixed up. I looked into every kind of an 'ology,' 'osis,' 'itis,' and 'ism' there was." He read spiritual guides, law books, medical books. And he joined the Church of Christ.

Guthrie doesn't mention his conversion in *Bound for Glory*. It doesn't come up in the later interviews with Lomax. It's not part of the Woody Guthrie myth that attracted and shaped Dylan. But in a small town like Pampa, to join the Church of Christ was a major commitment. It included a public confession of sins, a public acceptance of Jesus as the Lord, and a public baptism by full immersion. A strict, born-again denomination, the Church of Christ demanded belief in the literal word of the Bible. The goal was "to restore primitive Christianity." It eliminated any church hierarchy, encouraged members to conduct their own services, and restricted music to unaccompanied singing—no instruments allowed. Though it seems Guthrie attended church only for a little while, he never gave up his basic faith in Christ. Years later, asked who his heroes were, he'd answer, "Will Rogers and Jesus."

It was a joke—and it wasn't.

More than a decade after his conversion, he'd write a song called "Jesus Christ." Set to the tune of a 1920s ballad about Jesse James, it cast Jesus as an outlaw. He doesn't perform miracles or, for that matter, turn the other cheek. Instead, Guthrie's Jesus has a straightforward message: "Give your money to the poor." That's why, the song goes on, "the bankers and the preachers, they nailed him to the cross." That was the Jesus whom Guthrie considered a hero, and even toward the end of his life, when Huntington's chorea had ravaged his body, he'd still call Jesus "my best doctor."

Around the time he was wandering the streets of Pampa, wondering what to do, he took up the guitar. Like when Dylan found folk music, Guthrie discovered hillbilly music as its popularity was rising. A few years earlier, at a famous session in Bristol, Tennessee, RCA Victor recorded a number of rural acts, including a singing railroad worker named Jimmie Rodgers and a trio from nearby Virginia, the Carter Family. By the time Guthrie was learning to play, both were sensations. The Carter Family had hit with "Single Girl, Married Girl," "Wildwood Flower," "John Hardy." These are now called country songs or folk music, but those categories didn't exist then. At the time, it was hillbilly music: a genre marketed to an audience that once had or still lived outside of town.

Hillbilly music was meant to be familiar. It was the kind of playing and singing folks did at home, on the front porch, the kind Guthrie would have heard in Okemeh and Pampa. To find material, the patriarch of the Carter Family, A.P., became a collector. He went on music-finding expeditions throughout the South, uncovering tunes at family get-togethers, at hoedowns, at revival meetings, and in jails. He made a point of traveling with a black man, Lesley Riddle, who could get Carter across the color line into Negro America. "I was his tape recorder," Riddle recalls. The Carter Family's version of hillbilly music included a rich sampling of the blues.

The resulting records were Guthrie's main music school. Mother Maybelle Carter was the family's instrumentalist. She'd adapted her guitar style from banjo picking, playing the melody on the bass strings, using the high strings for accompaniment. It swung more than a simple guitar strum, drew people in, made it easier to sing along. Known as the Carter scratch, her method became the foundation for bluegrass and other kinds of country music. Listen to Woody Guthrie's guitar, especially on his early recordings, and you hear Mother Maybelle.

Sara, the Carter Family's lead singer, had a sharp, almost emotionless attack: a kind of modest holding back that made you lean forward. Some of that can be traced to church singing, where the object was to glorify God, not the singer. Alan Lomax would describe American rural ballad singing as a way of keeping emotion "in reserve. The singer does not color the story with heavy vocal underscoring: she allows the story to tell itself." Look at Walker Evans's Depression-era photographs, and you see the equivalent of Sara Carter's singing: her voice hung each note in its place the way tenant farmers placed their one washcloth next to their one plain bowl next to their one tin bucket. She sang with precision and modesty—no frills. When Dylan says Guthrie's voice was "like a stiletto," he could be describing Sara Carter's. It's the deliberately plain, deliberately simple sound of someone trying to tell the truth.

Guthrie soon knew enough music to help form a band. Their repertoire mixed old-timey songs with the kind of dour ballads his mother used to sing. "We played for rodeos, centennials, carnivals, parades, fairs, just bust down parties, and played several nights and days a week just to hear our own boards rattle and our strings roar around in the wind." Here's where his other hero, Will Rogers, comes in.

Born the same year as Woody's father, in the same part of Oklahoma, to a father who also worked cattle, Rogers—unlike Charlie Guthrie—was part Cherokee. When he emerged as a comedian, columnist, and movie star, his easygoing, everyman style included a sharp outsider's edge. "The difference between our rich and poor," he observed in one of his columns, "grows greater every year. Our distribution of wealth is getting more uneven all the time. We are always reading, 'How many men paid over a million dollar income tax.' But we never read about 'How many there is that are not eating regular.'"

"[E]very kid in the Southwest wanted to become another Will Rogers," wrote Lee Hays, one of Guthrie's later singing partners. Rogers was a local boy made good; newsreels showed him at his mansion in California, lassoing ponies. In 1931, he and hillbilly singer Jimmie Rodgers did a fifty-town goodwill tour of drought-stricken Oklahoma, Arkansas, and Texas. If they didn't play Pampa, they played close by, trying to bring laughter and music during hard times.

Guthrie aimed to do the same. When his band needed to fill time between songs, he'd launch into his Will Rogers act: telling tall tales with Rogers's innocent grin, scratching his head with the same corn-pone savvy. And as he began to write his own songs, they had some of Rogers's dry political humor. The year Guthrie turned twenty-one, Franklin Delano Roosevelt was inaugurated to his first term as president. "If I was President Roosevelt," Guthrie sang, ". . . I'd pass out suits of clothing / at least three times a week—/ And shoot the first big oil man / That killed the fishing creek."

In the spring of FDR's first hundred days, Guthrie started courting sixteen-year-old Mary Jennings, a daughter of sharecroppers, sister of one of Guthrie's musician buddies. He was now working five nights a week in the hillbilly band and bringing in extra money as a faith healer and fortune-teller. Total take-home: about four dollars a week, half of which went to groceries. But Mary was pretty, and the new president promised an economic recovery. The young couple married, and soon Mary was pregnant.

In the mid-1930s, in West Texas, there was no such thing as settling into a quiet, comfortable life. The drought was still fierce. And years of tenant farmers forced to plant and overplant the same acreage had taken its toll. On Palm Sunday, 1935, sixty-mile-an-hour winds began lifting huge clouds of gray-red soil and driving them across the broken prairie. The same way Dylan would feel he needed to sing about Guthrie, Guthrie saw these dust storms as "the most important thing that I had seen, so I had to write about them, or try."

Dylan wrote "Song to Woody" at age nineteen; Guthrie wrote his first important song at twenty-two. Hillbilly music had a tradition of commemorating storms and floods. "Any disaster that came along," the engineer at RCA's Bristol sessions recalled, "we'd have somebody write a song about it." The sinking of a ship, a mine disaster, a murder: the newspapers would report the facts, but to understand them—to feel the news—listeners turned to "event songs." Guthrie remembered how, when a cyclone hit, his mother had once taken him down into a storm cellar and comforted him by singing an old ballad about the Sherman cyclone of 1896.

Now Guthrie took that tradition and wed it to the melody from an outlaw ballad, the waltz-time "Billy the Kid." In 1927, Vernon Dalhart had sung "Billy the Kid" in a modified crooner's style. Eight years later, Guthrie delivered "Dusty Old Dust" in his unornamented Sara Carter voice and with Will Rogers's sense of humor. When the dust storm hit Pampa, he sings, people started talking about the end of the world, and the local preacher "folded his specs and took up collection." The repeating chorus is a farewell—"So long, it's been good to know ya"—but the waltz time keeps it funny and oddly hopeful: the song of a wry observer, interested in but a little detached from the human comedy. He's "got to be driftin' along."

By this time, Charlie Guthrie was on skid row, and the Depression had caught up with just about everybody. While FDR's first hundred days of relief bills and public works projects helped drop unemployment, some 17 percent of the population still had no work. Guthrie—with a daughter, Gwendolyn, born in November 1935—could barely support himself and his family. Soon, he was traveling: taking long trips away from Pampa to "look around for a place for us to go."

Millions were doing the same: Southwestern farmers beating their way toward California, Southern Negroes heading for Chicago, Detroit, Los Angeles. Guthrie knew—everyone knew—Jimmie Rodgers's hit, "Blue Yodel #1 (T for Texas)." It was all about leaving Georgia, where they treated a man "like a dirty dog," and heading west, "where the water tastes like cherry wine." The Guthrie family's "little bad luck" was getting folded into the larger issues of the day.

Bound for Glory begins and ends with the same scene. Guthrie's in a boxcar rumbling through California, one of dozens of drifters looking for work. The book doesn't mention his wife or baby, or that Mary is pregnant again. In the autobiographical novel, he's an unattached outcast, like the "Negro boy" he becomes friends with, a couple of kids who give him their shirts to keep his guitar dry, the whole "mixed-up bunch of blurred shadows and train smoke." All of them, rattling through the Western landscape, join in on an old gospel tune: "This train is bound for glory, this train." It's a moment of hope, of possibility, and part of the legend that would inspire Bob Dylan.

And it's true that Guthrie headed west at the beginning of 1937. It seems to be true that he brought his guitar and sang gospel songs, as well as Carter Family stuff and his mother's ballads, anything that might cheer up the displaced down-and-out and bring in some spare change. It's true that when his freight rolled down into the fertile valleys of California, he thought it looked like a kind of promised land, like glory. Though the water didn't taste like wine, there were "colors so bright, and the smells so thick all around, that it seemed almost too good to be true."

And it was. It was too good to be true.

The California he was about to enter was no Eden and held no brotherhood of man. That he'd have to fight for. He learned as much, he says, one day while bumming north, clinging to a freezing freight, trying to break "the lonesome whip of the wind." Alone, he suddenly realized his strength was about to give out, and when it did, he'd drop under the train wheels. His mind flashed back over "millions of things—my whole life was brought up to date, and all of the people I knew, and all that they meant to me. And, no doubt, my line of politics took on quite a change right then and there, even though I didn't know I was getting educated at the time."

The train slowed. He stumbled off. From then on, he writes, he was committed to a new course, a new definition of glory: "singing with the people, singing something with fight and guts and belly laughs and power and dynamite to it."

And that part is true: he did make that commitment. Not long after he arrived in California, a friend introduced him to actor and activist Will Geer. Geer's wife, Herta, introduced him to her grandmother, Ella Reeve Bloor. Guthrie found Bloor, then in her seventies, "peppery and friendly. . . . She looks like she comes every day upon something she has been hunting for all her life. That," he adds, "is because she knew what she was hunting for."

Ella Bloor will tell him the story of Calumet. And it will help Woody Guthrie understand who he is and what he wants.

SOME VISION OF THE FUTURE

fter writing "1913 Massacre," Guthrie explained why: "Any event which takes away the lives of human beings, I try to write a song about what caused it to happen and how we can all try to keep such a thing from happening again."

He was straightforward about how he worked—"I made up new words to old tunes"—and for "1913 Massacre," he took the melody of a seventeenth-century English ballad, "To Hear the Nightingale Sing." He probably heard it in New York City, where it was being passed around among singers in the 1930s, as it still would be when Dylan arrived, decades later. Guthrie said he preferred "a good old, family style tune that hath already gained a reputation as being liked by the people." That "hath" is a poke at the folk commandment that one must stay in the tradition, but a borrowed melody did help make a song sound authentic, linked it to the past, put listeners at ease. Guthrie often worked it like an inside joke, his new words bouncing off the old familiar ones.

For "1913 Massacre," he also borrowed the story. The Calumet disaster took place when Guthrie was only a year old. Like the house fire that started his family's run of bad luck, he wasn't actually there but writes about it like he was. A borrowed story grafted to a borrowed tune meant to uncover a history he'd only heard about from a third party, Ella Reeve Bloor.

She was known in labor circles as Mother Bloor. It was a sign of respect, the way older women at church were addressed, the way her fellow union organizer, Mary Harris Jones, became Mother Jones. Bloor's family history stretches back to the beginning of the United States. Her great-grandfather fought in the Revolutionary War, her father in the Civil War. When she was twelve, she regularly rode the ferry out of Camden, New Jersey, with a kindly, gray-bearded man who turned out to be Walt Whitman. In her autobiography, she quotes the poet: "I see the enslaved, the overthrown, the hurt, the opprest of the whole earth; / . . . give me some vision of the future; Give me, for once, its prophecy and joy."

As a young wife, Bloor kept searching for that vision, "earnestly trying to understand the world around me." Like the young Guthrie haunting the Pampa library, Bloor read Marx, Engels, Darwin. "It was then considered just as radical to be an evolutionist," she writes, "as it is to be a revolutionist today." Her search quickly brought her to socialism. She met Eugene Debs around 1895, not long after he'd served time for heading up the Pullman strike. "He spoke like an evangelist," she recalls, and the newly pregnant Bloor joined his utopian plan to start a model socialist community in the Midwest.

But the plan seemed too idealistic and impractical, and soon she switched loyalties to Daniel De Leon's Socialist Labor Party. She was impressed by "his analysis of the evils of the capitalist system." At the start of the new century, in what was known as the Progressive Era, Bloor became part of the same movement against big business that attracted Oklahoma's tenant farmers and immigrants. As America industrialized, as mine owners and factory owners and railroad barons built their fortunes, Bloor set as her goal (italicized in her autobiography): "*To unite and organize the workers so they could achieve the power they needed to own the machines themselves.*"

Young children in tow, she became a national organizer, rallying miners in Pennsylvania, becoming the first woman nominated for public office in Connecticut, helping Upton Sinclair research his exposé of Chicago's meat-packing industry, *The Jungle*. She traveled back and forth across the country, linking the various hot spots of radical activity. She not only had a vision of the future, but she believed it was about to come true. In 1912—the year Guthrie was born and Bloor turned fifty—Debs's run for president of the United States pulled a record-breaking 897,000 socialist votes. Woodrow Wilson won, but Bloor could see the beginning of a popular upsurge that would lead to the overthrow of capitalism.

The day before Wilson's inauguration, Bloor took part in an eight-thousand-person suffragette march on Washington. Then she headed up to Schenectady, New York, where the residents had elected a socialist mayor and were supporting a citywide strike against General Electric. When the GE workers won, they took up a collection to support other similar actions, to further the worldwide workers' revolution. In Calumet, Michigan, copper miners had been out on strike for almost five months; their families "owned little enough clothing even when the men were working," and they were now "in rags." The workers in Schenectady asked Bloor to carry their donations to the Upper Peninsula.

Mother Bloor saw the Calumet strike as part of what Eugene Debs was calling the battle for America's future: socialism versus capitalism. A few years later, World War I would signal to socialists that the old empires had begun to crumble. Only months after that came the Russian Revolution. Suddenly, as Bloor writes, "In a sixth of the world, workers had power!" Here it was: the time of change—of "new courage and inspiration"—and what happened in Calumet was part of that.

As Bloor explains the history, after the Civil War, a group of "Yankees from Boston" set up a "dummy company" in the wilds of Michigan. Called St. Mary's Land Grant, it was supposed to build a canal in the Upper Peninsula, but Bloor calls the canal "only a worthless ditch, a complete fraud." The real purpose was a land grab. The Boston financiers bought influence with local judges and legislators and eventually gained control of "lands that belonged to the people of Michigan." They then formed the Calumet & Hecla Mining Company and started looking for copper.

To Bloor, Calumet & Hecla was a perfect example of why there had to be a revolution. While the company's stockholders received 400 percent returns on their investment and the general manager of the mine got a salary of $125,000 a year (this in 1913), workers were paid "under a dollar a day." That day began by riding a thousand feet down into ill-lit, poorly ventilated mining shafts. There, the workers spent ten hours manning "widow-makers," 170-pound drills that they held overhead, gouging out rock in search of copper. The strike was for improved working conditions and better pay but especially for union recognition: the workers' right to own the machines.

When Bloor gets to Michigan, just before Christmas, she goes straight from the train station to union headquarters. She knocks on the door, and a woman's voice asks her for identification. Bloor shows a red Socialist Party card, and the door opens to reveal "a big fine looking Slav girl" called Annie Clemenc. Grinning at the red card, Big Annie says, "I have one of those, too."

After delivering the funds from Schenectady, Bloor decided she'd stay a few days and help. The ladies auxiliary had organized a Christmas party for the kids of striking miners. It was held in Italian Hall, "a big room up a long flight of stairs." There they set up a tree, and the children gathered, singing songs and getting presents. As Bloor describes it, a "little tow-headed Finnish girl of about 13, with long braids down her back," had just sat down to play the piano, "when a man pushed the door open and shouted: 'Fire!'

"There was no fire. But at the cry the children started to rush out of the hall in terror. . . . We around the platform did not realize how many had gone. . . . We tried to keep the entertainment going. The little girl kept playing."

Then a man came in carrying "a little limp figure in his arms." It was the first of many. "Little bodies [were laid] in a row on the platform beneath the Christmas tree. There were seventy-three of them. I can hardly tell about it or think about it even today. . . .

"What happened was this," Bloor continues. "In the panic," as the crowd rushed for the exit, a man with a child had fallen in the stairwell. The force of the fall threw the child out the ground floor exit doors. Outside stood a group of citizen deputies: enemies of the strike. "They themselves," Bloor declares, "had raised the cry of 'Fire!'"

Now, "someone," Bloor writes, "it was never known who . . . quickly closed the [exit] door, and both doors were held shut from the outside, so that no one could get out." The adults and children tripped and piled on top of one another. "The staircase was made an air-tight coffin pen," Bloor concludes, "by those who wanted to create panic and disaster in order to discredit the union."

"Afterwards," she continues, "I saw the marks of children's nails in the plaster, where they had desperately scratched to get free, as they suffocated."

Bloor includes the Calumet tragedy in her autobiography, *We Are Many*. She places it in a chapter beside her description of another miners' strike in Ludlow, Colorado, a year later. Miners' children were killed there, too, and the two stories form a chapter she calls "Massacre of the Innocents." In Bloor's vision—the socialist vision—the seventy-three who died at Italian Hall were martyrs in the battle for the future.

And that's how Guthrie read it, years later. He took the title to his song, "1913 Massacre," from Bloor, and it followed her description down to the smallest detail. It was, as he put it, "based word for word in the truth of bloody trade union history."

Except there are different versions of the history. The way they told it in the Upper Peninsula, the story began with pigs.

Everyone knew there was copper in Keweenaw. The hills that rose out of the swampy birch and tamarack forests were dotted with old Indian mines, some dating back four thousand years. Back in 1640, a returning traveler told the French government, "In Lake

Superior there is a great island . . . where there is a beautiful mine of copper . . . found in various places in large pieces, all refined." A century and a half later, when the area came under US control, the question remained how to get at it. As Patrick Henry told Congress, "The entire region is beyond the most distant wilderness and remote as the moon."

At the time, the whole of Michigan held fewer than nine thousand citizens, and the Territory was less interested in the Upper Peninsula than in laying claim to the valuable southern port of Toledo. The UP, after all, was sixteen thousand square miles of boggy wetland and ancient rock outcroppings. It extends out from Wisconsin on the west and is just a river-width away from Canada in the east; Michigan would have gladly let either claim it. But in 1837, when the territory became a state, it finally, grudgingly, accepted what it described as a "sterile region . . . destined by soil and climate to remain forever a wilderness."

Three years later, the state's first official geologist, Douglass Houghton, confirmed that the region held "rich and abundant ores of copper," but warned that it would take "skill, money and organization" to extract it. "I cannot fail to have before me the fear that it may prove the ruin of hundreds of adventurers. . . ." Plus, there was the problem of ownership.

The Chippewa still retained their rights to the land. Settlers moved in through a combination of "bullets, rum, and treaties, hardly worth the paper their terms were written on. . . ." In 1842's Treaty of La Pointe, the Chippewa ceded twenty-five thousand square miles to the US government. One of the provisions required that "The Indians residing on the Mineral district, shall be subject to removal therefrom at the pleasure of the President of the United States." When the last *i* was dotted, the Chippewa nation was reduced to about thirty-two square miles of reservation.

The spring after the Treaty of La Pointe was signed, as soon as the weather broke, hundreds of would-be miners stampeded in. It was like the land rush in Oklahoma, but here, prospectors traveled by dogsled, carrying basic supplies, hoping to stake claims quickly and worry about food and materials later. The US War Department was under orders to lease, not sell, land, and what followed was confusion at best, with prospectors staking overlapping claims and companies trying to cut deals.

UP copper was easy enough to find. In a lot of cases, all you had to do was clear some brush or dig a shallow trench. This "mass copper" turned up in solid chunks, from tiny reddish-gold bits to balls larger than a man's head, and almost 100 percent pure. But getting it to market was another thing. Copper is gummy. To split a chunk of mass copper into a manageable unit, it had to be hammered over and over again along the same line, one man holding the chisel, another swinging the sledge. Once divided, it then had to be hauled out of the wilderness. The mosquitoes and blackflies were so thick in the summer you could barely see, and most work had to stop by early fall as temperatures dropped to five degrees below zero. Winter would dump as much as thirty feet of snow on what passed for roads.

And that was for mass copper, the quickest and easiest to cash in on. Most of the Keweenaw lode—roughly three-quarters—was in "stamp rock," a mix of sand and stone. Only a percentage of stamp rock was copper, but there were huge seams of it underground. To get at it, shafts had to be dug, supported with timbers, then drained of groundwater that kept seeping in. Once the shafts were considered safe, men descended into a profound darkness. What light there was came from a tallow candle stuck to your hat. It flickered in the faint air that found its way down from above.

In that airless dark, workers swung picks and hammers. When you hit a section that wouldn't come away easily, you had to drill a blasting hole, hand-driving a chisel some four feet in. Then you'd pack the hole with black powder, light the fuse, and run back up the dark shaft. A roar, followed by deafening silence. After the dust and gravel had settled, you shoveled the loose rock into carts and hauled it to the surface.

Once aboveground, stamp rock had to be broken down. You

transported it to a stamping mill or "rock house," where it was fed into a mortar box and crushed over and over till it was in fine grains. The debris was then flooded with water: the heavier copper sinking while the crushed rock dust got leached out. Finally, the copper was melted down at the smelter, refined, and formed into bricks; the bricks barreled up and hauled to the lakefront; the barrels loaded onto ships; the ships sailed across Lake Superior, through the canal, and out to market.

That anybody kept at it was a testimony to the richness of Keweenaw's lode. And to the power, some would argue, of the American system. Capitalism might have its evils, but it drove men forward. Within four years of the first land rush, Michigan's Upper Peninsula was producing over 70 percent of all US copper. Or, more accurately, big business was.

Because it wasn't "the people" who organized Michigan's copper industry. In the prospector's dream, a guy could make it alone. He could break away from the pack, stake a claim, and make a fortune. While that vision of the future may have seemed plausible with surface copper, to get at the true wealth, hundreds of feet down, to extract and refine and get it to market, you needed capital. Four years after the land rush, over a hundred mining companies had registered land, but only a few had actually sunk shafts. Some prospectors lingered until seven years after the land rush; then news came of gold in California, and most packed up their kits and headed west. There they became forty-niners, still chasing the dream, still trying to beat the system—boomchasers.

Mother Bloor's version of the story has East Coast industrialists stealing copper that rightfully belonged to the citizens of Michigan. Others saw it as simply how the system worked: civilizing the frontier with the assistance and approval of the government. Through a bill called the Swamp Land Act, federal authorities gave the state of Michigan control of over five and a half million acres of "swamp and overflowed lands, made unfit for cultivation." That land was to be used as a reward for private individuals and businesses that improved the wilderness—which meant building roads and bridges and canals.

So in 1852, Congress granted Michigan 750,000 acres to build a ship canal connecting Lake Superior to the lower Great Lakes. The state, in turn, contracted out the job to the St. Mary's Falls Ship Canal Company, based in New York. Here was Bloor's "dummy company" and "worthless ditch." The canal opened the region to trade: during the decade, population rose from little more than a thousand to almost fourteen thousand. In return, the corporation became the owner of a vast stretch of the Upper Peninsula, some of which contained copper.

Enter Edwin J. Hulbert and (maybe) the pigs.

Hulbert was born in the UP. Son of one of the region's settlers, nephew of one of its early surveyors, he was raised five hundred miles southeast in Detroit. After graduating from what would become the University of Michigan, Hulbert spent a summer prospecting in Keweenaw with no luck. He returned to Detroit, where he got a job copying topographical maps. A "swarthy man, sinewy of limb and silent withal," he was back in Keweenaw by 1858, this time as a road surveyor for the state. The twenty-nine-year-old's professed goal was "to attain the dignity of a mine engineer." It's a modification of the prospector's dream: he still planned to strike it rich, but through or in partnership with the corporate system.

The way the Upper Peninsula version of the story goes, one of Hulbert's neighbors lost some pigs one day and asked for help finding them. Hulbert spotted the herd trapped in a large, bowl-shaped depression covered with brush. It looked to him like one of the old Indian mines. He scouted the area and, a thousand feet away, found a seven-by-nine-foot boulder of almost pure, high-grade copper. He took it as evidence of a major underground lode.

Hulbert's find stood on part of the St. Marys River Canal compensation and was now owned by something called the St. Mary's Mineral Land Company, offices on State Street in Boston. As Hulbert later wrote, "[T]hey would have held my discovery for their own benefit, paying perhaps one or two brass farthings for my study and search, and then 'good afternoon.'" If he was going to beat the system, it would take secrecy and patience.

A year later, he returned, alone. Though he didn't find any more copper or, for that matter, evidence of Indian mining, his geological training convinced him he was walking above a great frozen lava flow saturated with ore. Projecting a line from the pit to the boulder, he calculated a vein that continued to an adjoining two thousand acres. These were available, and he put down his deposit.

Hulbert now owned what he hoped was the right land, but he still needed capital to sink shafts, and capital was in the East. In 1861, as the Civil War was beginning, Hulbert went to Boston to strike a deal. He found what we might now call venture capitalists. By deeding them three-quarters of his newly acquired property, he bankrolled the Hulbert Mining Company. Then war interrupted. "Everyone supposed the end had come," wrote one Upper Peninsula resident, "that the mines must close down—that nothing was left to do but shoulder the musket and march to the South." Hulbert shouldered, marched, and quietly waited.

The Civil War was a boon to the North's economy and to the copper industry in particular. Armies needed cannons, cartridges, buttons, canteens. Copper prices rose from around eighteen cents a pound in 1861 to over forty-six cents by 1864. Though the vast majority of the region's early copper companies—eighty-six of ninety-four—never paid a dividend, a couple had managed to survive and now prospered. There was the Pittsburgh and Boston company at the northern end of the peninsula, and at the southern end, the Minesota Mining Company (misspelled by some busy clerk). With the war, these and companies like Quincy Mining started paying healthy dividends to their East Coast backers.

The problem was labor. The larger companies had been hiring skilled Cornish miners, the "immigrant elite," whose ancestors had helped make Cornwall the source for two-thirds of the world's copper. But the mines needed unskilled labor, too, and with so many

Americans pulled into the military, the owners imported Swedes, Norwegians, Finns. Speaking little to no English, the immigrants signed contracts that guaranteed passage. Few noticed that a monthly fee would be garnished from wages to pay for the trip. The contracts also stipulated that, due to the wartime currency shortage, wages would be paid in company scrip, negotiable only at company stores. When the new workers understood what they'd signed, "defiantly," as one historian put it, "many reneged on their contracts. They said they were not slaves and could not be made to work."

Hulbert got back to Keweenaw in 1862 and spent the rest of the war supervising various mines. Then in July 1864—eight months before the Confederacy surrendered—he returned to his boulder, relieved to find his secret safe. After getting the Boston backers to buy another two hundred acres, he gave his brother, John, a map and instructions to dig an exploratory pit at what would become the site of the Hecla mine.

Edwin, meanwhile, explored the area near his boulder. He found some twenty tons of pure mass copper at the surface, as well as preserved deerskins, sheets of birch bark, and oblong Chippewa baskets. But there was no sign of a prehistoric mine or of any more copper. Instead, the bowl-like depression turned out to be a storage unit. Apparently natives had mined copper elsewhere, stashed it here, and never come back.

Hulbert always maintained that he'd discovered his lode scientifically, but there had been no Indian mine, and it was pretty much luck that the ancient hiding place had a copper lode underneath it. To locals, the pigs became a symbol of that luck, of the prospector's dream that anyone could hit it big, that the little guy could beat the system, that you could stumble into a depression and come out with a copper mine.

The Hulbert Mining Company uncovered surface rock that was about 15 percent copper and, below ground, a dark red conglomerate that was 5 percent copper—more than double the richness of any other lode in the area. They sent a barrel of samples east, convincing their backers to place more acreage into a company called Calumet Mining and to form a third company, Hecla Mining, for land they might yet buy.

Then the war ended, and copper prices started a fall that continued into 1870. Stock in Michigan mines was hawked on the street and out in the backwoods as low as a dollar a share. When Hulbert asked for more investment to start large-scale operations, his backers backed off. He went East to argue his case, but got nowhere. Searching for a "delivering angel," he found his way to Quin Shaw and something called the Boston Associates.

Here are Mother Bloor's "Yankees from Boston." Here's how nineteenth-century capitalism worked.

Quincy Adams Shaw inherited a family fortune that began with an early nineteenth-century trader, Samuel Parkman. Parkman's import/export operation included everything from tar to snuff to women's shoes. One of his main commodities was human beings. When Congress banned the importing of slaves in 1808, merchants like Parkman looked for safe alternative investments. Starting in 1813, one group began following the lead of Robert Cabot Lowell, putting their money into textile mills that would turn raw cotton from the South into finished cloth. As one of the investors, Amos Lawrence, put it, cotton mills were a way to invest their fortunes with "*reasonable* assurance."

The Lawrence/Lowell/Cabot group became known as the Boston Associates, creators of America's first organized industrial system. By 1825, they'd built huge brick mills, created towns they named after themselves—Lawrence and Lowell, Massachusetts—and were realizing more than a 25 percent dividend.

But the Boston Associates saw themselves as doing more than making a profit. Their mills employed mostly young single women from the now mined-out New England farms. Textile jobs might be twelve hours a day, six days a week, but compared to farmwork, they were relatively safe, clean, and well paying. If the girls were thrifty, they could save enough for a dowry. Where Mother Bloor saw

exploiters of labor, the Boston Associates saw themselves as patri-
archs, helping create a new, more equitable, industrial America.

Profits from the Lawrence and Lowell mills stayed high till the
1850s. Then competition began to glut the market. Soon wages
were cut, and immigrants—mostly Irish—displaced the farm girls.
The post–Civil War generation of the Boston Associates—Quin
Shaw's generation—began looking for other places to invest. Shaw
had already put some money into Michigan copper mines. If it was
riskier than textiles, copper held the potential for even larger profits.
Shaw struck a deal with Edwin Hulbert where the local man still
controlled a majority of shares, but Boston held the financial power.

That first summer, it became clear the operation would need
even more capital, and Shaw upped the assessment on both the Calumet and the Hecla stocks. Local investors, including Hulbert, were
hard-pressed to come up with the extra cash. Even as his brother,
John, started to develop Hecla Number 1, Edwin was pushing to
get the maximum out of the nearby Calumet lode—and quickly.
He needed the money to keep his shares, and he needed to convince
Shaw that this was a going concern.

At first, the Hulbert brothers just took the mass copper off the
surface. Hulbert had promised Shaw he'd dig proper shafts to get
at the stamp rock and long-term profits. But that was slow, labor-
intensive work. They'd need timbermen to set up interior supports,
others to create a drainage system, ventilation, "cages" to transport
miners down and rails to bring the rock back up. Plus, steam engines
to power the whole operation. Hulbert had also promised an on-site
smelter, but he didn't make much progress on any of this. Instead,
as the little town of Red Jacket grew up around the mine opening,
the Hulberts continued to focus on the mass copper, carting it by
horse-drawn wagon to a smelter in Hancock, thirteen miles away.

Back in Boston, Shaw decided he needed eyes and ears in Keweenaw.
He asked his thirty-one-year-old brother-in-law, Alexander Agassiz,
to go west. Agassiz's qualifications included degrees in zoology, natural history, and civil engineering, but his only practical experience had

been overseeing a coal mine in Pennsylvania—which had failed. Still, he agreed to spend a month in the wilderness of the Upper Peninsula.

What he saw convinced him that the Calumet and Hecla lodes were going to make someone a fortune. But not the way Edwin Hulbert was going about it. When Agassiz got back to Boston, Shaw made him treasurer of the operation. Then the two of them agreed to raise the stock assessment again, and then again: by three dollars, then another five. That brought in more capital and, maybe more important, priced out the local Michigan investors.

The way the Boston investors told the story, Edwin Hulbert was too focused on short-term gain, hadn't kept his promises, had "lost his head." Agassiz was even fiercer: Hulbert was on a "suicidal course." The local Keweenaw version, on the other hand, was closer to Mother Bloor's: that the Bostonians had seen a good thing and were trying to grab it. Six months after Agassiz's visit, Shaw fired Hulbert and made his brother-in-law superintendent of the mines. Hulbert would sue. And he remained bitter the rest of his life, accusing Quin Shaw of being "a man who was not activated by principles of justice nor honor."

But Shaw was out to turn a profit. And so was Alexander Agassiz, although he claimed the mines were more a means to an end. Agassiz's true passion was science. He worked for his father at Boston's first natural history museum and had already published a monograph on starfish. But the museum job barely paid: he, his young wife, their four-year-old son, and a newborn had to live at his parents' house. When Agassiz met a friend on the street in Cambridge that fall, he declared, "I am going to Michigan for some years as superintendent of the Calumet and Hecla mines. I want to make some money; it is impossible to be a productive naturalist in this country without money."

Agassiz had been born in Switzerland, the son of an internationally known naturalist, his mother a scientific illustrator and hostess to a constant stream of distinguished visitors, the family home stuffed with specimens. To keep his research going, Alex's father,

Louis Agassiz, depended on patrons like the King of Prussia. When young Alex refused to salute the Prussian governor, his father caned him. There were, after all, rules and hierarchies in the world, and a boy had to learn to respect them.

When Alex was ten, his parents separated. Mother and children moved to Germany; father accepted a grant from the King of Prussia and headed to America. There, he's said to have "taken the Boston Brahmins by storm." He gave a series of sold-out public lectures on "The Plan of Creation in the Animal Kingdom." With his thick French accent, his broad-brimmed black hat, and a habit of smoking cigars at the podium, Agassiz was the exotic European expert. He quickly became, according to Ralph Waldo Emerson, "fat and plenteous as some successful politician." He was part theoretician (the first to propose the idea of an ice age), part popularizer, part fundraiser. William James, one of Agassiz's students, decided, "There is more charlatanerie and humbug about him and solid worth too, than you often meet with."

After a little over a year, Abbott Lawrence, of the Lawrence textile works in Lawrence, Massachusetts, gave Harvard the largest donation it had ever received from a living donor: $50,000, to create the Lawrence Science School. Louis Agassiz was named director. That summer, he led a research expedition to Lake Superior and Michigan's Upper Peninsula. He noted, in passing, the "very remarkable circumstance that the largest masses of native copper should occur upon Point Keweenaw." Then he headed back to Boston with boxes and barrels of specimens: the beginnings of what he hoped would be a world-class natural history museum.

When Agassiz arrived in the East, he learned that his wife had died. He sent for his children: Alex—thirteen, a "quiet, steady" boy, "prone to melancholy"—and Alex's two younger sisters. By the time they got to America, their father, forty-one, was courting Elizabeth Cabot Carey, twenty-six and a member of the younger generation of Boston Associates.

Like Quin Shaw's fortune, Lizzie's money can be traced back

to slavery. Her grandfather, Colonel T. H. Perkins, had been a successful slave merchant with a base in Haiti. After that trade was banned, he switched focus to China, where he'd turned as much as $50,000 profit on a single shipload of opium. Colonel Perkins was simultaneously known as "Boston's wealthiest merchant" and a man who "had never indulged his conscience till he could afford it." He eventually invested his gains in the Boston Associates' textile mills, as did Lizzie's cousins, the Cabots. On the other side of her family, the Careys had begun by running plantations in the West Indies but had "long been associated with the Lowell mills," as one historian puts it, "where profits depended upon low-cost cotton produced by slave labor."

Soon, Louis Agassiz had married into this fortune. And his children extended the ties. Alex's sister Pauline was nineteen when she married Quin Shaw, twenty years her senior. That same year, having graduated from Harvard, Alex married Anna Russell, daughter of "a prominent textile merchant." Three years later, Alex's other sister, Ida, married Henry Lee Higginson, who would become one of the city's leading investment bankers. Finally, Alex's best friend and Harvard classmate, Theodore Lyman, married Elizabeth Russell, the sister of Alex's wife. The Lymans' fortune fit the Boston Associates pattern: a merchant ancestor who diversified into textiles and railroads. Further thickening the interconnections, Lyman's sister married Quin Shaw's brother. If textile manufacturing was America's first industrial system, this knot of Boston families produced its first merchant kings and in Alex and Quin's generation its princes and princesses.

Louis Agassiz's constant fund-raising paid off. When Alex was twenty-two, his father opened the Harvard Museum of Comparative Zoology, popularly known as the Agassiz Museum. Soon he was lining its dark halls with his personal collection of specimens. His goal was to create "as complete a library of the works of God as it is humanly possible to make. . . ."

The museum was dedicated in June 1859. That November *The*

Origin of Species was published and within a month was, as Alexander's classmate Henry Adams wrote, "convulsing society." In the fight that followed, Louis Agassiz became America's best known anti-Darwinian. Professor Agassiz believed species were fixed; he called them "categories of thought in the Supreme Intelligence." By displaying specimens from all over the world, the Agassiz Museum would demonstrate the "intelligent and intelligible connections between the facts of nature [as] direct proof of the existence of a thinking God." Now his lectures drew even larger crowds. Here was America's scientific hero defending religion against Darwin's blasphemies.

In the battle Mother Bloor cared about—socialism versus capitalism—she considered Darwin to be on her side: a radical. *The Origin of Species* argued that the world was made of change, that Agassiz's carefully labeled specimens, organized by family and subfamily, weren't God's plan at all but man's, a convenient way for one species to make sense of others. Darwin convulsed society, in part, because if this was the truth, there were implications far beyond science. The theory of evolution suggested that the fortunes of people like the Boston Associates hadn't been divinely ordained, that no one was born to win, that the rich didn't automatically have God on their side, that nature was democratic.

Professor Agassiz called *The Origin of Species* "truly monstrous." It was shot through with a lack of respect for established hierarchy, but he was especially bothered by the racial implications. In his opinion, Negroes and whites had separate and unequal origins. "The brain of the Negro," he wrote when he came to America and saw his first black man, "is that of a seven month's infant in the womb of a White." It was perfectly clear, he wrote in 1863, that "the different races do not rank upon one level in nature." There were the "indomitable, courageous, proud Indian" and the "submissive, obsequious, imitative negro." He saw interbreeding—the mixing of God's categories—as "immoral and destructive" and thought "universal equality" threatened "the acquisitions of individual eminence, the wealth of refinement and culture. . . ." Darwin's idea undermined the very organization of society, and Agassiz was determined that his museum would be "a fortress against evolution."

It followed that he opposed the Civil War. An educated liberal man, he believed slavery an abomination. At the same time, it was "misguided" to think "that the future of the white race is with that of the black race." He not only forbade his students from enlisting in the war, he got furious if they even discussed it. At best, he thought the Civil War a huge inconvenience that could "cripple the advance of science in the new world."

His in-laws, the Boston Associates, mostly agreed. Known as Cotton Whigs, their textile mills depended on what one commentator called an alliance "between the lords of the lash and the lords of the loom." And as major donors to Harvard, their opinion helped determine the university's position on the war. As Emerson wrote about his alma mater: "Harvard College has no voice in Harvard College, but State Street votes it down on every ballot. Everything will be permitted which goes to adorn Boston Whiggism. . . ."

The younger generation was a little different. Sister Ida's husband, Henry Lee Higginson, fought in the war and was a fierce abolitionist. He'd go on to buy a plantation in the newly defeated South to demonstrate "that Free negro labor could be profitably and pleasantly employed." Alex claimed to be torn. "I am ashamed," he wrote when he was at prime draft age, "and have been ashamed any longer to stay home. And yet what is to become of father, if I go? I know the museum (no, not the museum) but father will go to thunder if I don't stay and hold on to his coat tails."

By this time, a lot of his father's students had left because of the professor's autocratic ways, his stand against the war, and because his refusal to consider evolution was making his science more and more outdated. The museum had become "rather a store-house," as Professor Agassiz admitted, "than a well-arranged scientific collection." The barrels and boxes were sitting in storage, unopened: for just one example, some twenty thousand lobsters and shrimp. Alex's father called it "a scientific fortune . . . an immense capital lying un-used." But it was only a fortune if you had real capital to catalogue, to employ researchers, to keep the museum open. During the war, with his father on an extended expedition in Brazil, Alex managed to keep the operation going only by putting the family house and library up as collateral.

Henry Adams called Alexander Agassiz "unrivalled" in their generation for "physical energy, social standing, mental scope and training, wit, geniality, and science. . . ." But by the time he ac-cepted Quin Shaw's offer, he'd learned, as Adams pointed out, that his chosen career of science "was helpless without money." Having grown up watching his father use "charlatanerie and humbug" in a constant search for donations, he refused to do that—or to depend on his wife's money.

Instead, in March 1867, he rode a train to the end of the line—Green Bay, Wisconsin—then spent days driving north on a dogsled till he arrived at what he considered "the unknown primeval forest" of the Keweenaw Peninsula. He was going to create the future that Guthrie—and Bob Dylan—would inhabit.

MEN POSSESSED
BY ANGER

When Woody Guthrie arrived in California in 1937, age twenty-four, he wasn't particularly opposed to capitalism. He wasn't even very political. What he wanted was a job.

The way he tells it in *Bound for Glory*, his political thinking changed on that freezing freight. When he jumped off it in Sonora, it was because his aunt lived there and he was hoping she'd put him up and maybe help him find work. In his autobiographical novel, he gets to her door but then turns away. It has to do with his new politics: "This wasn't what I'd hung that boxcar for. My belly is hard from hard traveling, and I want more than anything else for my belly to stay hard and stay wound up tight and stay alive."

That's Woody Guthrie the idol: stay hard, keep traveling, go it alone. Except the facts seem to be that he not only knocked on the door but stayed, and then rode down to Glendale with his relatives. And they did help him find a job.

His cousin Jack Guthrie was a handsome, blue-eyed, smooth-voiced tenor, three years younger than Woody. Known as "Oklahoma" or "Okie," his ambition was to be a singing cowboy. He'd bought a spangled Western suit and a white silk handkerchief; now all he needed was a partner. Woody signed on.

Peel back the myth, and you find both Guthrie and Dylan spent their childhoods in relatively prosperous, supportive, Middle

American families. Both ended up sounding like the people, in the words of one of Guthrie's songs, "on the edge of your cities." And both developed that sound in major music markets. Dylan went to New York City, the center of the folk revival, Guthrie to what one music historian has called "the mecca for country entertainers."

In Los Angeles, when Guthrie arrived in 1937, musical categories were mutating. What was labeled hillbilly had begun to incorporate the idea of the Old West. The fad of the day was singing cowboys. Every radio station in the city seemed to feature a cowboy group or two, and the trend had already spread to the movies.

The original singing cowboy, the man who'd pioneered this path to success, was Gene Autry. Born in 1907 in Texas, raised in Oklahoma, Orven Grover Autry picked cotton, played in patent medicine shows, and became a Western Union operator for the railroads. The story goes that Will Rogers went to send a telegraph and discovered the young Autry sitting at his desk, singing. It wasn't true, but Autry encouraged it: like Guthrie, he cherished any connection to the great Rogers.

In fact, Autry saved his wages and made his own way, first to New York City. There he cut a couple of tunes that went nowhere, returning home to appear on local radio as Oklahoma's Yodeling Cowboy. Autry wanted to be Jimmie Rodgers, the hillbilly star whose records were outselling the Carter Family's five to one. Rodgers's style was a hybrid: a tenant farmer's voice over music that swung like the blues and often featured yodeling that could be traced back via minstrel shows to the Swiss Alps. All this delivered by a white Mississippian dressed in a railroad brakeman's uniform. It was the sound of displacement, of Southerners finding their way out of the Old South to the Old West—Oklahoma and Texas—meeting and mixing with new cultures as they went. Call it post-Confederate music.

Autry modeled himself on Jimmie Rodgers, Guthrie more on the Carters, but you can hear how similar their beginnings are. In his early recordings, Autry emphasizes his Oklahoma twang, as if to nail down his credentials as the real thing. Six years older than

Guthrie, Autry returned to New York around the time Woody was playing with his hillbilly band in Pampa. The year Guthrie wrote "Dusty Old Dust," Autry was cutting his own version of what would later be called folk music: a political tune, "The Death of Mother Jones." It describes Jones as "a noble leader of labor" who "fought for right and justice" and "received a hearty welcome in every mining town." Here Autry's delivery sounds a lot like the style Guthrie came to: plain hard-edged singing over a simple strummed guitar. The song ends with Autry hoping, in Mother Jones's memory, that there might be "better conditions for every laboring man."

But the song didn't do much, and Autry eventually broke through by going in another direction. By the time Jimmie Rodgers died in 1933, the Depression had pushed migrating Southerners even farther west, into California. The Confederacy was still a proud memory for many, but it was a couple of generations old, and the Western landscape had begun to look like a new beginning. During a stay in Chicago, Autry started to sing more about, as he put it, "sagebrush and tumbleweeds." He admitted, "That sort of stuff didn't sound very glamorous to me, as my recollections of ranch life included aching muscles and endless days in the sun and dust." But he sensed there was a career to be made in "bright talk of the wind-swept plains, of coyote howls in the moonlight, and cowboys on galloping horses."

The result was less down-to-earth than Jimmie Rodgers—or Mother Jones. As Autry changed his subject matter, his delivery got mellow—more crooner than railroad man—and the arrangements began to feature strings and silkiness. Not far beneath the frontier settings of hits like "Tumbling Tumbleweeds" and "Mexicali Rose" were sophisticated pop songs. By the time he cut his theme, "Back in the Saddle Again," he was sounding like a cowboy version of Bing Crosby. And his vision of the future had become Hollywood's Wild West.

In this new, imaginary landscape, "a friend is a friend," "the only law is right," and though there's often a dusky forbidden love from south of the border, the cowboy always seems to end up "lonely but free." The movies Autry went on to make follow the same themes. The round-faced, genial-looking Autry became a good guy in a spotless white cowboy hat, a jaunty bandanna, glittering Mexican-style jackets. His characters didn't talk about the defeated South, the Depression, or the Dust Bowl. If they had a past, it was usually a secret: they appeared out of nowhere and rode off into the sunset. By turning the singing brakeman into the singing cowboy, Autry created a prototype for everyone from John Wayne to Garth Brooks.

The image and the music weren't particularly authentic. The high lonesome of a pedal steel guitar, for example, was Western only if the West included Hawaii, where it came from. But singers and producers and audiences agreed: pedal steel sounded like the imaginary place where singing cowboys wandered. The hybrid sound made Autry one of the best-selling artists of the midtwentieth century. By the time his biggest hit made the charts after World War II, the public had accepted his down-home cowboy delivery as the definition of sincerity. Never mind that it made "Rudolph, the Red-Nosed Reindeer" sound like he grazed on sagebrush.

Jack Guthrie wanted to be Gene Autry. When he and Woody teamed up, "Oklahoma" had already been in California five years. He was good looking, played a smooth guitar, and had learned to yodel and croon. In the spring of 1937, the duo booked their first public performance. A month later, they got a tryout on a small radio station and landed a fifteen-minute show at 8:00 each morning. It didn't pay anything, but they hoped the exposure would help them book gigs. They called it *The Oklahoma and Woody Show*. Oklahoma was the star, the singing cowboy, with Woody acting the sidekick, adding a little harmony, playing rhythm guitar.

The station, KFVD, could be heard for about five hundred miles: on a good day, that meant north past San Francisco and east into Nevada and Arizona. Within a few months, the show was doing well enough for the station manager to switch it to a more popular nighttime slot. That also made it easier for Oklahoma to keep his

day job, working construction. As part of the deal, the station offered Woody (who had no day job) their former morning slot. Here
was his chance to become a solo artist, a singing cowboy himself.

He had the chops. Listen to his version of Jimmie Rodgers's
"Muleskinner Blues." Or his smooth, sentimental way of singing the
old ballads his mother loved: "Pictures from Life's Other Side," "Put
My Little Shoes Away." And he could muster the looks, judging by
the early publicity shots of his country band in Pampa: the Corncob
Trio dressed either in respectable shirt and tie or in full singing-
cowboy regalia, complete with bandanna, white cowboy hat, chaps.

Guthrie was maybe a little too rough-sounding, too small, too
dark for the part, but as it turned out, he had the advantage of being able to write a country-and-western hit. Not long after team-
ing with Oklahoma, Woody borrowed the melody from a nostalgic
turn-of-the-century number, "The Girl I Loved in Sunny Tennessee," switched the lyrics to fit a romanticized version of his own past,
and came up with "Oklahoma Hills." It might as well have been
a Gene Autry song, the singer trading in his home "in the Indian
Nation" for his new occupation, a cowboy's life. Cousin Jack's version, with its catchy swing tune and calming lyrics, would become a
country-and-western hit in 1945. A few years later, Guthrie's friends
the Maddox Brothers and Rose, rode Woody's "Philadelphia Lawyer" up the country charts. A loping redo of a tune called "Jealous
Love," its story line comes from a newspaper clipping: a "gun-totin'
cowboy" returns from riding the range to find that a lawyer has
been wooing his "Hollywood maid;" the cowboy shoots the lawyer
dead.

If you were a hillbilly singer in Los Angeles, the singing cowboy
route offered a way up and out. For one thing, it was a lot more
respectable—and safer—than being looked upon as an Okie. As the
Depression kicked in, migrants out of the Southwest had begun arriving in California at a rate of twelve hundred to fifteen hundred a
day. By the end of the thirties, there were some 1.3 million, about
a quarter of the state's population. *Business Week* called it "one of

the greatest inter-State migrations since the gold rush." The back-lash was fierce. The year before Guthrie caught his freezing freight, the L.A. Chamber of Commerce set up border patrols to turn back "transients." An anti-Okie law was passed threatening anyone who transported "indigents" with six months in prison, and a petition opposing migrant housing got a hundred thousand signatures. As the *San Francisco Chronicle* put it, "We must stop this migration or surrender to chaos and ruin." There was talk of "white trash" and "half breeds" and "migrant hordes."

A lot of the opposition came from former migrants who'd worked their way to middle-class status and joined the American Legion, the Lions, the Kiwanis clubs. They planned to blend in, to achieve the dream you could hear in Gene Autry's croon. Maybe the world of good guys in white hats was make-believe, but it beat being white trash. For those who saw California as their new home on the range, Okie was a discouraging word, both a threat and a reminder.

So Guthrie had a chance to leave his bad luck behind; the fifteen-minute morning slot might take him from tramp to crooner, from sidekick to main attraction, a singing cowboy. First thing he did was get his own sidekick. A few months earlier, he'd met Maxine Crissman, the dark-haired, skinny daughter of one of Jack's work buddies. Hanging around her family's home, they'd begun to har-monize; twenty-two-year-old Maxine took the low parts—Guthrie described her voice as "rough and husky"—while he went high. Crissman would later call it their "crossnote trademark." It sounded something like the Carter Family: old-timey, reassuring. Now he invited Crissman to join him on the morning slot. They became an act: Woody and Lefty Lou.

Jack Guthrie only lasted a couple of weeks on the night show: it cut into playing dances and other evening gigs. When he gave it up, Woody and Lefty Lou began doing both morning and evening. They mostly sang older, more familiar tunes. Said Crissman: "It was exactly like Sunday-afternoon back-porch singing back home." And that was the idea. Instead of bright talk of windswept plains, Woody and Lefty Lou spoke what Guthrie would later call "workingman's lingo." They sounded, that is, like the migrant hordes.

Their first songbook was called *Woody and Lefty Lou's Old Time Hillbilly Songs: Being Sung for Ages, Still Going Strong.* Not quite the truth: about half the songs came from recent commercial records, including Tin Pan Alley and minstrel tunes. But a quarter of their repertory *was* hillbilly, or what would later be known as folk: public domain numbers their listeners knew from long ago. To fill the rest of their airtime, Guthrie began writing originals that *sounded* old: familiar tunes fitted out with new words, mostly humorous.

The down-home approach might not make them national stars like Autry, but they soon had a devoted local audience that treated them like part of the family, sending not only fan letters but birthday cakes and clothes and homemade cookies. By late 1937, Woody and Lefty Lou had signed a contract that guaranteed them twenty dollars a month plus whatever sponsor's fees they could drum up. It was a good living wage, enough for Guthrie to invite Mary and the kids to leave Pampa and come out.

Listeners recognized their sound as a link to an earlier, rural, pre–Los Angeles life. But some of the Sunday-morning back-porch tunes didn't play the same as they had in Oklahoma and Texas. That fall, Woody performed a song on-air called "Run, Nigger, Run." It seems to have struck him as just another hillbilly song, reflecting the way he'd grown up, the way his father talked, the way a lot of migrants saw the world. So he was startled when he got a letter from a listener: "I am a young Negro in college and I certainly resented your remark. No person, or person of any intelligence uses that word over the radio today. . . ." Guthrie quickly made an apology. It was a sign that, though Woody and Lefty Lou were singing old-timey music, times were changing.

Small, privately owned, KFVD had a radical lean. The owner had been a supporter of author and socialist Upton Sinclair, whose exposé of the meat-packing industry Mother Bloor had helped with and who had run for governor in 1934 on his "End Poverty in

California" platform. Sinclair believed the Depression was a "permanent crisis" brought on by the new machine age. In other words, it wasn't a fluke in the triumphant history of capitalism; it *was* capitalism. As a candidate, he argued that California's million-and-a-quarter unemployed would stay that way unless the basic system changed: the state had to tax the rich and use the proceeds to employ the poor in giant infrastructure and farming projects. Sinclair's vision was a more radical version of FDR's New Deal, and KFVD's listeners tuned in to a station that supported it.

By February 1938, Woody and Lefty Lou were on-air six days a week and receiving about a thousand pieces of fan mail a month. They mixed songs from Guthrie's childhood—like "Gypsy Davy" and the old Southern "Crawdad Song"—with contemporary numbers like Charlie Poole's eccentric "I'm the Man That Rode the Mule around the World." It wasn't singing-cowboy material but migrant stuff, Okie stuff. And Guthrie was busy developing a persona to match.

One of the songs Woody and Lefty Lou did was "Hobo's Lullaby," written in the twenties by Goebel Reeves. Reeves billed himself as the Singing Bum, pretending to be fresh off the rails. Jimmie Rodgers had done something similar when he cut "Hobo's Meditation" and "Hobo Bill's Last Ride," and up in San Francisco, Harry McClintock had been on the radio since 1925, calling himself Haywire Mac and claiming to have written hobo anthems including "Big Rock Candy Mountain" and "Hallelujah, I'm a Bum." Both Reeves and McClintock saw the Bum in political terms: both proudly claimed to be Wobblies, members of the International Workers of the World known as the IWW—that almost mythical "singing union" dating back to Mother Bloor's time.

The idea of the Singing Bum appealed to Guthrie. It offered a chance to talk about how the world looked to someone newly arrived and not particularly welcome. Plus, it left room to be funny.

Around this time, the twenty-five-year-old rewrote a 1931 Carter Family recording, "Can't Feel at Home." The original derived from a Baptist hymn, the kind of dutiful religious song whose melody appealed to Guthrie even as the lyrics irked him. The Carter Family sang about the treasures waiting "somewhere beyond the blue" and how "This is not [our] world;" we're only here temporarily. Guthrie took the notion of "just passing through" and decided there was another side to the picture, the Singing Bum's side. "Reason why you can't feel at home in this world anymore," Guthrie explained, "is mostly because you ain't got no home to feel at."

After speeding up the Carters' melody to jig tempo, he launched his hobo version: "I ain't got no home / I'm just a roamin' round / Just a wanderin' worker / I go from town to town." The singer of Guthrie's song isn't waiting on treasures in heaven; he needs a job, now. And he has a good idea who to blame for not having one: "Rich man took my home / and drove me from my door." That most of his radio listeners would know the Carter Family's "Can't Feel at Home" only added to the bite of Guthrie's version: "I Ain't Got No Home."

He soon found a song form that made a nice fit with this laid-back Singing Bum approach. In 1927, when Woody was fifteen, Christopher Allen Bouchillon had a hit called "Talking Blues." The song was structured as a twangy four-line verse followed by a spoken punch line or two. It was as much conversation as music—the talking blues—and became popular enough for Bouchillon to become known as the Talking Comedian of the South. Guthrie took the structure, applied a little Will Rogers, and vamped on the details of a migrant's life. His "Talking Dust Bowl Blues," for example, is a comic take on a farm family's journey out of the Dust Bowl and over the mountains to California. After engine trouble and roadside accidents, they arrive on the West Coast broke. Its politics are mostly implied, until the last spoken line—about that soup so thin "some of these here politicians coulda seen through it."

Guthrie hadn't come west that way, but he was singing for an audience that had. He didn't consider himself an Okie—his father's former wealth made him "a little bit different"—but he sounded like one. And if he drew out the accent and lengthened the pauses, he became the ultimate Okie, larger than life: "Th' Dustiest of Th' Dustbowlers," as he'd bill himself. Woody's version of the Singing Bum was part Wobbly, part tenant farmer, part drifter. With Lefty Lou playing his sweeter, more level-headed sidekick, they created a sound their audience recognized and loved. Guthrie had found his voice.

They did twice-daily broadcasts for almost a year. Crissman discovered that behind Guthrie's laid-back delivery was some real ambition; he pushed them, even moving the act (briefly) to a Mexican radio station that had more range and a potentially larger audience. At the same time, he shied away from what Lefty Lou called "good money. . . . [W]hen we got into the big time, Woody didn't want any part of it." She'd gone on the radio mostly as a lark, and in June 1938, anemic and tired, she decided she needed a break. Guthrie agreed to take the summer off, but it left him with a wife, two small kids, and no job in the midst of the Great Depression.

The owner of KFVD offered a solution. He was the Southern California campaign manager for Culbert Olson, that fall's Democratic candidate for governor. Olson was a liberal state senator backed by FDR, and the station manager put out a weekly newspaper, *Light*, that endorsed the campaign. He offered Guthrie a job as a reporter, and the singer immediately dubbed himself *Light*'s "hobo correspondent."

It was a joke—his radio personality transposed to a newspaper column—but there was a serious side, too. California had elected Republican governors for forty years. Olson rejected their anti-migrant position, but he also rejected Sinclair's radical redistribution of wealth. Instead, he saw the Okies as a social problem, one you could solve with a liberal agenda. Guthrie set out to investigate this "problem." In essence, that meant visiting his radio audience: dropping in on migrant camps, working in orchards, learning how the Okies lived by living with them. At one point, he even re-created their migration, going back to Okemah to see friends and returning via Route 66, known as the Okie highway.

It changed him, and you can track that change by his language. Okie was a term many migrants disliked, and so did Guthrie, at first. He preferred *hillbilly* as more neutral, less demeaning. Then he'd started to develop his on-air persona and seen how *Okie* could be used to identify with his audience and poke fun at the powers-that-be. Now, during his summer of reporting, Guthrie started to talk and sing about "dustbowl refugees."

Germany had invaded Austria that spring. In July, FDR attended a thirty-two-nation conference to discuss the increasing number of Jewish refugees. To call Okies refugees was to put their situation into that bigger picture, to connect them to others who were being driven from home by political and economic forces. If they were dustbowl refugees, they weren't a local or even a national phenomenon but the result—some argued, the inevitable result—of an economic system.

In a way, Guthrie was late to the cause. Between 1929 and 1935, California had seen a series of strikes that have been called "without precedent in the history of labor in the United States." 1933 was when Congress passed the National Industrial Recovery Act, part of FDR's first hundred days of activism. It gave workers the right to organize and to bargain collectively, essentially making unions legal. In San Francisco, new members strengthened the already radical longshoremen's union, and the strike that followed turned into a general one, including some 140 actions related to farmworkers. Filipino and Mexican pickers had walked off work, affecting crops from the San Joaquin to the Imperial Valley. Protestors carried signs reading, "DISARM THE RICH FARMER or ARM THE WORKER FOR SELF-DEFENSE."

California newspapers called it a "Communist Party conspiracy." In 1929, the Communist Party USA (CPUSA) had formed something called the Trade Union Unity League. "Whenever a strike was reported," one reporter noted, "or wherever a strike was rumored, they would appear and attempt to organize the workers." As the organizing spread, the mass meetings started to be met by mass arrests.

Strikers were tear-gassed, their tents and belongings burned, and as a founding member of California's Communist Party wrote, "The Imperial Valley assumed the appearance of an armed camp."

While Guthrie was still in Pampa playing in his cowboy band and telling fortunes, John Steinbeck published *In Dubious Battle*, a novel about the 1933 agricultural workers strike and its causes. "It's anger," he has one character say, "that's what it is . . . Ever place I go, it's like water just before it gets to boilin'." Another explains, "My whole family has been ruined by the system."

For his follow-up, Steinbeck had begun researching what would become *The Grapes of Wrath*. At the same time, photographer Dorothea Lange was making her piercing images of migrant families. And journalist Carey McWilliams was investigating working conditions for a nonfiction exposé, *Factories in the Field*. All before Guthrie arrived on the scene.

McWilliams went back in history to find the origins of the migrant "problem." He traced it to post–Civil War industrialism. Around the time Eastern investors were taking over Edwin Hulbert's copper claim, California was dividing its land into large grants. By 1871, economist Henry George observed "the land of California is already to a great extent monopolized by a few individuals. . . . [It is not] a country of farms, but a country of plantations and estates."

The same way the copper bosses in Michigan needed miners (and the land barons in Oklahoma needed tenant farmers), California's big estates needed seasonal pickers. A large peach orchard might have twenty year-round workers, but that would balloon to two thousand at harvest time. These were McWilliams's "factories in the field," part of the shift from the family farm to corporate agribusiness, a preview of the future. "California is very important to me," Karl Marx wrote in 1880, "because nowhere else has the upheaval most shamelessly caused by capitalist centralization taken place with such speed."

The growers first took their workforce from the Native American population, but it was too decimated by war and disease. Soon they started importing Japanese, Mexicans, Filipinos. Immigrants had the advantage (to the owners) of being noncitizens: you could pay them minimal wages, move them from harvest to harvest, and they were too poor and too worried about deportation to protest. Then came the organizers, communist and otherwise, and the immigrant work force was suddenly striking for better conditions.

Enter the Okies. Or as Steinbeck called them in a series of reports for the *San Francisco Chronicle*, the "Harvest Gypsies." McWilliams—who may have coined the term "dust-bowl refugees"—believed their arrival amounted to "a day of reckoning . . . for the California farm industrialists." Because they were white, English-speaking, American-born, Okies came to California expecting a fair deal. They might have to start on the bottom, do day labor beside Mexican pickers, but they were US citizens and had a chance, maybe even a right, to get ahead.

At first, California seemed to agree. The *San Francisco Chronicle* headlined an editorial "Our Race Problems Vanish." During the agricultural strikes of the early thirties, some Okies sided with the big landowners, picking cotton in place of striking workers. But as FDR's economic recovery started sputtering out in 1935—and as the drought in the Southwest pushed more families west—even a farming industry that needed some two hundred thousand pickers a year began to find the sheer number of Okies too much.

As Guthrie began reporting for the *Light*, pickers of cotton were getting about fifty cents a day, and the average pay for migrants totaled less than four hundred dollars a year. They lived in cars or pitched tents or were put up temporarily in growers' camps. These were often without basic plumbing, and overseers sold workers drinking water at a nickel a bucket. In one county, in one harvest season, fifty babies died of diarrhea and enteritis.

When Guthrie arrived on the scene, guitar and notepad in hand, organizers were struggling to include this new wave of workers. America's Communist Party had grown from fourteen thousand members in 1932 to some seventy thousand. And the San Francisco

Bay area had the second largest number of paying party members after New York City. In fact, one party leader called California the state "showing us the way to victory."

That's exactly what worried the mainstream press, big business, state government. By 1938, they saw victory by the strikers as the downfall of the economic system, of Christianity, of the American way of life. The state sent National Guard troops to stop organizers. Growers and local merchants formed a group called Associated Farmers with a platform to "save America." Thousands of citizens were organized into "Citizens Armies," vigilante groups dedicated to ending protests by any means necessary. Strike leaders were sent to prison; barbed-wire stockades were built to contain protestors. "But of course," the landowners explained, "we won't put white men in . . . , just Filipinos." McWilliams called it "the mechanics of fascist control."

The first and best-known biography of Guthrie calls American communism "a largely irrelevant and laughable sect" and describes the midthirties as "probably the only moment in American history when being a Communist seemed at all plausible to more than a tiny minority of people."

Maybe.

The idea of some sort of socialist alternative didn't just spring up in the midthirties. Guthrie was familiar with it from Okemah, where the father of a school friend used to pass out socialist literature on the streets. In some ways, the strikes in California were just continuing what Charlie Guthrie's "kumrids" had been proposing twenty years earlier. McWilliams described it as "a collective agriculture to replace the present monopolistically owned and controlled system."

If the collective solution appealed to more people in the thirties, you could attribute that to one basic cause: jobs. At the height of the Depression, a quarter of the United States was out of work. "Next to war," the *London Times* wrote, "unemployment has been the most widespread, the most insidious, and the most corroding malady of our generation: it is the specific social disease of Western civilization in our time."

But while America and Europe were sunk in the Depression, the USSR had launched its first Five-Year Plan. From the Great Crash of 1929 till the start of the Second World War, Soviet industrial production tripled. To many—and not just believers—it seemed to be the one system that was providing people with what Guthrie called a living wage. Most Americans may not have known or cared much about Karl Marx, but they could see which economy was functioning and which wasn't.

Guthrie had found his voice; now, as hobo correspondent, he discovered what he wanted to talk about. "The starvation armies of wandering workers," he called them, "bewildered and flat broke." And he began to consider what kind of political and economic system might help them.

It wasn't the instantaneous revelation of the freezing freight. It wasn't even the slightly more gradual version he told elsewhere. In that one, he's passing by a bookstore in Sacramento in 1936. In the window, he sees a thin volume with the words *constitution* and *union* in the title. He buys it, only to discover that it's not the constitution of the United States but of the Soviet Union. As he glances through, he finds that the Soviets guarantee, in his words, "Women folk and men folk are the same and get the same pay for doing the same work. . . . Color of your skin can't keep you from working and voting. . . . Every smokestack and boiler belongs to the workhands. . . . Nobody hanging around the streets out of work."

Book in hand, he then walks over to a rally of cotton strikers in a nearby church. The rally is surrounded by a bunch of threatening local deputies. Guthrie looks at the strike and the deputies and decides the Soviet constitution holds the key to change. From then on, he writes, "[I] wore that little ten cent blue book out carrying it around in my shirt pocket. . . . The best thing I did in 1936," he ends his story, "was to sign up in the Communist Party. . . ."

Except there's no evidence Guthrie was in California as early as 1936. And no evidence he ever officially signed up as a communist. His second wife believed, "[H]e was not welcomed by the party because he did not want to follow a party line." The actor Will Geer, a communist himself when Guthrie met him, declared, "Woody never was a party member because he was always considered too eccentric by the party apparatus." Instead, Geer says, Guthrie became "a convinced socialist, positive that this country had to be socialist."

The conviction grew over the course of that summer. As hobo correspondent, he visited a model migrant camp, federally run, that Steinbeck and McWilliams had been to a few years earlier. All three men saw it as an example of how the government could make a difference, could set up cooperative worker-friendly institutions, could adapt and use some socialist ideas. In *The Grapes of Wrath*, Steinbeck has Tom Joad wonder why the whole country wasn't run like the government camp: "Throw out the cops that ain't our people. And work together for our own thing—all farm our own lan'."

Steinbeck, McWilliams, Guthrie may never have joined the Communist Party, but they were all sympathetic to its ideals. Looking back, McWilliams recalls, "I was interested in Marxism in the 1930's—as who wasn't . . ." As Steinbeck started work on *The Grapes of Wrath*, he declared, "The old methods of repression, of starvation wages, of jailing, beating and intimidation are not going to work: these are American people." One commentator called the two writers "men possessed by anger." That fit Guthrie, too.

He returned to KFVD that fall to discover the Woody and Lefty Lou Show was over: Maxine Crissman had decided to give up performing. The station brought Guthrie back as a solo act on a show he called *Woody, the Lone Wolf*. He'd introduce it by saying, "The old Lone Wolf is here to sing to you. The lonesomer I feel, the lonesomer I howl." Gone were the comforting, down-home harmonies, replaced by Guthrie's stiletto voice and deadpan delivery. He was still funny, but there was no one to bounce the jokes off. And the rambling monologues rambled more toward politics. "I never heard that," Lefty Lou recalled, "before he went up to the labor camps." The Lone Wolf didn't draw nearly the audience the duo had.

That January, Guthrie introduced himself to Ed Robbin, a news commentator on the station. A graduate of the University of Chicago, Robbin had supported the pickers' strikes, then gotten involved with union organizing at Douglas Aircraft. When Woody met him, he'd just become the Los Angeles bureau chief of the Communist Party's new West Coast paper, *People's World*. Robbin heard Guthrie's music and suggested he perform at a rally in Los Angeles. He supposedly told Guthrie it would be a Communist rally, and Guthrie supposedly replied, "Left wing, right wing, chicken wing, it's the same thing to me."

It's a good Will Rogers line: a good line for a ramblin' unaffiliated loner. Except the rest of Guthrie's life argues it wasn't true.

At the rally, he came on late—after the speeches—and sang some of his new, more political ballads. "Dust Pneumonia Blues" took its melody and point of view from Jimmie Rodgers's "T for Texas": a drifter somewhere in the Southwest looks to migrate to California. But Guthrie's drifter doesn't expect the water to taste like cherry wine. In fact, he already has what he calls "dust pneumonia," which may also be a slanted reference to Rodgers, known as the Blue Yodeler, who would die of tuberculosis in 1933, age thirty-five. Guthrie begins one couplet, "There ought to be some yodelin' in this song" and finishes "But I can't yodel for the rattlin' in my lungs."

Touching, funny, pointed, Guthrie won over the rally. He was cheered as "the very embodiment" of the Okies. Robbin soon became his informal booking agent, bringing him to a whole slate of Communist rallies and meetings. For a twenty-six-year-old singer with two kids and a wife, the five to ten dollars those gigs brought in meant a lot; the average Okie cotton picker was making about three dollars a week.

Guthrie began sharpening his political edge. He wrote a song called "Them Big City Wages" about a country boy who ends up on skid row, realizing too late that city hustlers can "trim you faster than a mowin' machine." And he reshaped his own "I Ain't Got No Home," adding the line "Many a working man is nothing but a slave."

A few months after Guthrie started performing at Communist functions, Steinbeck's *The Grapes of Wrath* was published. It became an instant best seller, treated more as a nonfiction account than a novel. As Eleanor Roosevelt praised it, California's big growers attacked it, and the book was banned in libraries around Bakersfield. Guthrie called Steinbeck "a feller that knew us Oakies [*sic*] . . . because early in the deal, he threw a pack on his back and traipsed around among us." It's exactly what Guthrie had done, but now he so identifies with the migrants that it's "us Oakies." By the time McWilliams's *Factories in the Field* came out a few months later, dust-bowl refugees had become a national issue, and Guthrie was in the thick of it.

Ed Gibbon introduced Guthrie to an old University of Chicago friend, Will Geer. Geer had just finished a New York run in the radical musical *The Cradle Will Rock*, directed by Orson Welles. The show—about a strike in a fictional Steeltown, USA—had proven too incendiary for FDR's Federal Theatre Project, which shut it down. Geer and Guthrie were soon working the political circuit together, Guthrie singing his "Philadelphia Lawyer," Geer acting out the parts. They played migrant camps, rallies, Hollywood parties. It wasn't long before Guthrie was performing for Steinbeck, who would later write: "[He] sings the songs of a people. And I suspect that he is, in a way, that people."

In a way.

Through Ed Gibbon, he began writing a column, for *People's World* Woody Sez. It owes a lot to Will Rogers: cornpone humor over a razor-sharp intelligence. "[A] policeman will jest stand there an let a banker rob a farmer. But if a farmer robs a banker—you wood have a hole dern army of cops out shooting at him." In another one-liner he writes, "You might say Wall St. is the St. that keeps you off of Easy St." It was his radio act put to paper; what's shifted is his audience—who he's talking to and why.

After Guthrie had been playing rallies and contributing to *People's World* for about a year, the Soviet Union signed a treaty with Nazi Germany. The Communist Party USA and many of Guthrie's new friends supported the alliance. From their point of view, the coming world war is a battle among imperial powers to divide and re-divide land that should belong to the people. To be loyal to the greater fight—against fascism—is to be loyal to the Soviet Union.

A couple weeks after the treaty, Germany overran Poland from the west. Then Russia invaded from the east. Guthrie, trying to explain, composed a talking blues about how "Stalin stepped in, took a big strip of Poland and give the farm lands back to the farmers." KVFD's owner didn't buy it. Within a couple months, Guthrie had sung himself out of his job. With another new baby—Will Rogers Guthrie—and no prospects in L.A., he and Mary headed back to Pampa.

He comes back from California not a singing cowboy but a folksinger. That, anyway, is what his radical New York friends will call him. They'll embrace Guthrie's singing hobo as a "Communist Joe Hill," a reincarnation of the famous Wobbly songwriter. Guthrie's flattered and excited, eager to be part of a larger movement.

Thirty years later, New York gives Bob Dylan a similar embrace, but he backs away from it. As his girlfriend recalls, "[He] wasn't Joe Hill, then or ever, and he did not want to be Joe Hill, then or ever." By 1964, Dylan reports that when asked, "What d you think a the communist party?" he replies, "What communist party?"

NO MARTYR IS AMONG YE NOW

J oan Baez sang "Joe Hill" at Woodstock. It was in her standard repertoire and, still it was an odd choice.

The first night of the "3 Days of Peace and Music," as it was billed, was mostly folk music—Richie Havens, Tim Hardin, Arlo Guthrie—as if to acknowledge rock & roll's past. Baez, once Bob Dylan's singing partner and lover, closed the evening. It was already raining, but the huge crowd was still arriving. A nearby section of the New York State Thruway had been closed by the traffic, and the promoters had given up charging admission as four hundred thousand people gathered in the muddy fields. The governor of New York was contemplating bringing in the National Guard to maintain order.

Baez stepped onstage alone with an acoustic guitar, dark hair cut short, eyes big, six-months pregnant. She looked out over the hordes of sleepless, trippy fans and apparently saw a chance to organize. That, anyway, was her material in the summer of 1969: antiwar counterculture songs sung in a throaty voice that was part Appalachian balladeer, part Mexican ranchera singer, part classical soprano. Dylan called it her "nightingale sound." After a few songs, including an old hymn and a Dylan cover—and some talk about her husband's recent arrest for draft resistance—she launched into "Joe Hill."

It was like throwing out a line, fragile but real, between Wobblies and hippies, communists and communes. Joe Hill was executed by the State of Utah in 1915, but "Joe Hill" is from Guthrie's era. It's structured as a dialogue between Hill's ghost and the singer—in this case, the passionate, innocent-sounding Baez. "'The copper bosses killed you, Joe. / They shot you, Joe,' says I." To which, his ghost (vision? spirit?) replies that he didn't die: "What they can never kill / went on to organize." It's a song about martyrdom and activism but also about the political potential of songwriting.

The words are by Alfred Hayes, a British-born novelist, poet, and screenwriter. In 1936, Earl Robinson, a twenty-six-year-old friend of Pete Seeger's dad, was working at a summer camp for red-diaper babies—the children of progressives and communists. Part of his job was to write tunes for the campers, which is what he did with Hayes's poem. "Joe Hill," Robinson would later say, was written "for a campfire program." The result, with its circling melody, straightforward words, and inspirational lift, impressed Woody Guthrie, who arrived in New York a few years after it was written. He liked the idea that Hill's spirit was still alive and that he and others might carry it on.

But the Woodstock festival was a quarter century after that. As haunting as Baez's version was, the song couldn't help but sound out of place—a call to arms at a Peace and Music gathering, more about the past than the present.

Bob Dylan lived near Woodstock at the time, and the rumor was, he'd make a surprise appearance. He didn't. In a sense, he'd made his position clear a couple of years earlier. His countrified 1967 LP, *John Wesley Harding*, included a song that put Earl Robinson's melody to new lyrics.

In Dylan's song, as drums beat what sounds like a funeral march, he dreams that a fifth-century Catholic saint returns to life only to find the souls he's looking to save "already have been sold." Where "Joe Hill" promises the fight will go on, "I Dreamed I Saw St. Augustine" mourns its passing. Dylan's voice, pitched high as a bluegrass singer's, sounds like he's announcing the end of an era. "No martyr is among ye now." The song ends when the narrator wakes "alone and terrified. / I put my fingers against the glass, bowed my head and cried."

That last image is borrowed. Dylan took it from the Guthrie song "Ludlow Massacre"—based, like "1913 Massacre," on Mother Bloor's book. In "Ludlow Massacre," the narrator's a mourning father; he watches a group of children mowed down during a miners' strike, then "I hung my head and cried." The paraphrase turns Dylan's "St. Augustine" into a farewell not only to Joe Hill's vision but to Guthrie's attempt to keep that vision alive.

Dylan claims he hadn't heard "Joe Hill" until he arrived in Greenwich Village at the beginning of the sixties. Then, he says he found it "preachy and one-dimensional." He also claims that while "I knew that Joe Hill was real and important I didn't know who he was. . . ." Maybe. Though by then he'd spent a year deep in the Dinkytown folk scene, and he'd grown up in Hibbing, with its own connections to labor history. He says that once he did hear it, he began to research and discovered Hill was "a Messianic figure who wanted to abolish the wage system of capitalism. . . . Joe wrote the song 'Pie in the Sky' and was the forerunner of Woody Guthrie. That's all I needed to know."

Joe Hill was born Joel Hägglund in Sweden, the same year as Will Rogers, the same year as Woody Guthrie's father. He sang at his parents' fundamentalist church and learned to play fiddle and piano. At twenty-six, the tall, thin, dark-haired immigrant landed in America and took (or was given) the name of Joe Hillstrom. He spent the next few years bumming from state to state, picking up jobs with the railroad, on the docks, in mines—living, like thousands of others, on the fringes of the new industrialism.

What Hillstrom discovered in his travels was an open war between workers and owners. It was especially fierce out west, where the need for cheap labor pitted, as one observer put it, "the capital of money [against] another of muscle." The owners—many of them East Coast financiers—paid a going wage of three dollars a day for ten hours of breaking and hauling rock. The miners in Colorado, Montana, Idaho—many of them immigrants—led wildcat strikes demanding basic safety measures, decent housing, fewer hours, and better pay. The strikes turned into labor wars, with the law usually taking the company's side. Local sheriffs deputized residents and helped bring in replacement workers—scabs—and the confrontations escalated from beatings and mass arrests to gun battles and bombings.

A decade before Hillstrom arrived in America, Western miners had decided their only hope was to form a "fighting union." The resulting Western Federation of Mines soon affiliated with the nation's largest labor organization, Samuel Gompers's American Federation of Labor. The AF of L proclaimed that it believed in change through "education, organization and legislation" and was against violence. But the Westerners soon decided their parent union was too East Coast, too polite, too focused on elite skilled workers. The AF of L's slogan—"A fair day's wages for a fair day's work"—might rattle owners, but to the Western miners, it was middle-of-the-road: "trades unions without action." "Do not think me egotistical," the president of the WFM wrote Gompers, "when I say that I think the laboring men of the West are one hundred years ahead of their brothers in the East."

Within a year, the two organizations split. Immigrants and itinerant workers (proudly calling themselves bums) pushed the WFM into becoming one of the "most militant labor organizations in the United States." The miners' union decided "the only salvation of the working classes [is a] complete revolution of social and economic conditions."

By 1905, the WFM had some thirty-five thousand members in two hundred chapters scattered across the West. But its decade of gains had come at an enormous price. The "capital of money" was only getting stronger, forming giant business syndicates like John D. Rockefeller's Standard Oil and J. P. Morgan's United States Steel. The WFM concluded that the best chance for its "complete revolution" was to form "one great industrial union" that would unite the working class. So it bankrolled the International Workers of the World.

The preamble to the IWW's constitution began: "The working class and the employing class have nothing in common. There can be no peace so long as hunger and want are found among millions of the working people and the few, who make up the employing class, have all the good things of life." Unlike a trade union, the IWW welcomed all, whether they were skilled or not, whether they even had jobs or not. In fact, its organizers went out of their way to recruit hoboes and day-workers like Hillstrom, the kind of surplus labor that helped keep wages low.

The goal, in the words of leader William "Big Bill" Haywood, was for "the working class . . . to take possession of and operate successfully for their own interests, the industries of the country." To own the machines. They believed the way to get there wasn't through voting or influencing politicians but by confronting the status quo through slowdowns, walkouts, organized strikes. "Political action," in Haywood's words, "leads to capitalism reformed. Direct action leads to socialism. . . . All aboard for the IWW. Death to politics."

Within a year of the IWW's founding, a former governor of Idaho was killed by a bomb planted in his mailbox. He'd been a fierce opponent of the WFM, and a double agent in the labor wars fingered Haywood, WFM president Charles Moyer, and a third union leader. The three were locked in the death house at Boise, and their cause became national news. Twenty thousand New Yorkers marched in their support. And when President Teddy Roosevelt called Moyer and Haywood "undesirable citizens," protestors throughout the country carried placards reading, I AM AN UNDESIRABLE CITIZEN.

Representing Haywood at the trial was the lawyer and socialist Clarence Darrow (who'd go on to fame in the Scopes trial for defending the right to teach evolution). Darrow declared that the defendants' only crime was "their loyalty to the working class." His summation speech—which went on for eleven hours—addressed the possibility that Haywood would end up a martyr to the movement.

> Wherever men have looked upward and onward, worked for the poor and the weak, they have been sacrificed. They have met their deaths, and he can meet his. But . . . don't be so foolish as to believe you can strangle the Western Federation of Miners when you tie a rope around his neck. . . . [H]e is mortal; he will die, but . . . a million men will grab up the banner of labor . . . [and] carry it on to victory in the end.

Echoes of that language ended up in Alfred Hayes's "Joe Hill" thirty years later—and in the film version of Steinbeck's *Grapes of Wrath*. "A fella ain't got a soul of his own," says Tom Joad as he faces death, "just a little piece of a big soul that belongs to everybody. . . . Wherever you can look, wherever there's a fight so hungry people can eat, I'll be there."

Haywood and the others eventually got off. Instead of uniting the movement, instead of a million men rising up and grabbing labor's banner, the leaders began to bicker. Legend has it that, while in jail, the soft-spoken Moyer lost patience with Haywood's temper and told him, "Put an ice-pack on your head." To which Big Bill supposedly replied, "Get it from under your feet first." Soon the majority of the WFM's twenty-seven thousand members had returned to the AF of L, resolved to negotiate, not confront, to deal with capitalists "in a straight-forward, business-like manner." That left a splinter group of about ten thousand hard-core Wobblies, which is the group Joe Hillstrom joined when he got his first IWW "red card" in 1907.

Hillstrom joined the IWW during what became known as the Bankers' Panic. A decade of rising prices and widespread speculation had led to banks calling loans and small depositors demanding their savings. Unemployment soared, and the Wobblies saw it as proof that capitalism didn't work. There was a surge in temp agencies that charged exorbitant fees to find out-of-work men day-labor. The Wobblies called them "employment sharks" and led rallies against them. The trouble was that as soon as they drew a crowd, the Salvation Army would show up. The proselytizers' hymns, promising a better world "by and by," would drown out the calls for revolution.

The Wobblies decided to fight back with music. Volunteers began to take the familiar hymns and re-write the lyrics. That way, when the Salvation Army struck up a tune, the Wobblies could sing along, keeping the melody but plugging in their own words. "We will have songs of anger and protest," they declared, "songs that lampoon our masters. . . . We want our songs to stir the workers into action, to awaken them from an apathy and complacency that has made them accept their servitude as if it had been divinely ordained."

Joe Hillstrom became one of the Wobblies' premier songwriters. Some credit him (not Haywire Mac) with turning the melody of "Revive Us Again" into "Hallelujah, I'm a Bum." The first tune of his to appear in a Wobblies' songbook was "Longhaired Preacher." To the melody of "Sweet Bye and Bye," it mocks the idea of a heavenly reward: "Work and pray, live on hay. / You'll get pie in the sky when you die." Funny, sacrilegious, it had the same perspective and helped inspire Guthrie's "I Ain't Got No Home."

The tune was signed "Joe Hill." Like Robert Zimmerman, Hillstrom decided he needed a name that was easier to remember and more mainstream American. His goal, after all, was mass appeal, a call to revolution that would reach everyone. "[I]f a person can put a few cold, common sense facts into a song," Hill proposed, "and dress them up . . . in a cloak of humor to take the dryness off, he will succeed in reaching a great number of workers. . . ." As fellow organizer Elizabeth Gurley Flynn put it, "Let others write their stately, Whitmanesque verse and lengthy, rhythmic narrative. Joe writes songs that sing, that lilt and laugh and sparkle. . . ." Flynn, a twenty-five-year-old IWW leader, feminist, and rabble-rouser, was the inspiration for Hill's song, "Rebel Girl," which became a model for one of Guthrie's songs, "Union Maid."

The IWW's plan to lead an American revolution peaked the year before the 1913 massacre. That's when the Wobblies took on the descendants of the Boston Associates in Lawrence, Massachusetts. By then, the city's twelve textile mills employed some thirty-two thousand workers, mostly immigrant Irish, Greek, Portuguese, Italian. The average wage was under nine dollars a week, and the week was fifty-six hours long. After a decade where dividends rose 100 percent, the owners finally agreed to shorten the workday by two hours. But they wanted to cut pay to match—the equivalent, workers said, of losing four loaves of bread. It was the women of Lawrence who led a spontaneous walkout under the rallying cry "Better to starve fighting than starve working."

At the time, only three hundred of the millworkers were dues-paying Wobblies, but Big Bill Haywood saw the walkout as a chance for the union to establish a foothold in the East. The IWW brought its strategies of confrontation to Lawrence. To avoid the local law against mass meetings, they came up with the idea of a moving picket line. Thousands marched daily, singing, "Hearts can starve as well as bodies. / Give us bread but give us roses." It soon became known as the Bread and Roses Strike.

The more conservative unions refused to support the action. Representatives of the AF of L testified before Congress that the Wobblies were organizing "a revolution, not a strike." Joe Hill, on the West Coast, promptly rewrote "A Little Talk with Jesus" to make fun of the AF of L's refusal to back immigrants: "But to his great surprise the 'foreigners' were wise. / In one big solid union they were organized."

Management brought in fifty state and local militia units—including a company of Harvard students who got course credit for union busting. But by the end of March, the Lawrence workers had won their demands. Haywood called it "the most signal victory of any organized body of workers in the world." It not only proved that one of America's oldest and largest companies could be unionized, but that the movement could be led by women and immigrants.

The trouble was sustaining the revolution. The IWW had sixteen thousand paying members in Lawrence when the strike ended but only seven hundred a year later. Its new total of twenty-five thousand members nationwide still paled compared to the AF of L's two million. And the grand total of all America's organized labor represented only a fraction of the nation's workers.

Joe Hill was committed to continuing the struggle. He went south and fought for land rights in the Mexican Revolution and helped organize strikes in San Diego and San Pedro. Threatened with deportation for his radical activities, he left the West Coast for Utah, hoping to find work at a copper mine there.

Early in 1914, he was arrested in Salt Lake City for attempted robbery and murder. His supporters were convinced the charges were trumped up, but he was found guilty. Twice his supporters convinced President Wilson to ask for delays of execution. There were rallies throughout the country, and celebrities like Helen Keller came to his defense. Even the AF of L weighed in on his side.

Hill didn't much relish becoming a union martyr or, as he put it, "a Tin-Jesus." But as he told the Utah Board of Pardons, "Gentlemen, the cause I stand for, that of a fair and honest trial, is worth more than human life—much more than mine." And he could see certain advantages to his execution: "Well, it don't do the IWW any harm," he told the press, "and it won't do the State of Utah any good."

Hill was shot by a firing squad on November 19, 1915. "I have nothing to say about myself," he'd written in a farewell letter, "only that I have always tried to do what little I could to make this earth a little better for the great producing class. . . ." Or as he put it in his last wire to Haywood: "Good-by, Bill. I will die like a true-blue rebel. Don't waste any time in mourning—organize." Joe Hill became that Messianic figure, famous more for his death than his songs.

Dylan says the story appealed to him, that he fantasized writing a less "preachy" version. "I thought about how I would do it, but didn't do it. The first song I'd wind up writing of any substantial importance was written for Woody Guthrie."

If he's telling the truth, Dylan wrote "Song for Woody" instead of a new "Joe Hill." There's some support for that in the lyrics. Guthrie had written his own tribute to Hill, which he called "Joe Hillstrom." It doesn't seem to have been recorded, but it was included in a Woody Guthrie songbook published in 1947 and reprinted in 1961, the year Dylan wrote "Song to Woody." "Joe Hillstrom" is in Joe Hill's voice and includes the lines "Hey, Gurley Finn, I wrote you a song / To the dove of peace, it's coming along." Dylan's "Song for Woody" took the couplet, switching out Guthrie for Gurley Finn and changing what was coming along to "a funny old world." It's a tip of the hat both to Guthrie and to Hill: a way of acknowledging the line of history the nineteen-year-old had come east to join.

It's astonishing how quickly Bob Dylan rose. He met his idol in late January/early February 1961. By mid-February, he'd written "Song to Woody." A month later, he was playing Gerde's Folk City: a thin figure in a short-billed cap, "full of energy," a fellow singer recalls, ". . . herky-jerky, jiggling . . . one of the funniest people I have ever seen on stage." By that fall, he'd gotten a rave in the *New York Times*. Within days of that, he met producer John Hammond—and had cut his first album by the end of October. Eight months after arriving in the city, he's playing a concert at Carnegie Hall's debut room: a new star in the relatively small sky of folk music. At the concert, he sang a tribute version of "1913 Massacre," but he's already become more than a Guthrie imitator; he's finding his own sound.

Listen to an interview done just before the first record came out, and you hear a giggly twenty-year-old determined not to be labeled. "I like more than just folk music, and I sing more than just folk music." He won't quite admit to caring about rock & roll but goes on to play covers of everything from Hank Williams to Muddy Waters to 1920s jug-band music. He'd already developed guitar chops that could go from Appalachian picking to bluesy slides, a thunderous harmonica style, and an expressive nasal voice that seemed to have more miles on it than he had years. He told the interviewer he was from Sioux Falls, South Dakota, and had spent a long time with the carnival. "At the carnival," she asks, "did you learn songs?" His answer: "No. I learned how to sing though. That's more important."

And it's true that what already marks him in 1961 is how he sings, his performance style. He liked extending songs; the longer they go, the more time he has to establish a mood and then play variations on it. Over repeating guitar riffs, he'd hold a harsh note, building tension, then break down into sharp, staccato phrases. On a Guthrie number, he adopted his idol's jaunty, slightly detached, Carter Family approach. On a Howlin' Wolf blues, he'd groan and fade as if he'd spent his life in the Delta. Around him, the Greenwich Village folk scene was full of traditionalists trying to play the old songs the old way, to sound like the records. Dylan seemed less concerned with getting it "right" than telling the truth, trying to put himself back in that time and place, to *be* the person in the song.

He described himself as "into . . . the traditional stuff with a capital T . . . as far away from the mondo teeno scene as you could get." But he sounded less capital-T traditional than a lot of his peers. At the same time, he wasn't Top Ten smooth, like the Kingston Trio. According to Peggy Seeger, Pete's half sister, many in the new folk revival sang "working-class songs [in a] middle class manner. Without that working-class anger, the music changes." Judging by his first album, Dylan kept the anger, but he made a calculated decision about how to use it.

He'd circled the idea of making a record, listening to himself on friends' home tapes and getting studio experience playing harmonica on a fellow folksinger's LP. But now he was supposed to cut on a major label with legendary producer John Hammond, and he had to decide who he was, how he'd present himself. He might have done his Guthrie repertoire or covered the kind of traditional ballads that

Baez and others specialized in or cut an album of topical political songs. Instead, he made something like a blues record.

Yes, there's "Pretty Peggy-O," an eighteenth-century tune done as a carnival whoop, a kind of goof on traditional folk. In the same way, the spoken intro to "Baby, Let Me Follow You Down," pokes fun at folk collectors, Dylan saying he picked up this Reverend Gary Davis tune "in the green pastures of Harvard University." And there's a straight-ahead nod to the Scots-Irish ballad tradition in "Man of Constant Sorrow." But the majority of the songs—eight of the eleven non-originals—are from fairly obscure black bluesmen like Davis, Bukka White, Blind Lemon Jefferson, Tommy Mc-Clennan, Jesse Fuller. And Dylan goes at them with some of the beat-heavy, emotional delivery of Big Joe Williams, a Mississippi bluesman he'd recently appeared with at Gerde's. The kid from Hibbing doesn't exactly try to sound black. But along with anger and humor, he tinges his voice with a kind of death-obsessed, Mississippi Delta sorrow. And focusing on the blues lets him show off his love of rhythm in his pumping harmonica, his guitar picking, the delayed timing of his vocals.

If that doesn't seem like a very commercial sound, it wasn't. A smart ambitious kid could see what you needed to do to sell records. Around this time, Albert Grossman, who'd helped pick the lineup for the first Newport Folk Festival, was putting together a commercial folk group. He plucked two men and a woman from what Dylan called the "subterranean world" of Greenwich Village. The men, both college graduates, got to keep their bohemian goatees but were put in proper jackets and ties; the woman kept her long blonde beatnik hair but always wore a dress. The resulting LP, *Peter, Paul and Mary*, came out the same time as Dylan's and did a lot better— going to number one and staying on the charts for over two years.

Folk music was built on authenticity, and both Dylan and Peter, Paul and Mary claimed the tag. Maybe Dylan's channeling of a black hooker in "House of the Rising Sun" was no more authentic than Gene Autry's singing cowboy, but the liner notes to his record still described him as "so goddamned real, it's unbelievable!" Meanwhile, the notes to Peter, Paul and Mary's LP declared, in boldface, "The **Truth** is on the record." If so, their version of the truth consisted of catchy, carefully harmonized tunes; their first hit was the calypso-esque, nightclubby "Lemon Tree." The follow-up had a little more political bite; a cover of a Pete Seeger/Lee Hays broadside against the blacklisting of American communists. But the original had carefully camouflaged its anger, speaking in generalities about danger, warning, love, and Peter, Paul and Mary sweetened it that much more by speeding up the tempo and adding soaring harmonies. The result, "If I Had a Hammer," turned into a Top Ten hit in the fall of 1962 and eventually won a Grammy.

That was the sound of mainstream folk, and the music was now popular enough to claim the cover of *Time* magazine: a neo-expressionist portrait of Joan Baez, barefoot and playing guitar. The magazine described her as "earnestly political" and tied folk music to a new, rising left wing of "peace marches and ban-the-bomb campaigns." It wasn't Seeger and Guthrie's union politics or the older radical left of Joe Hill and Mother Bloor, but an updated collegiate sound that tried to reflect the times. As a 1962 statement put it, there was now a "pervading feeling that there simply are no alternatives, that our times have witnessed the exhaustion not only of Utopias, but of any new departures as well." The statement came from Students for a Democratic Society, a group that had been financed by the labor movement to explore the future of unions. It found that organizing workers had little appeal to a younger generation "bred in at least modest comfort, housed now in universities, looking uncomfortably to the world we inherit."

With its pushy, dark, outsider's sound, Dylan's record had echoes of that pervading feeling, but it didn't sell well. He claimed that, even before he recorded it, "The thought occurred to me that maybe I'd have to write my own folk songs. . . ." He'd heard Pete Seeger's half brother Mike play "Delta blues, ragtime, minstrel songs, buck-and-wing, dance reels, play party, hymn and gospel . . . ," and he not only played them well, "he played these songs as good as it was possible to play them." You could cover the old songs brilliantly and still not touch on the contemporary. Or make much of a living. Dylan had been writing songs since high school, but now he focused on it, using Guthrie's technique of putting new words to old tunes. In 1962 alone, he'd produce some fifty originals.

About half of the second record, *The Freewheelin' Bob Dylan*, is made up of love songs: ruminations on an old girlfriend, on the kind of girlfriend he wants, on the kind he doesn't. They combine the hip and the traditional. So, "Girl from the North Country" takes its melody from "Scarborough Fair," a tune that can be traced back to seventeenth-century England, but Dylan's song was enough of a modern country ballad for Johnny Cash to cut it. Sweet, evocative, nostalgic, it's a long way from "Rebel Girl."

The other half of the album is more political, though it owes its own debts to a girlfriend. Dylan's first New York love, Suze Rotolo, was a self-described red-diaper baby. She was raised on Guthrie and Seeger, worked for the Congress of Racial Equality, cared about avant-garde theater and poetry, took part in protests. Her family had been in Greenwich Village for a while, and her sister was Alan Lomax's personal assistant. Rotolo could not only help her lover enter New York's folk circles but guide him through the issues of the day.

Freewheelin's protest songs focus on a couple of key areas. By 1962, America had declared commies the national enemy. The Berlin Wall had gone up dividing East from West; US troops had attempted an invasion of communist Cuba; President Kennedy had OK'd the first combat mission in Vietnam. "Talking World War III Blues" takes on Cold War paranoia in a funny, Guthrie-esque ramble. "Masters of War," on the other hand, is an angry, finger-pointing takedown of those "who build the big guns." Dylan uses the tune of the medieval "Nottamun Town" and transposes its description of a peasant village—where "not a soul would look up, not a soul would look down"—to the present. In Dylan's version, the surreal, disconnected feeling comes from the warmongers who've "thrown the worst fear that can ever be hurled." But it was another song on the record, "A Hard Rain's a-Gonna Fall," that his peers saw as the twenty-one-year-old's stylistic breakthrough.

Dylan borrowed the tune and the question-and-answer format from an eighteenth-century Anglo-Scottish ballad, "Lord Randall." That begins with a mother asking, "O where have you been, Lord Randall, my son?" then slowly reveals he's been poisoned by his true love. Over a bass-heavy acoustic guitar strum, Dylan asks the same questions—where have you been? what did you see? who did you meet?—but his answers come from a world gone wrong.

Dylan admitted that the October 1962 Cuban Missile Crisis had scared him and everybody he knew, but he claimed "Hard Rain" was about more than the nuclear face-off; it took on the larger feeling that there were no longer any alternatives. Compare the song to Guthrie's "This Land Is Your Land," and the freedom highway has turned into "a highway of diamonds with nobody on it." Instead of "wheat fields waving," we get "a black branch with blood that kept drippin'." And the "Gulf Stream waters" are now contaminated by "pellets of poison." This land is no man's land.

If "Hard Rain" is in the tradition of Guthrie and Joe Hill, its approach is more personal, the singer wading through a word-thick emotional landscape. And when it comes to the final question, "What'll you do now, my blue-eyed son?" Dylan's answer is to go back out under that hard rain and bear witness: "I'll tell it and think it and speak it and breathe it." His idea of taking action is less organizing, more testifying, as if the world might change if we could tell the truth.

The breakthrough came in how he tried to tell it. The dense, surreal-sounding language reminded some of Rimbaud, Baudelaire, Kerouac. But you could find the model much closer to home—in Guthrie's "diamond deserts" and in the old ballads. The "Hard Rain" line "ten thousand miles in the mouth of a graveyard" plays off "Nottamun Town"'s "ten thousand got drowned that never was born." As Dylan said a couple years later, "From folksongs, I learned the language . . . legends and Bibles, it goes into curses and myths, it goes into plagues, it goes into all kinds of weird things . . ." "[F]olk songs," he'd add, fifty years after that, ". . . gave me the code."

And the final breakthrough of "Hard Rain" is how he delivers that code: in long, breath-bending phrases only hinted at on his first record. Call Guthrie's voice a stiletto, and Dylan's is more open, broader—a scythe, maybe, sweeping everything it can reach.

The other major target of Dylan's anger was white supremacy. As he was cutting *Freewheelin'*, white students were rioting to prevent James Meredith from integrating the state university in Oxford, Mississippi. Dylan's "Oxford Town" is based on "Cumberland Gap," an old banjo tune that both Guthrie and Seeger had recorded. Cumberland Gap was the route white settlers first took into the South. Dylan slows the melody down and steers it into the new South. The song's a sharp take on the uses of skin color and violence, but the singer doesn't urge people to protest or organize the way Joe Hill might have. Dylan's conclusion is to steer clear: "Ain't a-goin' down to Oxford Town."

He's certainly capable of writing a more conventional protest song. In "The Death of Emmett Till," he reminds his listeners of the murder of the black teenager eight years earlier and urges them to "make this great land of ours a greater place to live" by speaking out. But "The Death of Emmett Till" didn't make it onto *Freewheelin'*.

It was clear by that spring of 1963 that if you chose not to speak out about civil rights, you were still making a statement. As Martin Luther King wrote from his jail cell in Birmingham, Alabama, "We have waited for more than three hundred and fifty years for our constitutional and God-given rights. . . . There comes a time when the cup of endurance runs over. . . ." That sense of waiting, of time ticking past, is the subject of the song that opens *Freewheelin'* and launched Dylan's commercial songwriting career.

For the melody, he borrowed the moan of a black spiritual that dates back at least to the 1870s, "No More Auction Block." He'd probably heard a version by Odetta, the African American singer represented by Albert Grossman (who by now was managing Dylan, as well as Peter, Paul and Mary). "No More Auction Block" is built on a contradiction: the lyrics celebrate the end of slave auctions and public whippings even as the melody descends to a lament for the "Many thousand gone." It's a song about American time: how long slavery went on, how long it will continue to affect the nation.

Twenty-year-old Dylan kept the theme and the tune's sadness while speeding it up and shaping it into three-line verses. Each verse asks a question: "How many roads must a man walk down . . . ?" "How many deaths will it take . . . ?" The chorus serves as the answer: that there is no sure answer, that it's "blowin' in the wind."

The result sounds like a deliberate attempt to write an anthem, a kind of variation on "If I Had a Hammer" with the same generalized, nonthreatening protest. If Joe Hill wrote pointed songs for specific direct actions, Dylan painted the big picture, making a song broad enough to apply almost anywhere. "Blowin' in the Wind" has a little of Guthrie's "blowin' down this old dusty road," and Dylan sings it without anger in an almost neutral voice, his version of Guthrie's (or Sara Carter's) deadpan. In the end, it comes across as less about injustice than our reaction to injustice. How many times will we let this happen? How long will we listen to people cry?

The song was an immediate sensation in folk circles. "Blowin' in the Wind" was featured on the cover of *Broadside*, a magazine dedicated to "topical songs." And before *Freewheelin'* was even released, Albert Grossman brought it to Peter, Paul and Mary. Their take sweetened the melody, added three-part harmony, and boosted the song's drive with a bass line and strummed chords. In other words, it ended up more like a pop song of the day. In the process, it seems to assume we all agree on the answer and becomes less about questions, more an invitation to join in. It was this version that reached number two on the charts. Peter, Paul and Mary went around the country that summer of 1963, introducing it as the work of "the most important folk artist in America today."

"I wasn't a pop songwriter, and I really didn't want to be that," Dylan commented fifty years later, "but it was a good thing that it happened." Onstage at that summer's Newport Folk Festival, the thin, intense, slightly hyper young man deflected attention. Smiling shyly, he exited the stage almost before his songs were over. He acted with the backcountry modesty of some of the older performers at the festival: Maybelle Carter, the Reverend Gary Davis, Dock Boggs. And he tried to look the part. Where the audience was mostly college-age kids (which is to say, Dylan's age) in sport shirts and shorts, Dylan wore the dark work pants and button-down work shirt that amounted to the folk uniform. Pete Seeger, Doc Watson, Ramblin' Jack Elliott dressed the same. It's a look you can date back to Joe Hill and the idea of the singer as worker—though Dylan's soft, pale skin suggested indoor work at most.

If he looked and acted a lot like the older generation, Dylan didn't sound like them. Take the version of "Gospel Plow" he performed at Newport. Seeger had been singing the spiritual since the forties and had made it into a communal experience: leading the audience in his choir director's voice, driving it forward with high harmonies, cajoling the crowd by insisting that everybody could and should sing. A master performer, Seeger played the regular guy in front of other regular guys, and his version of "Gospel Plow" acts as a kind of moral lesson: we're all in this together.

Dylan, on the other hand, doubled the pace to a gallop. He sang it solo, in a tour de force of speed and breath control. When he shouted "Hold on to that plow!" it was the voice of a juggler wowing the crowd with all the balls he could keep in the air. At the end, he turned modestly away, but Dylan's performance was a lot about the performer, and the audience cheered accordingly.

That year's festival ended with a tribute to the civil rights struggle: a group-sing of "We Shall Overcome." Leading up to it was an all-star version of the movement's new anthem, "Blowin' in the Wind." Out came Seeger, Baez, Peter, Paul and Mary, and the Freedom Singers, a young black group fresh from the protests in

Georgia. The crowd loved it. But Dylan's version of "Blowin' in the Wind" doesn't really work as a sing-along. The phrasing is too personal, too eccentric. So, while the others modulated behind like a gospel chorus or a doo-wop group, Dylan ended up standing in front, singing lead—a little like a pop star.

Dylan already knew he was breaking away from traditional folk music. In that year's festival program, he published a poem in the form of a letter back to Dinkytown. It's as much apology as explanation. "Hey man—I'm sorry—/ I mean I'm really sorry." He describes "the songs we used t sing an play / The songs written fifty years ago / The dirt farm songs—the dust bowl songs / The depression songs . . . / Woody's songs . . ." Back in those days, it goes on, "When there was a strike there's only two kind of views / . . . Thru the unions eyes or thru the bosses eyes." But now, Dylan says, "them two simple sides that was so easy t tell apart" have become—and he capitalizes for emphasis—a "COMPLICATED CIRCLE." He acknowledges his debt: "The folk songs showed me the way / . . . An I got nothing but homage an holy thinkin for the ol songs and stories." But those days are over. He's now "singin an writin what's on my own mind . . . / Not by no kind a side / Not by no kind a category."

It amounts to another farewell. He couldn't keep singing about One Big Union in a world that had become a COMPLICATED CIRCLE. If there was going to be protest, it had to take another form. And in declaring that, he also leaves room for contemporary love songs—some might call them pop songs—like "Don't Think Twice, It's All Right." Peter, Paul and Mary would have another Top Ten hit with it.

In fact, part of "singin and writin what's on my mind" included the pop music he grew up with. In late 1962—as he was cutting *Freewheelin'*—he spent part of two recording sessions trying to record Elvis Presley's 1954 hit, "That's All Right." The sound that Dylan was after fell somewhere between the original rhythm-and-blues version by Arthur "Big Boy" Crudup and Elvis's version. To his own jumpy harmonica and strummed acoustic guitar, he added a band: slap bass, drums, and honky-tonk piano. "I want to do it again," he announced after one take, "fast!" It was as if he'd gone back to the beginning of rock & roll, kicking its tires, seeing if it'll restart.

He also wrote and recorded his own rock & roll. "Mixed-Up Confusion" is the portrait of a man caught in the COMPLICATED CIRCLE: "hung over, hung down, hung up." Powered by long-held vocal notes in front of the same slap bass, piano, and a needling guitar, the song infuriated and baffled its singer. After some twenty-five tries over three sessions, Dylan finally came up with a version that his label released as a single, only to withdraw it. The trouble is "Mixed-Up Confusion" doesn't sound mixed-up: the jump band arrangement seems stapled onto vocals that never quite take off. In the end, he didn't include it on the album; the closest Dylan's second LP came to rock & roll was the gentle drumming behind the traditional tune, "Corrina, Corrina."

He was trying to find a sound to match the times. He didn't want to go back to Joe Hill. In a sense, that's what he left when he left Hibbing. The Iron Range was "a historic center of the American labor movement," saturated with the failures of the past. There'd been a major strike when Dylan was eight, another a few years later, and then there was the older Wobbly history.

Hibbing was the birthplace of the Finnish Socialist Federation. Its 225 locals had eleven thousand members, both on the Mesabi and across Lake Superior in Upper Michigan. Miners on the Iron Range were living, as one Wobbly described it, "hived in stationary railroad cars" and "thronged in filthy and poorly lighted shacks. [Misery] drifts the miners beastward and sends their women to haghood." In June 1907, seventeen thousand iron miners walked out, demanding an eight-hour day, better pay, the end of under-the-table kickbacks to the mine bosses. Scabs were brought in, and the strike was broken. But "in all of the towns," a historian writes, "there remained those who didn't forget."

A decade later, during the labor shortage brought on by World War I, Finnish, Croatian, and Italian miners led a spontaneous walkout. The mines were controlled by a subsidiary of U.S. Steel, and protestors marched through Hibbing with signs reading THIS VILLAGE IS NOT GOVERNED BY THE STEEL TRUST. When the company brought in a thousand troops to break the strike, the strikers countered by calling in the Wobblies.

To a Duluth paper, that amounted to treason. "The I.W.W. is not a labor union, and the condition faced on the range is not a labor strike. The I.W.W. is a revolutionary organization whose sole aim is to overthrow government and take possession of all properties for the use of its members." In June 1916, on the streets of Hibbing, a thousand deputized mine guards fought a thousand protestors. By July, the city was being patrolled by sharpshooters in armored cars. "All that summer," a visiting Elizabeth Gurley Flynn wrote, "the strike dragged out a dogged existence." In the end, the Wobbly leaders were jailed, and the effort collapsed. The strike officially ended in September 1917, a month before the Bolsheviks took power in Russia.

President Woodrow Wilson's Department of Justice proceeded to raid forty-eight IWW meeting halls throughout the country. Their members were accused of being German allies. The US attorney general, A. Mitchell Palmer, sure that radicals were trying to import the Russian Revolution, led the 1919 Palmer Raids. Five hundred Wobbly leaders were indicted for "treasonable conspiracy," including advocating draft resistance. Though the IWW struggled on, it had been "effectively suppressed."

In Hibbing, while that history might have been buried, it wasn't forgotten. People had stood up, confronted the bosses, and been crushed. Dylan remembered the Iron Range as "an extremely volatile, politically active area—with the Farmer Labor Party, Social Democrats, socialists, communists. They were hard crowds to please. . . ." As he was working on *Freewheelin'*, Dylan reminisced how "the town I grew up in is the one / that has left me with my legacy visions." It was a legacy not only of what had been but of what might have been, a legacy of loss.

The Joe Hill/Woody Guthrie union dream had failed. The result: "No martyr is among ye now." Wind out of that quarter no longer carried answers. The question: why?

TO HANDLE MEN

lexander Agassiz had to deliver. His family, his friends, his own future depended on it.

When his brother-in-law, Quin Shaw, made him the new superintendent of the Calumet copper operation, he included "a substantial gift" of company stock. On top of that, Alex invested even more, borrowing from his other brother-in-law, Theodore Lyman, some $10,000, the equivalent of about $160,000 in early twenty-first-century currency. Plus, he convinced his sisters to do the same. Pauline was already in through her husband, Shaw. Ida's husband, Major Higginson, had been left "an unexpectedly large bequest," part of which he, too, invested in copper. The Calumet and Hecla mines had become the family business for the next generation of Boston Associates.

With Quin Shaw's initial investment, Calumet stock leapt from a dollar a share to seventy-five dollars: an extraordinary instant profit. But by the spring of Agassiz's arrival in Keweenaw, prices had begun to drop. Soon it was hard to get capital out of "an increasingly skeptical community," and Shaw was—in Agassiz's words, anyway— "at the end of his financial resources, pressed by his creditors, and loaded with law-suits."

On the ground, Agassiz found, "Everything was in confusion. Supplies were exhausted and cash was low. Lines of authority were tangled. . . ." One of his first letters back to Cambridge described "huge open pits . . . sunk in the middle of the lode. No attempt was made to support the roof, timbering was entirely neglected, and the mine was strained to its utmost capacity to produce rock at any price and regardless of the consequence." It was so disorganized that, as he put it, "Even if the pits were full of gold, it would be of no use."

His job, then, was more than getting at the copper. He had to set up an entire industry. Most of Keweenaw was low birch and tamarack forest, marshes filled with moose, rocky shorelines. In the few months he had before the snows started, shafts had to get dug, hoists erected, a smelter built, a railway laid to get the stamp rock to a smelter, and a dependable water supply established for the separating process—the Hulberts had been relying on a small pond created by a beaver dam. He had to bring civilization to the wilderness.

Agassiz's biggest challenge was the workforce. While there were some Upper Peninsula locals, most of the mine workers were immigrants. And many of them were familiar with Agassiz's brand of old-country "refinement and culture." In the words of one biographer, the new superintendent had a "cold demeanor and ferocious temper . . . not a forgiving man." No wonder the workers showed "nearly unanimous sympathy for Hulbert"—the local, recently fired—"and distrust and suspicion of the inexperienced intruder from Boston." As a result, Agassiz faced a slowdown verging on a work stoppage. "The thing I drive and look after is the only that goes," he wrote Shaw that first summer, "and just as fast as I pass from one thing to another, just as fast do things move." In addition to the workers' resistance, Agassiz believed Hulbert had "served his notice to be a nuisance."

The new superintendent had the miners dig exploratory shafts; that way he could provide samples for potential investors. And he got construction started on a rolling mill. But it was frustrating work. "I get fearfully blue up here at times all by myself and feel often like choking anybody who crosses my path." There was a year's worth of work to do in the few months before winter, and funding had dried up. "If Quin had ever known when he was beaten," Agassiz later wrote, "we would never have pulled the thing off." At the last moment, Shaw managed to secure additional capital from a New York speculator—and Agassiz got some from his father-in-law, Thomas Cary.

By August, the new superintendent was "trotting between" workplaces and supervising construction of five miles of railroad to haul stamp rock to the smelter. By late September, he'd gotten the mill at Hecla running. Still, in Agassiz's words, the locals "laughed at everything that was done." In an outpouring to Shaw, he wrote, "I get perfectly frantic with the men here: nobody seems to take any interest in what is doing, all simply here to live on you, and when any attempt is made to prevent chances of slighting work, seem determined to put all possible obstacles in your way, and instead of attempting to help you, seem bound to see if they cannot compel you to yield and do as they want."

Here he'd bet everything on the mines—and talked his family and friends into joining him—and the workers weren't interested. They treated it like . . . a job. "I don't wonder mines don't pay," Agassiz reported back to Cambridge, "for the people up here care very little whether they do or not as long as they stay open."

In November, as the snows began, the battle of wills got worse. Agassiz discovered that the railroad track he'd pushed all summer to finish was an inch wider than the locomotive's. Operations came "to a dead standstill." Agassiz blamed his assistant, but it was more pervasive than that. Why hadn't anybody noticed? Why hadn't anybody said anything? In the superintendent's mind, the laughter, the slighting of work, the slowdowns now verged on sabotage. "I am in such a rage," he concluded a letter to Shaw, "that I cannot write better."

The workers didn't care. And they wouldn't obey him. Now it was December, and winter had come "in earnest." Still, he got the men to redo the railroad till it was successfully hauling stamp rock to the mill. Then came another setback. "We tried the mill today," he wrote Shaw, ". . . and I am sorry to say I am awfully disappointed." The ancient Michigan stone was too hard, the mill too weak: it couldn't crush the stamp rock.

"I have done the best I could," he wrote Shaw, "but I am satisfied from the results that I have made many blunders . . . simply from my want of experience of the ways of the men up here. . . . If [things] don't improve materially, my advice would be to sell out the whole thing in a block. . . ."

He'd failed. The rock and the weather and the men were all too hard.

Spring came slowly. When the ground thawed and work could recommence, the new shafts finally began to yield copper. The new locomotive hauled it on the new rails. And the improved mill crushed it. Agassiz had even managed to secure a dependable water supply by replacing the beaver dam with an earth-and-rock construction. It seemed his constant driving of the men had worked.

Then on a Saturday night in June, when the mines were shut down for the weekend, there was an explosion. Someone had blown up the dam. Water flooded the new mill, the mineshafts, the whole operation. "The watchman," Agassiz reported, "must either have been scared off or got asleep. I don't know which yet . . . no one knows how the thing took place."

The watchman told Agassiz that "the Irish" had done it. By that, he meant the Hulbert brothers. "I wish I could just get my hands on them," Agassiz wrote Shaw. "I should shoot either one of them with perfect satisfaction." But it wasn't just the Hulberts. To Agassiz, the workers in general, no matter where they came from, were "the Irish"—those who stood in the way of progress, too hard to fit into the system, the unrefined.

Agassiz put "all men we could get on dam repairing damage." By Sunday night, they had enough water pressure to get the mill started back up. It turned out to be the last major hitch. By late summer, the operation was running smoothly enough for the Hecla mine to produce about 185 tons of ingot a month; Calumet, 140.

Part of that was the result of modernization. Agassiz had upgraded the operation: from sledgehammers to mechanical drills, from dimly lit tunnels and rope hoists to underground railroads and steam-powered lifts. Soon, he'd dotted the wilderness of the Upper Peninsula with red sandstone mills, hoists, smelters, and "a collection of steam engines second to none in the world."

Between 1866, when Quin Shaw became Calumet's delivering angel, and 1869, when Agassiz turned things around, Michigan's output of copper doubled. Soon the dominant producer in the world copper market was no longer England but the seventy-mile-long Keweenaw Peninsula. Much of that was from the Calumet and Hecla mines. In five years, the two shafts would go from producing just over 8 percent of the state's output to over 60 percent.

It would be hailed as a great American success story. Man conquers nature, wrestles value out of the frontier, creates an industry and a civilization. The towns of Red Jacket, Hancock, Houghton sprang up and prospered, thanks, as some people saw it, to one man: Alexander Agassiz. "Called as a last resort to prop up a failing enterprise," one historian wrote, "he transformed it into one of the most prosperous and extensive mines known in the history of industry."

Though Yankee determination—and capital—got credit for the success, it wouldn't have happened without political power. Even as his workers were repairing the sabotaged dam, Agassiz was in Washington with Shaw, lobbying for a copper tariff. In an open market, Michigan had to compete not only with European copper but potentially, a South American product that could be mined with cheaper labor. In 1869, the influence of the Boston Associates helped pass a tariff that doubled the duty on imported copper and added three cents a pound on imported stamp rock. That guaranteed US copper would dominate the domestic market. More, it effectively closed East Coast smelting plants, which depended on imported ore. For the next fifteen years, most of the world's copper would come out of and be processed in Michigan's Upper Peninsula.

There, the Keweenaw copper companies formed what was known as a corporate pool. Competing mine and smelter owners met and agreed to set prices and levels of production. One of the pool's first acts was to dump five million pounds of copper abroad.

The resulting scarcity drove domestic prices up, a profit margin the pool then guaranteed by agreeing to take only so much copper out of the ground.

In 1871, a merger produced Calumet, Hecla, Portland and Scott Mining Companies, known as C&H. Agassiz was elected president. He owned about 10 percent of the stock, and his extended family controlled around 35 percent. As the nation's growing electrification program doubled the demand for copper wire, C&H played "an increasingly important role" in the copper pool. It helped create what one analyst calls "a substantial subsidy for the industry at the expense of consumers in the United States."

Agassiz took care that these manipulations of the market stayed private. "The company does not give detailed figures to its stockholders," one observer noted, but "the stockholders content themselves with a minimum of information . . . and the maximum of profits." Or as Agassiz wrote a friend, "As long as the stockholders have faith in the management of the Companies, let them keep quiet and ask no embarrassing questions. . . ." And why shouldn't they have faith? In the fifteen years between 1869 and 1884, stockholders would receive some $25 million in dividends.

One of the first things Agassiz did with his money was to pay for the publication of his monograph on sea urchins. "I shall take this out of the Dividend," he wrote, "and never know it." He then went on a tour of Europe that included a visit to Charles Darwin. In a letter of introduction, his father, Louis Agassiz, wrote, "You will find Alex far more ready to accept your views than I shall ever be." When he returned to America, Alex rented an estate in Cambridge. But he insisted, "I want to go down as a man of science and not be known by a kind of cheap notoriety as an American millionaire."

He dedicated himself to the support and expansion of his father's museum. In 1872, Quin Shaw donated $100,000 to the cause, and Harvard's Museum of Comparative Zoology went on to double in size. The barrels of specimens could be sorted, labeled, displayed. Alex donated several million dollars to Harvard and built a research center in Newport, Rhode Island. His brother-in-law, Thomas Lee Higginson, donated so much of his C&H profits to the college that, by the 1920s, Upton Sinclair would refer to it as "The University of Lee-Higginson." And Louis Agassiz's young wife—Alex's step-mother—would go on to co-found and become first president of Radcliffe College.

Five years after Agassiz got the mines up and running, his father died of a massive stroke. That night, Alex's young wife caught cold, and she died a week later of pneumonia. Rich, successful, he suddenly lost all purpose. "I can find no incentive for anything," he wrote a friend. "I feel as if I were acting a constant lie, but it is a harmless one which I must make up my mind to keep for many a weary year." He started traveling, going from the Galapagos to the Great Barrier Reef, gathering evidence to disprove Darwin's theory about the origin of coral reefs. "[It] does not make any difference," he declared, "and all I can do is try and distract myself." He was, in his son's words, a "permanently saddened man."

He still had the mines to run. "We are accustomed," wrote Agassiz's son and biographer, "to think of the man who devotes himself to pure science as aloof from the world, with but little interest or ability in the practical concerns of our complex modern civilization. Agassiz is a striking exception." Though he spent most of each year traveling on his scientific expeditions, he was described as managing C&H "as though his eyes were ten-power field glasses." He'd visit Calumet every fall and spring to keep the operation, as he put it, "in apple pie order and running as smooth as clockwork."

The key to that clockwork was labor relations. According to the company's official history, "What Mr. Agassiz accomplished was in a great measure due to his ability to handle men, to make them like and respect him." Keweenaw had only one real business—copper—and C&H was by far the largest employer. The company created and controlled thousands of jobs. It considered its operation "an object lesson of what may be accomplished when the workman is treated with understanding, sympathy, justice and intelligent consideration."

Agassiz set the tone. A contemporary called him a "curious combination of democrat and autocrat." On the one hand, he was "appalled at the squalor produced by Western Europe's and early America's industrialization." He was determined that the corporate civilization he brought to Keweenaw would be different. Yes, he was in the UP to turn a profit, but in the process, he hoped to use his liberal education to establish "worker satisfaction and civilized communities."

It was a lot like the goals of the old Boston Associates. Back in 1810, Francis Cabot Lowell had visited the vast cotton mills in Manchester, England, to study (some say steal) their manufacturing methods. He returned to set up his own American textile factories but was bothered by the conditions that came with industrialization: the streams clogged with industrial slime, the air yellow with smoke, the cramped and unsanitary tenements often decimated by cholera epidemics. Friedrich Engels, who worked as a textile agent in Manchester, believed this "Hell upon Earth" was "the grim future of capitalism." One of the goals of the Communist Manifesto, which Engels wrote with Marx, was to imagine an alternative to "the great factory of the industrial capitalist."

Lowell and the Boston Associates also wanted an alternative. But instead of communism, they envisioned a modified, enlightened capitalism. They turned to what was known as the Scottish model, where the factory owner thought of himself not as an oppressor or a profiteer but as an "improving landlord." Years later, Agassiz set up something similar in Keweenaw.

As the copper mines prospered, C&H put up workers housing: more than seven hundred plain but livable homes, "all alike and painted red." The company provided running water and connected almost half the houses to the company's sewer system. This company housing rented out monthly for a dollar a room, and that included water, garbage pickup, repairs. About a third of C&H workers leased houses from the company, while another third boarded in those houses' extra rooms. C&H bought wood and coal in bulk to keep the price down for its employees.

The company also provided education, recreation, and health care. It funded company bands, company ball teams, company skating rinks, company bowling allies. It built a fully equipped company bathhouse and, nearby, an impressive library that held thirty-five thousand books. It also built ten public schools, soon considered among the finest in the United States. True, the curriculum tended toward vocational training. And few students went on to high school. But that's partly because their futures were all but guaranteed. Their company education prepared them for a company job. C&H built and ran a hospital, which, like the schools, mirrored company values. Its doctors refused to treat venereal disease, for example, because Agassiz considered it a "self-inflicted wound."

Red Jacket, Hancock, Houghton, Laurium, Ojibway were company towns that upheld company morals and depended on the company's benevolence. In America's Gilded Age, Agassiz built what some observers saw as a "self-sufficient empire . . . wherein the corporation and the men worked harmoniously for the common welfare according to the most advanced ethics of the 19th century . . ." Those ethics were seen as "laissez-faire and . . . absolute individualism," but C&H's model of capitalism incorporated collective benefits. The company set up one of America's first workers' aid funds, paying half the cost of injuries and rehab (the other half taken out of workers' wages). It ran a broom factory to employ disabled workers, and it established a pension system (again, half funded through workers' wages). According to the Michigan commissioner of mining statistics, "No mining company in the world treated its employees better than Calumet and Hecla." Or as the wife of one C&H worker put it, "The company was wonderful—a man always came and fixed the toilet."

If that was Agassiz's democratic side, there was also the autocrat. Like his father, Alex believed in a social hierarchy, in "individual eminence . . . wealth and culture." After taking over sponsorship of the Agassiz Museum, he came to resent its emphasis on educating the general public, especially as the museum got "more and more absorbed in undergraduate instruction." In 1898, he wrote, "I am sick to death of supplying the means of running a big machine. . . ." He preferred focusing on specialists doing advanced work. The man who had stayed "in a rage" that first summer in Keweenaw, "perfectly frantic" with the locals and ready to shoot "the Irish," would storm at trespassers on his Newport estate: "[T]he way everybody drives all over the place and ties his horses everywhere is perfectly outrageous. The worst of it is that when they are spoken to, they are so insolent."

Agassiz wanted an alternative to capitalism's grim future, wanted to be an improving landlord, but he expected to control which improvements happened and who received them. That's why the list of C&H pensioners was never made public: so management could decide in private whose twenty years of work would be rewarded and whose wouldn't. In the same way, management had the final say on who got to rent company housing. Even if workers could afford to buy their own place, C&H stayed in control. It owned some seventy-five thousand acres in Keweenaw, which meant many homeowners had to lease the land their houses stood on. If they displeased management—showed questionable morals, asked for better pay, talked union—they could be ordered off. It then became their problem how to pick up and move their houses.

At work, the company decided who got which job. Almost all crew captains were "native-born." Underground, the Cornish were the "immigrant elite": they directed the mine crews, gauging which way a lode was running, where to drill the blasting holes, how much powder to use. After the explosion, a lower level of employee—trammers—mucked out the rock, loaded it by shovel or hand into a tram car, pushed the car down an underground track to a lift, unloaded it, pushed it back to where the miners were drilling, and started over again. By the early twentieth century, trammers were moving about a thousand pounds of rock a day, and almost all were first-generation immigrants: Austrians, Italians, Croatians, Finns.

The company kept the distinctions rigid. Non–English speakers made up the majority of the workforce and of the local population—two-thirds of Red Jacket's residents, for example. Only a little over 10 percent of the residents of Keweenaw were what was called "native white of native parentage." But management claimed that the few times it named foreigners (other than the Cornish) as crew heads, "We got more criticism from these nationalists than if we had promoted a man not of their kind." Under Agassiz, then, C&H organized its labor force in the sort of strict ethnic categories that would have fit smoothly into his father's theory of racial types.

There was some fightback early on. As C&H's dividends rose, workers began agitating for better wages. And an eight-hour day. On May 1, 1872—five years after Agassiz arrived in Keweenaw and less than year after he'd been appointed president of C&H—they struck.

Agassiz urged his manager to approach the strikers in a spirit of "cheerful cooperation." But the strike spread to other Keweenaw mines, and within a week, Agassiz and C&H asked Michigan's governor to send in troops. The combined punch of big business and state militia quickly ended the action. The company later increased wages by 10 percent but insisted it wasn't in response to the strike. And the work day stayed ten hours long.

The next year, enormous corporate debt and a string of financial scandals brought on the national panic of 1873. Prices plummeted, banks and railroads failed, the stock exchange was closed for ten days. Unemployment soon soared, so those businesses that weren't hurt by the panic—the copper industry, for one—could hire when they wanted and on the terms they wanted. So when C&H workers called another strike in early 1874, their second in two years, Agassiz had no patience for it. "We cannot be dictated to by anyone," he wrote his manager. "The mine must stop if it stays closed forever. . . ." In his estimation, "we have always treated our men fairly and honestly." He was a widower by then, and his father had died, and he took the workers' action personally. "I have attempted formerly to try and get their good will. . . . They spit in my face as it were. . . . Wages will be raised whenever we see fit and at no other time."

The company broke the strike in less than a week. "It is high time," wrote the local *Mining Gazette*, "a class of men in this country were taught that the rights of a corporation are just as sacred as those of an individual."

There wasn't another strike for thirty years. In 1877, during nationwide labor battles that became known as the Great Uprising, when President Rutherford B. Hayes felt he had to send out federal troops to stop strikes, Keweenaw remained quiet. In 1886, when bombs went off in Chicago's Haymarket Square during protests to establish the eight-hour day, Keweenaw remained quiet. Surveying the scene in 1902, Michigan's commissioner of mineral statistics confidently reported, "The copper miner is the best paid wage-earner in the world, is assured of steady work the year-round, and the companies are always zealous for his comfort and safety. Naturally the labor agitator has poor picking in the copper district."

The answer to unrest—and so the key to prosperity—was the improving landlord. C&H went from employing 1,200 men at the beginning of the 1870s to 3,500 in 1890 to over 4,000 by 1910. Many were born in company homes, left company schools for company jobs, died in company hospitals. Keweenaw had become "an industrial Arcadia," as one historian put it, ". . . secure, productive, healthy, and benevolent." Within that industrial Arcadia, there were ways to get ahead. A man (no women worked in the mines) could advance from drill boy to trammer to miner and then, if he was the right nationality, to captain. But there the ladder ended. People who lived in the UP were the workers: they blasted, hauled, smelted, and transported the copper. Meanwhile, those who owned it—over 90 percent of the stockholders—lived outside Michigan. From its beginnings in the Gilded Age into the Progressive Era, the company maintained "a well-ordered social pattern . . . with a few elegant Bostonians at the top."

People started calling it the Copper Country Empire. "With a

lavish Boston aristocracy and the well-being of 66,000 Keweena-
nawans resting on their shoulders," an analyst concluded, "Alexander Agassiz and his board of directors may be pardoned if they
occasionally forgot some of the democratic principles their forefa-
thers fought for in the American Revolution." Democracy is fine
and good, but you don't run a business that way. You need someone
at the top to make decisions and take responsibility. Experience had
convinced Agassiz that workers weren't really interested, that unions
only made trouble, that to succeed a company couldn't be dictated to
by the masses. If, as a sympathetic journalist wrote in 1912, ". . . the
system verges on paternalism, it is the kind of paternalism that kills
unionism and, in one generation, builds out of foreigners, ignorant
of Anglo-Saxon institutions, citizens that any community can well
be proud of."

C&H, then, was making good Americans. Out west, the heavy-
handedness of the mine owners had turned workers' complaints into
labor wars that had led to organized opposition: the WFM. Agassiz
steered C&H in a different direction. Maybe he—as the improving landlord, as the company's founding father—was willing to take
the cane to his workers, but wasn't that his right and responsibility,
the "sacred right" of a corporation? Wasn't that part of what made
America great?

In C&H, Agassiz created a corporate model, an "object lesson,"
that would lead the way to modern business methods. In the process,
it made Alexander Agassiz one of the richest citizens in the United
States. And in Woody Guthrie's eyes, an enemy of the people.

TILL THE WORLD
IS LEVEL

A s far as Woody Guthrie's wife, Mary, was concerned, "He never should have been involved in politics. . . . [It was] his downfall as an entertainer." And in a sense, it was—if his goal was to be an entertainer.

Politics cost him his job at KFVD in Los Angeles. Around Thanksgiving 1939, Woody, Mary, their four-year-old, two-year-old, and month-old baby headed back east on Route 66 to Pampa: reverse migrants.

There wasn't a lot to come back to. After a little over two years on the radio, Guthrie had a career, but it was mostly in and around southern California. He tried working in Pampa's drugstore for a little bit while he figured things out. Even if he got on local Texas radio or restarted his cowboy band, it wasn't going to be like Los Angeles. There, between his show, his live appearances at rallies, playing with Will Geer, touring the migrant camps, writing his column, he'd felt part of something larger.

That something larger was a specific brand of communism, a Depression-era phenomenon known as the Popular Front—"Popular" because (like pop music?) it hoped to appeal to a wide spectrum of Americans. And a "front" as in the front or frontier of a larger battle. As Guthrie was playing his first Communist rallies in California, the main front was in Spain. To communists, the Spanish Civil War pitted the democratically elected government against General Francisco Franco's fascist troops, backed by Hitler and Mussolini. While England, France, and the United States stayed officially neutral, the Soviet Union opposed Franco's coup as part of the larger fascist threat. That battle had to be fought everywhere—in Madrid, in Berlin, in the fields of California: a worldwide Popular Front.

Before Guthrie arrived in California, the American Communist Party had been a relatively small, tight-knit organization. Its national membership was estimated at seventy-five thousand, much of it foreign-born and unemployed, almost a third living in or near New York City. The party took a hard line: capitalism would fall; communism would triumph; you were either a supporter or the enemy. So in the summer of 1934, when the San Francisco general strike began, the party attacked Upton Sinclair as a "faker and forthcoming fascist" and described FDR's policies as "demagogy."

But within a year, the Communist International had changed tactics. It now recognized the need for allies in what it was calling a "People's Front Against Fascism and War." The new front welcomed socialists, New Dealers, organized labor. Within the AF of L, American communists helped form the Committee for Industrial Organization (later the Congress of Industrial Organizations), which tried to pick up where the Wobblies had left off. Two decades after Joe Hill's execution, it called for industrial unionism for all workers. Appealing to lettuce pickers in California, textile workers in New York, auto workers in Michigan, the CIO became part of "the largest sustained surge of worker organization in American history."

The communists Guthrie met in West Coast migrant camps saw themselves fighting for basic American ideals. The Popular Front presented itself as homegrown: the next step in a line that ran back through Whitman and Lincoln and Tom Paine. It was a line of anger. And it was a line of loss. Modern America, it argued, had lost sight of its ideals and needed to reconnect. The country once had "golden sunsets" and "virgin prairies wide," as a Wobbly poet had written, but now "new dismal cities rise . . . / And freedom is not

there nor here." They could almost be Gene Autry lyrics. In appealing to that streak of American nostalgia, the Popular Front offered
"the promise of a different road beyond modernism." After the flap-
pers and fast cars and hot jazz of the Twenties, the sizzling American
economy had collapsed. Now, the Popular Front argued, you had to
look back to see the future; you had to build on traditional working-
class values, on folk values.

Some of Guthrie's friends believed that the revolution would
grow "within the womb of the disintegrating two old parties."
Earl Browder, leader of the American Communist Party, saw the
New Deal as "an essential part of the developing democratic front
against monopoly capital." For all its "weaknesses and inadequacies,
its hesitations and confusion," FDR's program championed unemployment compensation, social security, food stamps, job programs.
If this sounded like what C&H had done in northern Michigan—
offering benefits that tempered but didn't fundamentally change
capitalism—the Popular Front maintained these were steps on the
path. FDR, consciously or not, was incorporating collective, socialist ideas: getting the State to intervene and help people when the free
market couldn't or wouldn't. The Works Progress Administration
used federal money to hire artists to paint murals in small-town post
offices; the Tennessee Valley Authority built dams to provide electricity to the rural South. It wasn't a revolution (yet), but the Popular
Front argued that you could both support radical change and be a
mainstream New Dealer. "Communism," as Browder put it, "was
Twentieth Century Americanism."

The new approach called for new language. There was less talk
about "the proletariat"—a term that maybe sounded too foreign
(the same way Hägglund or Zimmerman did?)—and more about
"the people," as in Guthrie's phrase "singing with the people." And
the people included not just the awakened masses but the unskilled,
unemployed, disenchanted. Not just whites, but Asians, Hispanics,
blacks. As African-American author Richard Wright described the
Popular Front, "It did not say: 'Be like us and we will like you,

maybe.' It said: 'If you possess enough courage to speak out what you are, you will find that you are not alone.'" What Guthrie, the Lone Wolf, had found in Los Angeles was a "culture of unity," a home.

But another definition of a front is a false face, and that's how many Americans saw this new brand of communism. To them, the Popular Front was a mask, a cover to let the Soviet Union insinuate itself into America. Even as Guthrie read his little blue book copy of the Constitution of the Soviet Union, reports emerged of purges in Russia: political executions in which thousands—some said hundreds of thousands—were killed. And when the Soviet Union signed its nonaggression pact with the Nazis, the *New York Times* declared, "Hitlerism is brown communism, Stalinism is red fascism."

Guthrie, meanwhile, supported what he saw as the Soviet Union's neutrality. "Now," he wrote his sister, "it looks like there are some wars breaking out around over the world. This is between the rich people. Us poor folks have nothing in the world to do with these wars, because, win, lose, or draw, we are poor to commence with, and will be poor to end with." That was the crux of it. He declared himself in the fight ". . . till the world is level—and there ain't no rich man, and there ain't no poor man, and every man on earth is at work and his family is living as human beings instead of like a nest of rats."

It was that kind of talk that had landed him back in Pampa, where there was nothing popular about the Popular Front. If Congress reflected the country's mood, the fight wasn't to make the world level but to defeat Communism. It passed the Hatch Act, denying federal jobs to anyone advocating the overthrow of the government. Soon the Voorhis Act would mandate that all groups with "foreign affiliations" had to register with the government. And popular media was often supportive: William Randolph Hearst, head of a nationwide newspaper chain, began calling the Democrats "the party of Karl Marx and Franklin Delano Roosevelt."

In this wave of anti-communism, New York was an island of

Popular Front support. After Guthrie had spent a couple months in Texas, he got a letter from Will Geer inviting him to come to New York, where Geer promised him a place to stay and the kind of radio work and live shows he'd been doing in L.A. It meant he could return to the fight and reach an even larger audience. Guthrie jumped.

But he didn't jump freight. Or hitchhike. Contrary to the legend that would grow up around him, Guthrie much preferred driving his own car. So he left Mary and the three kids in Pampa and headed east. He got as far as his brother's in Oklahoma before the car broke down. He sold the wreck for twenty-five dollars and bought a bus ticket as far as Pittsburgh. There he ran out of options. In January, in the Allegheny Mountains, in a raging snowstorm, he put his thumb out. There wasn't much traffic, and it took a long time to make a couple hundred miles. Finally, some strangers picked him up and, feeling bad for him, donated enough money for him to get back on a bus. Which is how Woody Guthrie entered New York City.

The Geers put him up for a week. Then he found a room in a beat-up hotel off Times Square. Here, having spent the past three months crossing the continent (in stages) from California to the New York Island, he wrote what would become "This Land Is Your Land." It's the song of a man fresh to the big city, about to reinvent himself, his political faith still strong. "This land belongs to you and me."

It's also an answer song. Back when Guthrie was starting his Lone Wolf broadcasts on KFVD, the number-one pop singer of the day, Kate Smith, had created a sensation by singing Irving Berlin's "God Bless America" on national radio. Almost instantly it became a patriotic anthem, so popular that Smith reprised it weekly on her own program for the next year. Guthrie would have heard it in California, in Pampa, on the radio coming east, and on that new invention, the jukebox, in New York City. Finally, he had to respond.

Israel Isidore "Irving" Berlin was from Joe Hill's generation of immigrants. His Russian Jewish family fled the pogroms for New York's Lower East Side. Like Hill, Berlin saw America as a land of opportunity, but where Hill decided the promise was mostly "pie in the sky," Berlin believed in the dream. A few years after Hill was executed, Berlin was serving as a soldier in World War I and wrote a testimonial to his adopted motherland.

At the time, the tune didn't do much. But just before the next world war, Smith—known as "the Songbird of the South," came to Berlin looking for material. She was going to be on an Armistice Day broadcast and wanted, she explained, "more than an Armistice Day song. I wanted a new hymn of praise and love and allegiance to America. . . ." It was 1938. Hitler was in power and had taken over Austria and parts of Czechoslovakia. Smith's spoken intro sets the stage: "While the storm clouds gather far across the sea . . ." Then she launches into Berlin's lyrics.

They tell a classic story of immigrant success. America begins as "the land that I love" and ends as "home, sweet home." On the page, the words read like a supplication, requesting that God stand beside and guide the nation. But add the martial strain of the music and Kate Smith's big voice, and it becomes a declaration of triumph. she marches the tune forward, slowing to tremble at the country's majesty but ending with a ringing affirmation. God has—and always will—bless America. The song's patriotic fervor helped make it a bipartisan sensation, used at the 1940 conventions of both Democrats and Republicans.

As Guthrie kept hearing the tune on the radio, it made him angrier and angrier. To his ears, its horns were a call to join a war he didn't believe in, a war among capitalists for capitalism. The triumphant beat celebrated a lie. And Kate Smith's strident, emotional voice was rallying people to defeat change and defend the status quo. "God Bless America" was a self-satisfied anthem for a nation that belonged only to certain people—who believed a certain way and in a certain god.

In his room off Times Square, Guthrie wrote his answer. He called it "God Blessed America." In the first written draft, he doesn't question God's existence or His power to anoint a nation. But where Berlin asks for God's blessing, Guthrie says it's already happened.

"This land," he begins, "is your land." Where Berlin skims from mountains to prairies to ocean, Guthrie gets more specific: "from the red-wood forest to the Gulf stream water." For the melody, he borrowed an old Baptist hymn the Carter Family had recorded, the apocalyptic "When the World's on Fire." The old tune declares that on Judgment Day, we'll be wanting God's bosom to be our pillow. Guthrie plays off that, insisting we don't have to wait till then for the world to get better and we don't have to pray to God to make it happen; there's already a voice around us, sounding.

In this first version, the chorus is "God blessed America for me." But who exactly is this "me"? The verses clarify. It's someone who's walked America's highways, who's roamed and rambled, who's watched people waiting in line at the relief office. God blessed America, in other words, for them that don't have, including the Singing Bum.

Four years later, when Guthrie recorded the song, he eliminated God altogether and changed the chorus to "This land is your land." It isn't a question or a prayer but a present-tense reality. Where Kate Smith's voice calls to the back row of some Broadway theater, Guthrie sings with the unemotional, understated delivery of a reporter. At the bottom of the original copy of the lyrics, he made a note: "All you can write is what you see." His song is based not on patriotism but observation: the truth.

Woody Guthrie's New York success came as quickly as Bob Dylan's would. Two weeks after he hit town, at the end of February 1940, there was a benefit for Spanish Civil War refugees. Guthrie sang some dust-bowl songs and a brand-new number about FDR. A few days earlier, the president had denounced the Soviet Union as "a dictatorship as absolute as any other dictatorship in the world." Guthrie's tune struck back, describing European "war lords;" while "they butcher and they kill / Uncle Sam foots the bill." Then he mocked FDR's advice to a group of young Communist protestors: "You gotta make your resolution through the U.S. Constitution." Listeners were impressed not just by the sharpness of Guthrie's anger but by its speed. It was a skill he'd honed with "event songs." As Dylan said years later, "He wanted to bring the news very quick to people."

One amazed member of the audience saw "this little guy, big bushy hair, with this great voice and his guitar . . . [a] ballad-maker [in the] pure country style," playing a mix of "ragtime, hillbilly, blues . . . all the currents of his time." Together, he thought it added up to "a new idiom . . . [with] the sound of movement in it . . . the sound of a big truck going down the highway with the riders bouncing around in the front seat." The listener was twenty-five-year-old Alan Lomax, and the sound of Woody Guthrie was what he'd been looking for.

Square-faced, dark-haired, bright-eyed, with a wide, hungry-looking mouth, Lomax was an enthusiast. That night when he first heard Guthrie, he was simultaneously an anthropology student at Columbia University, a producer of national radio shows promoting America's "authentic music," and an assistant to his father, John Lomax, at the Washington, DC, national Archive of American Folk Song. In Guthrie, Lomax heard the culmination of a search that had begun decades earlier.

John Lomax was the son of a horse rancher. While Charley Guthrie was busy snapping up farms in Oklahoma, John was collecting cowboy songs in Texas. He didn't graduate from college till he was thirty, and then when he showed his manuscript of Western ballads to his professors, they dismissed it as "tawdry, cheap and unworthy." He promptly went behind a dorm and burned it. But eight years later, when he got a fellowship to Harvard, the nearly forty-year-old student was encouraged to go back and resurrect *Cowboy Songs and Other Frontier Ballads*.

Lomax, Sr. had a particular take on cowboys. To him, they were "roving and restless young blades from all over the South" singing "the song heritage of their English ancestors." The British connection is what interested Harvard. Back in 1855, poet James Russell Lowell (distantly related to the Lowells of the Boston Associates) had given a public lecture in Cambridge, declaring, "The ballads are the only true folk songs that we have in English. There is no other poetry in the language that addresses us so simply. . . ." In the audience was Francis James Child, a Chaucer expert. Inspired, Child began collecting songs (mostly from old manuscripts) for an exhaustive ten-volume set of English and Scottish ballads.

It was the same era and at the same university where Louis Agassiz was collecting for his museum, and the two shared some beliefs. Where Agassiz saw his fossils as evidence of God's master plan, Child saw old ballads as links to a pure Anglo-Saxon past. They were the "true voice" of the people. In the romantic, nineteenth-century German concept of *Volk*, folk songs were a way back into the unadulterated soul of mankind. Joan Baez would include ten Child ballads on her first five albums. And the dream of a "lost England," of "the old simplicities and candours," helped feed Dylan's notion of folk music as a mythical realm.

It was in that tradition that Harvard welcomed John Lomax. America's musical past might be shorter and messier, but it could be traced back to England's pure musical wellspring. As Louis Agassiz did with species, Lomax tried to categorize folk music, dividing the songs of lumbermen from railroaders from "the negro, and . . . the tramp." Like Child, he believed the older the song, the purer, so he tried to collect in the nation's remotest regions, where the music was less likely to be tainted by modern civilization. But the genealogy was more complicated. The nation's first compilation of folk music, for example, was *Slave Songs of the United States*: African rhythms and singing techniques applied to Baptist hymns and who knew what else. John Lomax's most famous discovery came from a black cook in a "low drinking dive" in San Antonio, who was singing something he called "Home on the Range."

Lomax's son, Alan, both followed his father and rebelled against him. Enrolling in Harvard in the midst of the Great Depression, the sixteen-year-old found his academic courses filled him with "cold indifference and anger." Soon he was writing his father that he was "soaked and soaking in theoretical communism." He left college after a year. "Communism," he told his sister, drawing flames on the capital C, "& low grades & monetary deficiency will keep me out of Harvard indefinitely." To his father, he wrote, "I think now that, unless I go red, I should like to look at the folk-songs of this country along with you. . . ." As it turned out, he did both.

The Lomax father-and-son team collected throughout Texas, the Deep South, the remote Appalachian hills, in prisons and other isolated areas. The summer Guthrie was reporting on California's migrant camps, for example, Alan Lomax was in Michigan's Upper Peninsula, documenting what the Finns and Swedes and Italians were singing near Calumet. Like his father, Alan was interested in the remote and the pure, but where his father was politically conservative, to Alan folk songs were "summaries of the great proletarian population." What he saw hidden in that mythical realm was a radical past, a vein of protest. "My job," Alan Lomax would write, "was to try and get as much of these views, these feelings, this unheard majority onto the center of the stage."

The Lomaxes became not just collectors, but promoters. One of their greatest discoveries followed Guthrie onto the stage that night at the Spanish refugees benefit. Huddie Ledbetter, known as Lead Belly, was a two-time offender who the Lomaxes first heard at Louisiana's Angola Prison in 1933. John Lomax admitted that what Lead Belly sang wasn't "folk songs entirely." He mixed blues, jazz, spirituals, hillbilly, even pop songs of the day. Those last were, Alan declared, "my worst enemy . . . wiping out the music that I care about—American traditional folk music." But with his deep rich voice, an astonishing repertory that included songs like "Goodnight, Irene" and "Midnight Special," and his ragtime twelve-string guitar, Lead Belly was too exciting to deny.

The singer signed on as the Lomaxes' driver. In a newsreel Lomax, Sr. produced re-enacting their first meeting, the musicologist declares, "I never heard so many good Negro songs." To which Lead Belly replies, "You be my big boss, and I'll be your man." Soon Lead

Belly was performing at Lomax's lectures, including a triumphant appearance at Harvard. Lomax Sr. saw it as a benevolent arrangement. But after six months, Lead Belly quit, furious over what he saw as an exploitative management contract that included partial copyright on his songs. Alan, however, stayed his "young admirer." Lead Belly was as close as he'd come to finding a singer who could evoke America, "the wild land and the heart-torn people."

Then he heard Woody Guthrie.

It was lucky the Spanish refugee concert happened when it did. A year earlier, Alan Lomax was dismissing hillbilly music—the commercial sound of the Carter Family and Jimmie Rodgers—as "Anglo-American, blond, blue-eyed sentimentalism and musical gaucherie." He hated that it was being fobbed off as traditional, describing a "stupid hill-billy show" as "masquerading under the title of 'folk festival.'" In the months before Guthrie came to town, Lomax became a copyright advisor for the RCA label. His job was to determine if songs had been previously recorded, and that meant going back and listening to all the hillbilly music cut in the twenties and thirties. To his surprise, Lomax discovered mountain ballads, blues, cowboy songs. He came to the conclusion that the labels— and artist/collectors like A. P. Carter—had actually done "a broader and more interesting job of recording American folk music than folklorists. . . ."

By the time Guthrie appeared on his first New York stage, Alan Lomax was taking a Popular Front approach to music: all types and all allies were welcome. He appreciated how the little man with the bushy hair seemed to mix musical influences. A week later, Guthrie did his second benefit show: the John Steinbeck Committee's "Grapes of Wrath Evening" to help farmworkers. Will Geer had organized it and was performing; so were Alan Lomax and his sister, Bess, Lead Belly, and Lomax's young assistant, Peter Seeger. It was the core of New York's still small folk scene.

The other performers watched as Guthrie "just ambled out" onstage, "offhand and casual . . . complete with western hat, boots, bluejeans, and needing a shave. . . ." The *Daily Worker* was already promoting Guthrie as "a real dust bowl refugee . . . straight out of Steinbeck's [book]." For the big-city audience, he threw in an extra helping of Will Rogers, declaring, "New York sure is a funny place. . . . [The subways] were so crowded today, you couldn't even fall down." To Earl Robinson, "It was an act, obviously, but it felt so fantastically real." To Alan Lomax, it confirmed his first impression. And Guthrie's originals were "ballads," as Lomax put it, " . . . that will fool a folklore expert."

As soon as the concert ended, Lomax began making plans. Within two weeks, he had Guthrie down in DC recording for the Library of Congress. The idea was to create an "oral autobiography" of the singer, a technique borrowed from Soviet folklorists. Mixing Guthrie's songs and stories, Lomax hoped to capture a history of America, the "wild land and the heart-torn people."

So Guthrie's first record wasn't a commercial release like Gene Autry's or Jimmie Rogers'. But the format was enough like his old radio show that he could relax. If he sounds a little uncomfortable talking about his personal history, especially his family, the confidence kicks in when he gets to the material he's done before— dust-bowl songs and stories. They aren't *his* story—in a typical introduction, he tells Lomax, "I kept looking at all these people, and it just struck me to write this song. . . ."—but they are his interpretation of the American scene. Lomax leads him from the dust bowl into songs about hard times, outlaws, bankers, the men's shared politics helping to shape the conversation.

When Lomax asks for a definition of the blues, Guthrie answers "just plain old being lonesome." Then he adds, "A lot of people don't think that's a big enough word, but you can get lonesome for a lot of things. People down around where I come from are lonesome for a job. . . ." Guthrie, in his Okie drawl, talks with Lomax, with his Texas drawl, about the Negroes he knew back in Okemah. "Ever since I was a kid growin' up, I've always found time to stop and talk to these colored people. Because I find them to be full of jokes. And wisdom!" He does an imitation of the "big bare-footed boy" who taught him how to play harmonica. "I'd never hardly pass either an Indian or a colored boy where I . . . learned to like 'em." You can hear him trying to find his way from "Run, Nigger, Run" to the Popular Front's goal of racial equality.

During his first days in New York City, in the same Times Square hotel room where he wrote "This Land Is Your Land," he composed a song called "Hangknot, Slipknot." It attacks vigilante mobs who "tied the laws with a hangknot." Charlie Guthrie's son dedicated it "to the many negro mothers, fathers, and sons alike, that was lynched and hanged under the bridge . . . seven miles south of Okemah, Okla., and to the day when such will be no more." Guthrie maintained "The best way to knowing any bunch of people is to go and listen to their music . . ." and he was now making a point of studying the blues, which he called "rock bottom American music." Bess Lomax remembers him in her brother Alan's D.C. apartment, poring over Blind Lemon Jefferson and other blues singers. "[A] bout eight records he listened to absolutely continuously. Sitting in the kitchen you could hear him play the record, and at the end of the cut, he'd pick up the needle and move it back to the beginning. He'd play these songs maybe a hundred and fifty times, until he drove us crazy."

After the Library of Congress recordings, Lomax brought Guthrie back up to New York City, where he sang "poor farmers' songs" on Lomax's CBS radio show, *American School of the Air.* To Bess Lomax, Guthrie's version of the unread, unwashed Okie was too much: "Everybody knew it was an act." But the Communist *People's World* was delighted: "Karl Marx wrote it and Lincoln said it and Lenin did it. Sing it, Woody. . . ." He performed at a second Grapes of Wrath concert, this one a benefit for Oklahoma's Communist Party. And on April 26, less than three months after Guthrie arrived in New York, Lomax arranged for him to go into RCA Victor's studios to cut his first commercial record.

The project was timed to take advantage of the nationwide

publicity about the Okies that came with the release of the movie version of *The Grapes of Wrath*. Guthrie produced *Dust Bowl Ballads*, twelve tracks that formed a single, unified statement: a concept album. Some of the material he'd been performing for years: "So Long It's Been Good to Know You," "Talkin' Dust Bowl Blues," "Blowin' Down This Road." Some were brand-new, written for the recording session. RCA wanted to capitalize on *The Grapes of Wrath*? Fine. At Lomax's apartment, Guthrie played and re-played the Carter Family version of "John Hardy," a song about the hanging of a West Virginia outlaw, "a desperate little man." Now he took the rise-and-fall of the melody, Maybelle's distinctive pick, and Sara's dour vocal and spent all one night writing a long ballad about another kind of outlaw, Steinbeck's Tom Joad.

RCA let him cut the six-minute song in two parts—both sides of a 78. The first half takes the story from Oklahoma to California, from exodus to the edge of the promised land. Flip the record, and you heard the other side of that dream: how a deputy sheriff shoots a woman in the back, how Tom Joad ends up clubbing a "vigilante thug" and going on the run. Guthrie's Joad is a political outlaw; he swears to be "Wherever little children are hungry and cry / Wherever people ain't free." Condensing the movie intensifies Steinbeck's (and Guthrie's) vision of "one big soul," of people "fightin' for their rights" not through but outside the law.

In the liner notes to *Dust Bowl Ballads*, Guthrie begins by saying, "This bunch of songs ain't about me. . . . They are 'Oakie' songs, 'Dust Bowl' songs, 'Migratious' songs, about my folks and my relations, about a jillion of 'em. . . ." Not only aren't they about him, but in the spirit of singing for the people, he also insists he isn't the real author. "These here songs ain't mine . . . you made 'em up yourself." In the *Daily Worker*, he's more explicit: "They came out of the hearts and mouths of the Okies. On no occasion have I referred to myself as either an entertainer or a singer and I'd better not start now. . . ."

To entertain is to be part of show business—is to bend the truth. Guthrie sees himself as a messenger, transmitting the news. In

California, he'd looked into "the lost and hungry faces of several hundred thousand Oakies, Arkies, Texies, Mexies, Chinees, Japees, Dixies and even a lot of New Yorkies . . ." he writes in the liner notes. "And I got so interested in the art and science of Migratin' that I majored in it. . . ." *Dust Bowl Ballads* is the product of that study. There's no call to join a movement or to protest, no explicit party politics. Instead, Guthrie tries to re-create what he's seen: from the first black dust-storm cloud of 1935 to the bands of refugees wandering "like the whirlwinds on the desert." His villains are bankers and vigilante thugs; his heroes, outlaws like Joad and Oklahoma's Pretty Boy Floyd. To re-create these characters, Guthrie ranges from despair to humor to defiance: "I ain't a-gonna be treated this a-way."

"I'm sure Victor never did a more radical album," he wrote in the *Daily Worker*. *Dust Bowl Ballads* didn't sell well: fewer than a thousand copies. Just as Dylan's first LP mostly got heard in the small circle of folkies, Guthrie's mostly circulated within the Popular Front, on campuses, and among a kind of folk intelligentsia. But he hadn't set out to be Kate Smith or Gene Autry; his was a more underground path, chipping away to get at the truth.

Many who did hear the record became convinced—despite Guthrie's explanation—that it was autobiographical. "They say I'm a dust bowl refugee," he sang in his stiletto voice, and that's what he became: not an increasingly sophisticated songwriter who could create a world. Or a performer who could inhabit it. But the real thing.

More radio shows with Lomax followed, more live performances. After three months in New York, he had enough money to go west to see his family. He invited young Peter Seeger to come with him. "The car was not paid for by a long shot," Seeger recalled. "Woody called the trip 'hitch-hiking on credit.'" To Seeger, it was a chance to see the world. And learn how to be a folksinger. To be, that is, Woody Guthrie.

Seeger, like Lomax, was a Harvard drop-out and the son of an academic musicologist. Except Peter's father, Charles, was a New

England radical who'd lost a professorship at Berkeley because of his association with Wobblies. Before the Popular Front, Charles Seeger had followed the Bolshevik model: intellectuals formed an enlightened cadre that educated people about the revolution to come. His composers' collective in the early thirties included Aaron Copland, Earl Robinson, and others; they wrote futuristic, avant-garde "songs for the masses." In those days, the American Communist Party dismissed folk songs as "a badge of servitude . . . , complacent, melancholy, defeatist." Then came the Popular Front. "Unquestionably," Charles Seeger was soon declaring, "the musical soul of America is in its folk music, not in its academic music. . . ." He started working within the system, becoming director of FDR's Resettlement Administration, and began taking his teenage son to folk festivals. Peter became fascinated with the six-string banjo. He also joined the Young Communist League.

"Pete," instead of "Peter," was an attempt to be one of the guys, to be folksy. He was, he'd write, "trying my best to shed my Harvard upbringing." But Pete Seeger never pretended to be the real thing. "Of course I'm not authentic," he'd later say. "All I can be is authentically myself." Tall, thin, patrician-looking, he was shy except when singing; then it was chin up and Adam's apple bobbing. He'd studied the Grand Ole Opry's premier banjo player, Uncle Dave Macon (who had recorded "Run, Nigger, Run"), the down-home styling of the Coon Creek Girls, and the Carter Family. Now, the twenty-one-year-old would have a chance to study the twenty-seven-year-old Guthrie.

Boarding school and Harvard may have kept him separate from "the people," but through his father's connections, Seeger knew more about the national Communist Party and local leaders than Guthrie. As they traveled west toward Texas, he brought the older singer to Tennessee's Highlander Folk School. Highlander was helping to collect folk tunes to use as organizing tools: it was through Highlander that Seeger would hear a song used by a Southern tobacco workers' union that would become "We Shall Overcome."

In return, Guthrie showed Seeger how to make meal money playing in bars along the way. And how to write a Contemporary Folk song. Seeger had been there the night Guthrie turned out "Tom Joad." Now, spurred by meeting grassroots radicals in Oklahoma and elsewhere, Guthrie sat down to create a ballad for and about organizers. First, he took a popular early twentieth-century tune, "Red Wing," which began "There once was an Indian maid," and changed it to "union maid." Then he constructed a catchy chorus: "Oh, you can't scare me, I'm sticking to the union." The tune would become one of Guthrie's most popular.

The trip was a turning point for Seeger. He became a student of Guthrie's, maybe the first, certainly one of the most important. "The most valuable thing I learnt from Woody was his strong sense of right and wrong, good and bad, his frankness in speaking out, and his strong sense of identification with all the hard-working men and women of this world." At the 1963 Newport Folk Festival, when Dylan and the other youngsters dressed in work clothes, they were dressing like Pete Seeger—who was dressing like Woody Guthrie.

While Guthrie and Seeger were hitchhiking on credit, Hitler invaded France. By the time the two got back to New York, Paris had fallen. "We read the *Daily Worker*," Seeger recalls, "and took it as our main guideline in what our politics should be." The Communists continued to maintain their neutral stance: let the imperialists fight it out. In America, that made the Popular Front less and less popular. After Guthrie played a downtown New York club, the newspapers called him "a communist and a wild man," he wrote Lomax, "and everything you could think of, but I don't care what they call me. I ain't a member of any earthly organization. . . ."

Maybe. But a lot of his work continued to come through people who supported the Popular Front. He became a regular on Lomax's latest radio concept, *Back Where I Come From*. Designed as a songfest, it featured some of Lomax's favorite New York folk singers: Lead Belly, Josh White, Burl Ives, Pete Seeger, Guthrie. They all sympathized with Lomax's politics, as did the director, Lomax's apartment mate in DC, Nicholas Ray. Ray had joined the Communist Party in the early thirties, collaborated with the New Deal's Federal Theatre Project, then worked with Charles Seeger, which is how he and Lomax met. Together, Ray and Lomax designed *Back Where I Come From* to look back, three times a week, on small-town USA. What it found there, largely through music, was a history of rebels fighting for what would become Twentieth Century Americanism.

Guthrie's climb to success culminated when he was asked to host the Model Tobacco Company's *Pipe Smoking Time*. Another nationally broadcast radio program, this one's politics were closer to "God Bless America." From the start, the producers made it clear they wanted Guthrie, in his own words, to "act the fool": sing hillbilly songs, tell hayseed jokes. By now, Guthrie had learned that New York used *hillbilly* as a sort of slur: country people were amusing but not too bright. It's part of why the Lomaxes had helped invent an alternative term—*folk*. That was Dylan's joke, years later, about the coffeehouse that wouldn't hire him because he sounded like a hillbilly: "We want folksingers here."

Pipe Smoking Time wanted hillbilly. And Guthrie—whose Singing Bum could sound like a variation on that theme—was willing to provide. He dropped his *Daily Worker* column. He rewrote his own "So Long, It's Been Good to Know You" to add a plug for the sponsor. In return, "They are giving me money so fast," he told Lomax, "I use it to sleep under." He bought a new car, moved to a better apartment, sent for his wife and kids. It was like his success in California but that much bigger.

Maybe Guthrie believed, in the spirt of the Popular Front, that he could bore from within. That by playing the hayseed, he could get a national radio show to focus on "the hungry folks . . . [who] get the credit for all I pause to scribble down." Maybe he just wanted to make a decent living. Maybe he recognized that whatever he did to pay the rent, there'd be some compromise. Even Lomax's *Back Where I Come From* had to adjust to the demands of the market. Around this time, director Nicholas Ray tried to reduce Lead Belly's role on the show, claiming the black man's Louisiana accent was "incomprehensible" to the audience. Guthrie, with his developing sensitivity about race, threatened to boycott if Lead Belly wasn't on.

He soon realized *Pipe Smoking Time* was up to something similar, although the racial stereotype its sponsors wanted was a white one. "I got disgusted with the whole sissified and nervous rules of censorship on all my songs and ballads. . . ." More and more, he saw how show business was like any other business: he was getting paid not to sing for the people but to cater to the market, to act out preconceived ideas of what was real. He lasted seven shows. On New Year's, 1941, not quite a year after he'd arrived in New York and a month after he'd brought his family east, they piled into his new car and headed back west.

KFVD had fired him; this time he'd quit, but it was the same result. As an entertainer, Guthrie was a man caught between: trying to make a living in a system he didn't agree with, that he wanted to tear down. He believed there was a new day coming when people would, as he put it, "own everything in Common. That's what the Bible says. Common means all of us. This is pure old commonism." But until that day, he was an unemployed husband, driving his wife and three young kids from the New York Island back to California.

The Guthries returned to Los Angeles, where Woody thought he might revive his local career. Instead, he spent four months "depressed, unhappy, angry and drinking." He still wanted to make the world level, but after his stint in New York, there are signs he'd lost patience with the Popular Front strategy of slowly boring from within. "I ain't in favor of bloody revolution," he wrote that spring. "You ain't either. But I'm high in favor of a Change in things that'll give you and me and all of our folks plenty of what they need to get along on. . . . I hope to God that you don't have to hurt nobody in getting your fair and honest share. . . . But in case anybody tries to step in and stop you from changing things into a better world—use your strength."

WE ARE THE BOSSES NOW

The fear was violent revolution. That's why James MacNaughton, the new manager of Calumet and Hecla, went out of his way to avoid hiring Finns. Too many of the Finns he knew were socialists, out to overthrow capitalism. Some scientists claimed they weren't even Anglo Saxons—but belonged to a separate racial category, *Homo mongolicus*. And in 1901, when Alexander Agassiz hand-picked MacNaughton to run C&H, it was to minimize trouble and maximize profits.

The son of a local mine employee, MacNaughton had begun as a water boy on the C&H docks and grown up with the corporation. At nineteen, he'd gone downstate to the University of Michigan, returning as a qualified surveyor and civil engineer. For a while, he ran another local mining operation. Then, when he was thirty-seven, Agassiz put him in charge of C&H.

MacNaughton wasn't a prospector, laborer, or delivering angel. He was a new breed for the new century: a corporate manager. Experienced and disciplined, he believed wholeheartedly in the company and in the dignity of his position: he went to work in pince-nez glasses and a stiff collar, his blonde hair neatly parted down the middle.

MacNaughton brought a modern scientific approach to business. The days of the prospector's dream, of dogsleds and land grabs, were long gone. As manager, he enlisted a Harvard geologist to survey the Keweenaw Peninsula and conducted time-and-motion studies to get the most production out of his workers. With an annual salary of over $100,000, Superintendent MacNaughton kept a certain distance from the miners and trammers, many of whom didn't speak English. His policy was to "try and get out of [them] as much regarding . . . their general situation . . . and the progress of the work . . . [as] I can," but his first loyalty was to his Boston bosses. Agassiz, by now in his midsixties, declared, "I like him, and I now feel as if my orders would be carried out promptly. . . ."

Some forty years after the Boston Associates had taken over Edwin Hulbert's claim, the labor hierarchy around the Calumet lode had stayed essentially the same. Eastern financiers still owned most of the stock, with Quin Shaw as the prime investor and Alexander Agassiz remaining as president. Middle management was still local: MacNaughton the most recent example. And those going down into the earth each day were still mostly foreign-born. What had changed was who filled those categories.

In the 1870s, the majority of America's two and a half million immigrants had been Western European: English, Irish, German, Scotch. They'd done much of the country's hard labor, from the textile factories of Lawrence to the iron mines in Hibbing to the copper mines of Michigan. In the next decade, as American industrialism expanded, another million immigrants arrived, but now they began to come from Eastern Europe. Between 1891 and 1910, twelve and a half million people entered the United States, 70 percent of them from Italy, Poland, Hungary, Greece, Finland. All told, Eastern Europeans went from 1 percent of the US population in 1860 to almost 40 percent by 1910.

At C&H, that change helped push the more established, second-generation immigrants, like the once reviled Irish, into positions of authority. So, MacNaughton was accepted by the Boston Associates, where Hulbert had been driven out. It also changed the political nature of the workforce.

Many of the Finns, for example, had been radicalized before coming to America. In 1809, Russia annexed Finland as a Grand Duchy. By the late nineteenth century, the Russian czar had quashed signs of rebellion by censoring Finnish newspapers, limiting the power of local legislators, and conscripting Finns into the imperial Russian army. Many young men left for the United States, bringing with them a sympathy for socialism and an anger against patriarchal rule. In 1900, there were over 7,000 Finns in Michigan's Houghton County; a decade later, there would be 11,500.

As well as a new kind of workforce, the other change MacNaughton faced was increased competition from out west. There, mines were starting to produce more high-grade, low-cost copper. C&H, with its capital reserves, considered simply buying them out. But as Agassiz wrote, "Mr. Shaw was getting old and hard to move to anything new and . . . I was always away and couldn't run anything new." Instead, they tried to include the Western mines in the copper pool but were turned down. C&H profits remained astonishingly high: the electrification of America doubled and tripled the price of copper stock. But Western production kept rising. In the last two decades of the nineteenth century, Michigan went from producing 80 percent of US copper to less than 25 percent.

By 1900, C&H had followed its main lodes down some three thousand feet. At that depth, there was less copper in the rock, and it cost more to get out. Mechanization helped; air drills and better explosives produced 20 percent more ore with 20 percent fewer miners. But the new technology and increased production also brought more danger. During the 1870s, there had been about a hundred mining-related deaths in Keweenaw. That rose to nearly two hundred in the 1880s and almost three hundred in the 1890s. In the first decade of the twentieth century, over five hundred men died in the Michigan mines: on average, a death a week. Forty percent of those killed were young men between the ages of eighteen and twenty-nine; the majority were married. It was like a war—an unseen, below-ground war.

As a result, Michigan's industrial Arcadia began to hear murmurs of complaint, especially among the low-paid, immigrant trammers. Agassiz wrote his manager, "We must be prepared to do our tramming in some other way than man power very soon for the men, judging from scraps in the paper, are beginning to talk about the use of men as beasts of burden. I shall be very glad not to have any of them." This was the modern corporate dream: to improve the technology till you could get the work done without workers. That would not only cut costs, but eliminate the growing threat of unionization.

Out west, the WFM had added fifty-five new locals and ten thousand new members just between 1900 and 1902. Agassiz became convinced that, despite thirty years of labor peace, C&H had been too lenient with its employees, had "coddled" them, had shown a "lack of force." As unions gained popularity and the national pressure for workers' rights built—as people started talking about a worldwide revolution—Agassiz decided he needed a more hard-nosed management style. That's when he hired James MacNaughton.

MacNaughton took over the same year Mother Bloor joined the Socialist Party of America. "[S]ocialism is coming . . . like a prairie fire," the party's paper announced, "and nothing can stop it . . . you can feel it in the air, you can hear it in the wind." It was a decade before Woody Guthrie was born, when his father, Charlie Guthrie, was fighting Oklahoma's "kumrids." The seeds of a radical American labor movement were being carried in the Western Federation of Miners. When Keweenaw's workers began to press C&H for a larger share of the profits—and a larger say in the company—they asked the WFM to come to Michigan and help. "The working class," they wrote, "must become the dominant class."

The leaders of the WFM, Big Bill Haywood and Charles Moyer, were eager. Western mines had been importing Michigan workers as strikebreakers. If the union could get a foothold in Keweenaw, it might stop that—and add new members—and help establish a better industry standard for hours and wages. Soon, Mother Jones was leading a rally in Red Jacket. "You say you cannot join the union," she prodded the crowd, "because you would lose your job. Poor, dreary wretch. You never owned a job, for those who own the machinery own the job, and you have to get permission to earn your bread and butter."

Agassiz's first reaction to the WFM's arrival was to tell Mac-Naughton not to let any Westerners on the premises and "not to take Colorado men on any account." Then he added, "The only thing we can do is to sit still and wait developments and to try to keep our heads cool. . . ." MacNaughton reassured him: "I don't think there's anything in the entire situation to cause us worry. . . ."

Maintaining his role as the benevolent father—and without appearing to accede to or even notice the workers' demands—Agassiz began increasing benefits. 1903 was when C&H set up its broom factory to provide jobs to disabled miners. The following year, it inaugurated its pension program. All of this helped undercut the WFM, which was distracted anyway, between trying to organize out west and putting together its new national union, the IWW. By 1905, the first organizing push in Keweenaw had faded. Soon, total WFM membership in the region fell to fewer than thirty workers. The president of Michigan's WFM local wrote Haywood, "unionism in this place a failure."

Agassiz's ability "to handle men" had once again triumphed. But the threat of unionism wouldn't go away. A year later was when the WFM started organizing around Hibbing. It was now a less radical union, having just split from the Wobblies, but an expanding one. In July 1907, when it called for a "strike but no violence" on the Iron Range, the WFM was supported not only by the Finns in northern Minnesota, but also by their counterparts across Lake Superior in Michigan. As one historian points out, "The many Finns, Slavs and Italians of the Copper Country were linked to those on the Mesabi by ethnic newspapers, organizations, and migration between the two ranges." When Hibbing struck, a solidarity parade wound through downtown Hancock, violating the municipal ordinance against displaying "the red flag of anarchy" and leading to mass arrests.

C&H stock, meanwhile, was hitting an all-time high of $1,000 a share. The company began buying up other mines in the region. By now it was paying, on average, about three dollars a day. While those were the highest wages in the district's history, they were still lower than you could get in mines out west—where the days were eight hours, not ten. Many of Michigan's English-speaking workers left for Montana and Idaho. To them, Keweenaw's paternalism—its company homes, libraries, baths, schools—paled beside the chance for more money, for less time below ground, for something that felt more like freedom.

Quin Shaw died on June 12, 1908, age eighty-three. His obituary called him "the heaviest individual taxpayer in Massachusetts, the largest individual owner of Calumet & Hecla stock in the state." The next year, Alexander Agassiz made his usual spring and fall visits to Calumet, checking to see that the clockwork was still running smoothly. He spent that winter in Egypt, the spring in Paris, writing his never-to-be-finished book on the origin of coral reefs. He died suddenly on March 27, 1910, on a ship headed back to America. He was seventy-three.

Quincy Shaw Jr. was promoted from second vice president to head of C&H. A Harvard graduate and US Open tennis player, Quin Jr. was about MacNaughton's age. So was Rodolphe Agassiz, Alex's son, who became vice president. He was a noted polo champion. From now on, C&H would be headed by a third generation of Boston Associates, tennis and polo players who had grown up taking astonishing wealth—and paternalism—for granted. More and more, decisions would be made by the supervisor. It was, as one congressman called it, "A little kingdom [where] James MacNaughton of the Calumet and Hecla is the king. . . ."

During MacNaughton's first decade running the copper empire, the push for workers' rights kept getting stronger. In the presidential election of 1912, Socialist candidate Eugene Debs would get almost nine hundred thousand votes. And many would consider the union movement key to Woodrow Wilson's victory. Wilson was opposed to what he called the "dictation of labor organizations," but he needed the support of Samuel Gompers's AF of L, so he campaigned on the promise "that property rights as compared to the vital red blood of the American people must take second place. . . ." And after his victory, Wilson appointed the nation's first secretary of labor. But he also had his Department of Justice begin prosecuting Western union leaders for trying to form a so-called "monopoly of labor."

In Keweenaw, the most important politics remained local. For years, miners had used big 300-pound drills to gouge out the stamp rock. They were called two-man drills because it took two men to lug them down the shafts, brace them upright, and operate them in the half-dark. Now the Michigan mines started experimenting with smaller, more powerful one-man units, weighing around 150 pounds. Management believed the one-man drill, by upping production and lowering labor costs, would keep Keweenaw competitive with Western mines.

But workers saw it as another weapon in the underground war. Drilling up into hanging rock was bad enough with a two-man crew, where one could at least keep an eye out for faults and slides. How many more would die per week if men were operating these new widow-makers alone? And the one-man drill meant higher production out of fewer men, which was bound to have a ripple effect on those at the bottom of the mine's hierarchy. Drill boys and trammers, mostly immigrants, would have less chance to advance or get hired in the first place. To the foreign-born workforce, the one-man drill was part of a larger plan to (literally) keep them down. "Though few would express the belief publicly," writes one historian, "many saw the copper district in 1913 as a battle-ground where Anglo-Saxons, Celts, and Teutons, challenged by new blood, sought continued dominance over Finns, Slavs, and Latins."

In 1912, seven Keweenaw mines decided to switch over to the one-man drill. That change did more for the union, according to one analysis, than "years of speech-making." Workers up and down the peninsula resolved to organize, to assert their rights, to break the peace. In early 1913, the WFM returned to the copper kingdom, sending in a dozen organizers who succeeded in enlisting a thousand new members. Around Red Jacket, the Finns began singing a rewritten version of one of their old folk songs: "We have slept enough already and been slaves / Just kissing MacNaughton's whip."

Michigan's mine managers accused the WFM of being the instigator: outsiders who "preached the gospel of discontent." But it was the locals who were pushing. The thirty-eight-thousand-member WFM was now in some twenty-two states—and less interested in "complete revolution." It had recently realigned with the more conservative AF of L, a move "as useful to the labor movement," old Wobblies sneered, "as a gold ring in a hog's nose." President Moyer cautioned about "the absolute necessity of deferring action" in Keweenaw until the local chapters were stronger. But the action had already started. As the manager of the Quincy mine wrote, "It is practically impossible to get the Finnish miners and trammers to do anything . . . 'they just simply won't work.'"

By June, local enrollment in the WFM had tripled, and members were demanding the union take a stand. Led by the Finns, they voted nearly unanimously to send a letter to the copper companies. The letter outlined their demands: a ban on the one-man drill, better hours and working conditions, wage increases, and recognition of the union. "We hope you realize that labor has just as much right to organize as capital, and that at this age these two forces, labor and capital, while their interests are not identical, must get together and solve the problems that confront them." That getting-together part sounded like the new, more moderate WFM. But against the wishes of national leadership, the letter ended, "Your failure to answer this will be taken as proof that you are not willing to meet us and to have the matters settled peacefully."

It was delivered in mid-July. By then, union membership had doubled again to some seven thousand, about half the mine employees in the region. MacNaughton consulted with Quin Shaw Jr. "My present feeling," the manager wrote, "is that I shall not acknowledge the letter in anyway whatever, for by . . . acknowledging the receipt of this one I would be in a measure recognizing the Union." On July 18, Shaw telegraphed back, "Approve not acknowledging union letter."

The rest of Michigan's copper companies followed suit. Throughout Keweenaw, the workers' request to negotiate was met with silence. Five days later, the workers walked out—against the WFM's recommendation and while its president, Charles Moyer, was out of the country at a conference. According to President Wilson's newly appointed secretary of labor, that silence "precipitated the strike."

On the morning of July 22, 1913, MacNaughton telegraphed Shaw, "Everything very quiet. We are beginning to swear in deputies to protect the property. . . . No cause whatever for worry." But the next day, when it was time for the second shift to begin, strikers grabbed sticks and pipes off the ground and lined the route from the shaft to the "dry" (the changing house). They jeered those who tried to enter the mines, threw rocks, bottles, fists. At least five men were hospitalized. As MacNaughton reported it to Shaw, "A mob of between four and five hundred is going from one engine house to the other demanding that the fires be drawn."

And as the giant steam engines shut down, the strikers began to shout, "We are the bosses now."

It was the moment management had feared and workers dreamed of, the moment when they claimed ownership of the machines. What followed was a long strike; what had preceded were years of organizing; but here, in this moment, was the vision of the future come to life: the world made, briefly, level.

MacNaughton was furious. It's what he and the Boston Associates had worried about all along, "the very humiliating experience of turning over our property. . . ." This wasn't just workers looking for better pay but "red socialism," a militant demand for power, for changing the system itself.

MacNaughton ordered the local sheriff to begin deputizing non-strikers and issuing them cheap handguns. By nightfall, Houghton County had some six hundred armed deputies. He also had the sheriff telegram Michigan's governor requesting military support.

Armed rioters have begun to destroy property and have threatened the lives of men who want to work. I am unable to handle the situation. . . . The strike is on in 20 mines, with 15,000 idle men. . . . I am convinced that the situation will become worse and will result in great destruction of property and possible loss of life unless I receive the aid of State troops.

Maybe. But as MacNaughton later admitted, "There was practically nothing destroyed." According to a Department of Labor report, "No attempt was made by the strikers to damage property." And at a strike rally the next day, speakers exhorted the workers in English, Finnish, Croatian, Italian, and Polish "to avoid all acts of violence and respect property and personal rights." The striking workers didn't want to ruin the mines; they wanted to run them.

To MacNaughton and the other managers, the union was "a foreign body preaching socialistic doctrines, and inciting class hatred and disloyalty." The state seemed to agree. Within twenty-four hours, despite his reputation as a progressive, Governor Woodbridge Ferris dispatched all 2,500 National Guard at his disposal. Thirty-six infantry companies, two cavalry troops, a mounted signal corps, and three brass bands pitched their white pup tents beside the tall, dark, and suddenly quiet hoists of C&H.

But the immigrant strikers refused to be intimidated. "We served in the army in the old country, and we can fight the boy soldiers here."

As a final show of power, the county Board of Supervisors, led by MacNaughton, directed the sheriff to hire some fifty professional strikebreakers from the Waddell-Mahon Company back east. Waddell-Mahon was a private security force, armed and with the reputation of being dangerous. The Finns called them hounds, set on the workers by C&H; Guthrie would call them gun thugs.

MacNaughton, his troops assembled, declared that "the Union must be killed at all costs." Not just stopped, or blocked, or even broken. Killed.

That first week, strikers and their supporters began to organize regular morning protest parades down the streets of Red Jacket. The local newspapers reported and MacNaughton telegraphed Shaw about "riots and mobs," but the six a.m. marches were peaceful. The men dressed in dark jackets, ties, bowler caps; the women, in their Sunday best. They were often led by a huge American flag carried by Annie Clemenc, a "tall, straight-backed woman, beaming confidence."

Meanwhile, the mines stayed shut. And MacNaughton claimed to want it that way. "I feel convinced that an absolute shut-down, with no effort on our part, is the only answer." No work meant no pay meant no food meant a short strike. "The grass will grow on your streets," MacNaughton announced, "before I ever give in." But it was snow, not grass, that he was betting on. Once winter came— and it comes early in northern Michigan—it would be almost impossible for the strikers to hold out. Meanwhile, C&H turned off its pumps and let its shafts flood. The streets started filling with displaced mine rats "too big for a cat to tackle."

The strikers soon refined their demands: abolition of the one-man drill, an eight-hour day, a three-dollar-a-day minimum for underground work, a formal grievance procedure, and recognition of the WFM. A week after the strike began, union officials met with Governor Ferris; they also approached the federal Department of Labor. But MacNaughton refused all offers to negotiate: "If the Governor and the Labor Department in Washington and the U.S. Senate would keep their respective noses out of our affairs we would get along a good deal better."

MacNaughton laid all blame for the unrest on the WFM and its "campaign of violence and riot." After all, he wrote Shaw, "the great majority of the strikers are like children." Like children, that is, who had defied their father's will. "Industrious, loyal men," he wrote, ". . . they have been influenced by Western Federation of Miners' organizers and hired men who have been here in some cases for years. Constant dripping will wear a stone."

By early August, the protest parades had swollen to where they were often some eighteen hundred strong, complete with hand-painted signs and marching bands. "Where in the name of liberty did they all come from?" a national guard supposedly asked.

"I guess they must have gotten up out of the graves," another answered.

"Oh, no," said a striker, "just up out of the mines."

The governor sent a representative to investigate. He reported that, among other issues, the companies' policy of refusing to consider rehiring the protestors was "wrong fundamentally and wholly wrong in principle. . . . [I]f an employer can do this, he can, with like propriety, compel withdrawal from any political, religious or social body as a condition of employment. It is basically un-American." The governor concluded the workers had "real grievances," and that "the employers should be the first to offer the olive branch." With the strike less than a month old, he began pulling out the National Guard.

A week later, on a sultry hundred degree day, four of the Waddell-Mahon private security guards and two local deputies attempted to bring a striker in for questioning. When he refused, they fired through the doors and windows of his boardinghouse. According to one of the women inside, "Nobody didn't have any guns, they didn't have anything to shoot with except the spoons they had in their hands while they were eating." Two men were killed.

At the funeral the next Sunday, thousands showed up. A WFM speaker blamed "Boston coppers" and went on, addressing the Board of Supervisors: "Long have you boasted of your mines of wealth untold. Long have you grown fat by keeping us lean." MacNaughton described it to Shaw as a "very large demonstration. The killing of these men," he added, "has given a serious setback to resumption of work." Now there were martyrs.

By the end of August, the WFM had secured major contributions from the AF of L and the United Mine Workers, among others, allowing them to begin paying out strike benefits. Single men collected three dollars a week; married men, ten. Though they'd been reluctant to call the strike, the WFM now recognized it as a chance to take on a corporate giant and garner national attention. Members of its more radical wing—like Wobbly leader Big Bill Haywood— saw greater possibilities: "There is a nucleus here that will carry on the work and propagate the seed that will grow into the great revolution. . . ."

C&H's plan to wait out the strike didn't seem to be working. The early-morning parades expanded until MacNaughton was admitting to Shaw, "More picketing by strikers today than at any time." So in early September, the company changed tactics. It decided to reopen the mines. The problem was that, of the roughly fourteen-thousand-man workforce in the region, the company estimated that only four thousand were willing to defy the strikers and go back into the mines. C&H's solution was to bring in replacement workers.

The outsiders arrived by the trainload. As they got off the trains and tried to enter the shafts, the wives of strikers shouted, "Scabs!" and hit them with broom handles dipped in manure. A thousand strike supporters marched through Yellow Jacket chanting, "You can't stop us! You can't stop us!" When mounted guards with drawn bayonets closed in on the marchers, Annie Clemenc wrapped herself in her big American flag and cried, "Kill me! Run your bayonets and sabers through this flag! Kill me! But I won't move back! If this flag won't protect me, then I will die with it!"

Afterward, as strikers retreated to Calumet's Italian Hall and displayed the huge gashes cut through the Stars and Stripes, the mine owners got a court order prohibiting all protests and public gatherings. The union papered Keweenaw with posters: "Don't be a scab. . . . No real man will come to the copper district until a settlement is made." Many of the three thousand outsiders left when they realized why they'd been brought in. But some stayed. And C&H brought more.

By late October, winter had begun. It was a relatively mild one; still, protestors were already throwing snowballs. The local sheriff and his deputies began making more arrests—over four hundred by mid-November. Then management added another weapon. It undercut key union demands, announcing that, starting January 1, it would institute an eight-hour day and new grievance procedures. It still wasn't budging on the one-man drill, calling it "imperative for the continuance of operation," and there were still no wage increases. But the company had compromised. What more did the strikers want? What were they really after?

As the editors of a pro-strike newspaper wrote in early December, "[It] is not that the miners are shockingly underpaid, though their wages certainly are not adequate." Nor, it went on, are "the conditions in the mines . . . extremely dangerous or unsanitary, though they ought to be improved in both respects." Those issues could be worked out. But, the editorial concluded, the strike was really about something more fundamental. "What should give us concern is the undoubted fact that Houghton County, Michigan, in the heart of what purports to be the purest democracy on earth, is being governed by an oligarchy."

There was the crux of it: the strikers wanted the company—wanted business—to function as a democracy. They wanted to be treated as equals, as grown-ups, as at least part owners of the machines. And that the company wouldn't allow.

To defeat the strike—to kill the idea of a union—management helped form something called a Citizens Alliance. The name and the concept came from out west, where the mining companies had used not only the state militia, but businessmen and other local supporters to defeat the WFM. Members of Keweenaw's Citizens Alliance signed a pledge that "the Western Federation of Miners is a menace to the future welfare and prosperity of this district and that therefore . . . [it] must be eliminated. . . ." The Citizens Alliance began holding rallies and handing out distinctive white lapel pins to show you were pro-business, anti-union.

According to a representative of the governor, the area was tense enough to be "on the verge of a little civil war." The workers had been out four months now, surviving on seven dollars a week in strike benefits, about half what they'd been earning. It had turned cold, and the AF of L had begun to cut back its contributions, refusing to further deplete its national treasury for what had begun to look like a losing cause. MacNaughton now claimed union leaders knew "they were whipped."

The WFM made a new proposal to management: if it would "reemploy without asking surrender of union cards [those] strikers who had committed no violence," the WFM would withdraw from the district. It was an almost total surrender: there would be no recognized union, no wage increase, no blocking of the one-man drill, only the concession that men who carried union cards could work.

MacNaughton rejected the proposal outright as being "conceived in iniquity and born in sin." The union—the idea of union—had to be eliminated.

On the night of December 7, three more men died when another boardinghouse was shot into. But this one was occupied by English-speaking Cornishmen: some of the replacement miners the company had brought in. They were "murdered," according to a pro-company paper, "because they chose to work." Union organizers were blamed, with headlines blaring, FOREIGN AGITATORS MUST BE DRIVEN FROM THE DISTRICT AT ONCE.

Four strike supporters were eventually arrested for the crime, but the local prosecutor suspected "imported guards had a hand in this atrocious killing." He believed Waddell-Mahon gunmen had killed the substitute workers in order to keep the region divided and prolong the strike. Management didn't want things to just peter out; they wanted what one congressman called "a war of extermination."

By the holiday season, almost all the Cornish, Scotch, and Irish had gone back into the mines. Along with the scab workers, that brought C&H to about 80 percent capacity. Still, more than two-thirds of the Finns and Croatians held out. They called MacNaughton the *tsaari*—the Czar—of the copper empire. Governor Ferris wrote MacNaughton privately about a settlement, hoping "thousands of mothers and children would have a real Christmas instead of a day of despondency, doubt and hate." MacNaughton's response was to continue to blame "alien agitators and strike leaders." As he put it, "If we want to be insured against a repetition of this thing within the next 15 or 20 years we have got to rub it into them now that we have them down."

The Citizens Alliance rallies grew larger and larger. At one, a speaker declared that a supporter of the WFM "has no right to the protection that the flag affords. That man has no right to live in a country where that flag floats." The cheering audience proceeded to ransack a union headquarters. These vigilantes—as Guthrie would call them—raided homes, confiscated weapons, closed businesses. On December 18, Keweenaw's mining companies announced that employees had until the end of the year to return to work or be replaced. And that management had the right to refuse "absolutely and unqualifiedly," as MacNaughton put it, "to re-hire union members and their supporters."

The WFM was out of money. The mines were back up and running. Winter had descended. After almost five months without work, not only had the strikers failed to become bosses, it looked like they had permanently lost their jobs. The strike was essentially over, the dream in tatters. Trying to lift spirits, if only temporarily, the WFM's women's auxiliary came up with an idea: a Christmas party, to be held at Italian Hall.

THE TRUTH JUST TWISTS

A plain acoustic guitar strum, and then a neutral-sounding voice asks us to gather round: there's news. Things are changing: the ones on top will soon be last, the old order is fading. Bob Dylan considers it big enough news that he opens his third LP with it. As 1963 ends, he tells his parents' generation—the generation in power—that it needs to get out of the way.

The song is a call to pay attention. A kind of follow-up to "Blowin' in the Wind," it's another nonspecific anthem, asking passionately but politely ("please," Dylan sings a couple of times) for politicians and parents to listen up. It says farewell to the old without naming the new and talks about how the loser will someday win but not who's been losing—or what winning might look like. For all its defiance, there's a built-in sadness to "The Times They Are a-Changin'." Dylan adapted the melody from a World War I bagpipe tune, "Farewell to the Creeks," which he probably heard Peggy Seeger's husband, Ewan MacColl, sing as "Farewell to Sicily." It's a march tune—and Dylan's song has that martial air, his voice rising to the call—but a specific kind of march: a retreat.

"There's a battle outside," is how Dylan puts it, "and it's ragin'." By 1963, violent opposition to the civil rights movement had gone from Dr. King being thrown in the Birmingham, Alabama, jail to that city attacking young protestors with police dogs and fire hoses.

Over the next few months, there were some 750 civil rights protests in 186 cities. In mid-June, President John Kennedy gave a televised speech on what he called "a moral issue . . . as old as the Scriptures and . . . as clear as the American Constitution. The heart of the question is whether all Americans are to be afforded equal rights and equal opportunities." The evening after his speech, the NAACP's Mississippi field secretary, Medgar Evers, was shot in the back and killed.

Within a few weeks, Dylan has written a song about it. Unlike "The Times They Are a-Changin'," it's specific and pointed. After a quick description of the assassination, he shifts his focus to the assassin, the nameless "poor white" who pulled the trigger. Instead of attacking the killer, "Only a Pawn in Their Game" tries to understand him. How he's been taught to "hang and to lynch" and to "walk in a pack," how he's ended up a tool in the hands of politicians—which the song implies, we may all be. It's a protest against the shooting, but it also questions the standard protest song, cutting through the black-and-white conventions of Greenwich Village and the folk world to emerge not far from the old Popular Front idea that racism is a product of the larger economic system.

Dylan premiered the song at the front lines of the civil rights movement in Greenwood, Mississippi. He, Pete Seeger, and folk singer Theodore Bikel went there to support a voter-registration drive being led by the Student Nonviolent Coordinating Committee. Four months earlier, the local KKK had ambushed a SNCC car, riddling it with machine-gun fire, wounding one organizer. A month later, SNCC's office was firebombed. When organizers James Forman and Bob Moses led a protest march to the police station, "They met us there with the dogs and with guns and so forth," Moses recalled, "and I guess, as Jim says, they simply went berserk for a little while."

Not far from where Evers was shot, Dylan sings "Only a Pawn in Their Game." Though Peter, Paul, and Mary's "Blowin' in the Wind" is climbing the charts, he's still little enough known for the

New York Times to identify him as "Bobby Dillon." The local black audience listens to the young New York singer politely enough, and they clap at the end, but his song is asking them, in essence, to try to understand and empathize with the people who are hunting them down.

SNCC leader John Lewis calls the event "the first time in the history of the Delta that black and white are standing and singing together." Afterward, Dylan hangs out with, among others, Bernice Johnson, founding member of SNCC's Freedom Singers "We all thought," she'd say, "those of us in the movement and those of us in the Freedom Singers, that Dylan was fantastic as a songwriter and as a person."

Back in New York, Dylan has broken up with his girlfriend. "[T]rouble between us," Suze Rotolo would write, "slowly grew out of his facility for not telling the truth." He's spending time with SNCC member Dorie Ladner, who'd worked with Medgar Evers. Ladner is helping to organize a march on Washington planned for August. Many in SNCC think the march is a kind of sham. It's nonthreatening, nonrevolutionary, and backed by the kind of big, middle-of-the-road unions that have shied away from SNCC's more radical, grass-roots organizing.

When Dylan's invited to perform at the march, he does it again. Before Dr. King's "I Have A Dream" speech, Joan Baez sings "We Shall Overcome," and Peter, Paul and Mary serenade the crowd of three hundred thousand with "Blowin' in the Wind." Dylan chooses to duet with Baez on his promise-filled "When the Ship Comes In," then intones "Only a Pawn in Their Game," that wordy, thoughtful, complicated look at why whites and blacks are being pitted against each other.

Three weeks after the march, opponents of the movement bombed a Birmingham church, killing four young black girls. A month or so later, Dylan completed his last session on the new LP, *The Times They Are a-Changin'*.

The majority of the songs could be called protest music, but the anger isn't aimed where you might expect. In the accompanying poem that serves as liner note, Dylan asks, "where t go? / what is it that's exactly wrong? / who t picket? / who t fight?" This in the midst of one of the great social uprisings in American history: the largest mass protest since the heyday of the labor movement. If it seems obvious who to picket, Dylan insists—his poem and the songs on the record insist—"there is no truth."

Most of the melodies were taken from old folk tunes, but it's different from Guthrie's technique. Where Guthrie's audience knew the Carter Family songs and got the joke, Dylan's references are obscure to anyone outside the folk scene. His songs may be New Words to Old Songs, but they come across as Contemporary Folk: originals that respect but pull away from tradition, from the old truth.

"The Lonesome Death of Hattie Carroll" traces the senseless killing of a maid by a rich man. It has some of the rage, high drama, and working-class perspective of Bertolt Brecht's "Pirate Jenny": the death is lonesome because it's overlooked. But as the song continues, it's less about the murder than our reaction to it: we shouldn't weep just for her brutal death, but for the larger issue of a justice system that doesn't provide justice. In the same way, "Ballad of Hollis Brown" asks us to shift attention from the front-page news of the civil rights movement and the beginnings of the Vietnam War to a farmer starving in South Dakota, another kind of lonesome death.

"North Country Blues" is another take on the overlooked, going back to Dylan's memories of the Iron Range. Based on the late nineteenth-century "Red Iron Ore," it's narrated by a mother of three who recalls the days when "the iron ore poured." Now cheaper foreign wages have closed the mines and put whole towns out of work. Dylan's droning, stubborn performance is all clenched teeth and quiet, as if the tune—like the young mother—might not make it through. It's the sound of hidden poverty, of desperation.

The Times They Are a-Changin' isn't intended as a concept album like *Dust Bowl Ballads*, but you can hear Dylan using the LP format as a way of trying to talk about the big picture. And the big picture is that something's gone wrong, something larger even than civil rights or the Cold War. Protest songs are one way to talk about that, but Dylan also includes tunes that mourn a broken affair and others that try to get at the more generalized, pervasive feeling of uneasiness.

Included is Dylan's take on "God Bless America" or on God blessing America. He borrows his melody from an Irish tune, "The Patriot Game," that the Kingston Trio had covered a year earlier. That song begins with a fighter in Ireland's civil wars announcing his name and age: "I've just gone sixteen." Dylan's tune starts off the same, except he says his name "is nothing / my age it means less." And where the narrator in "The Patriot's Game" explains how "love of one's country" can be a terrible thing, Dylan's Midwesterner has been "taught and brought up" to believe that God is on America's side. Taught and brought up, that is, in Irving Berlin's version of history, not Woody Guthrie's.

Over a stuttering acoustic guitar, "With God on Our Side" proceeds chronologically through America's wars, from the extermination of Native Americans to the atomic age. In every case, America claimed that God was standing beside her, guiding her toward victory. How do we know that? "The history books tell it / They tell it so well." The song's less about patriotism, finally, than education. Or reeducation, because as it builds, the narrator loses his Midwestern innocence and realizes that what he's really been taught is to "never ask questions." By the last stanza, confused and "weary as Hell," he decides that "if God's on our side / He'll stop the next war."

In the debate of "God Bless America" versus "This Land Is Your Land," Dylan comes down on Guthrie's side. But it's almost as if he's writing about a different country. There's no sign of a voice sounding through the fog or of a freedom highway. Dylan's song is sadder than that. Even though it's laced with anger and frustrated by the lies that pass as history, "With God on Our Side" ends up a slow reveal of how things are; it barely tries to evoke how they might be. The lyrics, the creaky tune, the breathy harmonica solos sound traditional, but like the rest of *The Times They Are a-Changin'*, the song's from a new world, one that's hardly been born.

In October, reviewing his Carnegie Hall concert, the *New York Times* called Dylan "a social protest poet, a latter-day James Dean who knows what he's rebelling against. . . . He is assuming the role of radical spokesman with music as his vehicle." But his new record wasn't rallying anyone to a cause and refuses to suggest what to do or believe. Its final tune, "Restless Farewell," is set in a bar at closing time, the melody borrowed from an Irish drinking song, "The Parting Glass." Where that original is all about saying good-bye to lovers and old friends, Dylan starts there and then extends his farewell to the causes he's believed in and even the career he's begun. He dismisses them as a "false clock," a distraction. The last words on the record are a vow to "remain what I am / And bid farewell and not give a damn."

The world the LP constructs doesn't have much humor or optimism. The closest it gets is "When the Ship Comes In," a celebration of some future victory that manages to combine Brecht and Joe Hill. But there aren't many whoops or wild harmonica swings. By now, the twenty-two-year-old Dylan has all but perfected a deceptively simple folk delivery: measured singing over clear, forceful guitar work. His pleasure in long-held notes has begun to stretch Guthrie's Okie accent into something edgier, more emotional, more interior. But if the lyrics challenge some of the assumptions of the folk world, the music doesn't. It's a mostly somber, sober collection of rewritten traditional melodies. What some might call grown up. No sign of rock & roll.

A month after the record was finished, President Kennedy was assassinated. Dylan's reaction: "Something had just gone haywire in the country. . . ." That December of 1963, Dylan received the Tom Paine Award from the National Emergency Civil Liberties Committee. The committee was a splinter group formed when its parent organization, the American Civil Liberties Union (ACLU), backed down from defending victims of the recent anti-communist Red Scare. Gathered together to honor the young folksinger were some of the more radical survivors of Woody Guthrie's era. By recognizing "distinguished service in the fight for liberty," the award amounted to an initiation into the Old Left. Or, as Dylan later put it, "They were trying to make me an insider. I don't think so."

He did offer a tribute to Guthrie: "I wish sometimes I could have come here in the 1930s like my first idol. . . ." But then his brief acceptance speech quickly switched to talk about changing times: how this celebration was about balding "old people" when it should have been about "youngness." He goes on to critique the March on Washington, how the Negroes on the podium with him didn't look like "none of my friends. My friends don't wear suits." Finally, he swerved to the Kennedy assassination: "I got to admit that the man who shot President Kennedy, Lee Oswald . . . I saw some of myself in him."

He saw himself in the man who shot the president? Applause turned to boos. Dylan quickly ended his speech, accepting the award on behalf of, among others, SNCC's James Forman.

Excuses were made: he was drunk; he wasn't used to making public speeches. Later, Dylan tried to explain. "I am sick at hearin' 'we all share the blame'," he wrote in a long poem/letter to the committee. "[I]t is so easy t say 'we' an bow our heads together / I must say 'I' alone an bow my head alone / . . . if there's violence in the times, then there must be violence in me. . . ." The gray-haired Civil Liberties audience had spent years trying to forge coalitions, fighting for the idea of collective unity, and were still being attacked for it. Dylan's speech and his recent songs distanced him from that old "we," that us-against-them . In his letter, he tries to explain: he's not abandoning the Left's history as much as trying to see it fresh: "once this is straight between us, it's then an / only then that we can say 'we' an really mean / it . . . an go on from there to do something about / it. . . ."

"I am with you more'n ever," he assured the publishers of the folk magazine *Broadside*. This was early in 1964, after a summer and fall of appearing with Joan Baez, after playing Carnegie Hall and being featured in *Newsweek*, after he's become, as he put it, "famous by the rules of public famousity." The quality of his music, its ability to reflect what was happening—Dylan's public reticence, and his insistence that all idols could be shattered combined to make him an idol. He doesn't reject fame. He doesn't walk away from it the way Guthrie left *Pipe Smoking Time*. Times, after all, have changed, and Dylan's success came not against the background of the Great Depression but in a period that would come to be seen as America's "golden age of capitalism."

From Dylan's childhood to this, his early twenties, the US economy had thrived in unprecedented ways, till it was churning out about three-quarters of the world's manufactured goods. After the Second World War, the Marshall Plan in Europe and the recovery in Japan helped create new international markets for US products: the fifties and sixties saw a tenfold increase in world trade. On the ruined post-war landscape, America erected a world in its own image, a market that it dominated the way Calumet & Hecla once controlled world copper.

At home, the per capita output between 1950 and 1973 would grow three times faster than in the previous 130 years. Fordism—the mass-production assembly-line approach associated with the Ford Motor Company—turned out everything from plastics and nylon to transistor radios and magnetic recording tape. In 1955, when the fourteen-year-old Robert Zimmerman first heard Little Richard's "Tutti Frutti," US consumers spent $277 million dollars on recordings. Four years later, when he was heading to college as Bob Dillon, that had jumped to $600 million. And by 1970, it would climb to $2 billion. There were more teens, and they had more money. For one thing, their parents were doing better: from the war years to the midfifties, union wages rose by half—and by half again from then till the late sixties.

In many ways, this golden age was the result of victories and losses in the thirties. So, the triumph of California's big growers (you could also call it the defeat of the Steinbeck/McWilliams/Guthrie position) led to a new industrial agriculture: more factories in the field, more food produced by fewer people. That cut the cost of groceries from about a third of the average household's expenses to under 15 percent. But it also cut the number of farmers, from a quarter of the US workforce to less than 5 percent. So in 1938, when Guthrie went out to report on all that he could see, he found refugees fresh off the land. Dylan, twenty-five years later, found "Hollis Brown," a farmer whose family was starving because he'd stayed on the farm.

Between the mid–fifties and early sixties, technology and automation (think the two–man drill) helped boost production: more cars being made, for example, but 17 percent fewer workers to turn them out. And half the number of steelworkers to produce the same amount of steel. So in 1941, Guthrie looked at the Grand Coulee Dam and saw the potential for a new industrialism, but by the fifties, Dylan found mines closing and a widening gap between rich and poor: the "North Country Blues."

Dylan predicts, "The loser now will be later to win," but did the Golden Age promise that? If he wanted to test how things had changed and where he fit in, he couldn't have arranged a much better itinerary than his trip west in February 1964. He left New York City in a station wagon with a few friends. First, they went down to North Carolina to try to meet seventy-four-year-old Carl Sandburg, born the same year as Guthrie's father. A socialist and a populist poet, Sandburg had also been an early champion of folk music; his 1927 collection, *American Songbag*, helped lay the groundwork for the Lomaxes, and he was one of Guthrie's favorite writers. Sandburg, in other words, was the Old Left. When the twenty-three-year-old Dylan showed up on his doorstep, the white-haired Sandburg greeted him politely enough and accepted a copy of *The Times They Are a-Changin'*, but had no idea who the singer was. If Dylan was trying to connect with America's tradition of poetry and protest—that line that stretched back to Walt Whitman—it doesn't seem to have worked.

Backtracking to Kentucky, Dylan and friends entered the town of Hazard, where a coal miners' strike was in progress. The strike was straight out of Joe Hill's era: miners fighting for decent wages. The strike had already attracted folk singers like Carolyn Hester and Judy Collins, and both Tom Paxton and Phil Ochs would write songs about Hazard. But when Dylan arrived, there was no rally, no singing, no sign of One Big Union. Though the local organizer knew who Dylan was, he didn't have time to talk. The singer dropped off some clothes and supplies and pushed on.

Next stop was Atlanta. It was a center for organizers of the civil rights movement, which was, in some ways, an updated version of the old labor wars, using thirties' techniques like picket lines and sit-ins, recycling thirties' anthems like "Which Side Are You On?" At Emory University, Dylan gave a concert to a crowd sprinkled with SNCC friends, including Bernice Johnson, now married to fellow organizer Cordell Reagon. He gave another, similar concert at historically black Tougaloo College near Jackson, Mississippi. At these stops, the young protestors, black and white, not only knew who he was but welcomed him as part of their extended community.

Still, the COMPLICATED CIRCLE was more . . . complicated than the Movement, less linear. When the car full of friends swerved down to New Orleans for Mardi Gras, they discovered "everything out of shape," as Dylan wrote: "blazin' jukebox / gumbo overflowin' / . . . everything's wedged / arm in arm / stoned galore." From there, they kept heading west, stopping briefly at the JFK assassination site in Dallas, the spot where the country "went haywire." Then, at a sparsely attended folk concert in Denver, Dylan played a new song he'd been composing in the back seat during the trip.

For all he'd talked about hard travelin', the twenty-three-year-old hadn't actually done that much. For the past few years, he'd been in New York City, living in Greenwich Village apartments, writing tunes made to sound like they've come off a thirties' freight.

"Chimes of Freedom" is his first song from a speeding car. A word-drunk portrait of a thunderstorm, it's as much chant as melody and less a narrative than an attempt to describe a sound. The sound—like Guthrie's voice in the wilderness, like Whitman's prophecies—is all-encompassing and almost indefinable: a "mad mystic hammering" that chimes for everyone, "for the countless confused, accused, misused, strung-out ones and worse." The sound, maybe, of a new world.

It's when he reached Berkeley, California, that Dylan found a crowd eager to hear that or any other sound he might make. "They had come with a sense of collective expectancy," wrote one member of the audience, ". . . attracted by already implausible legend. . . ." They cheered his set, getting even louder with the surprise appearance of Joan Baez. And he followed that with an appearance on Steve Allen's TV show that introduced him to a national audience. It's as if the trip across the country had carried him from the past to the future, from Woody Guthrie's New York Island and the fading memory of thirties' radicalism through Kerouac's "On the Road" to sixties California, where everything was arm in arm and stoned galore.

The soundtrack to that trip was a new sound on the car radio. When Dylan left New York, the Beatles' "I Want to Hold Your Hand" had reached number one. The song was a hybrid: a countryish guitar intro followed by familiar folk chords, handclaps like the pop girl groups of the day, and a chorus that climaxed in Everly Brothers (which is to say, hillbilly) harmony. The words weren't exactly poetry, but who cared? It sounded joyful and doable (thousands of garage bands soon tried) and full of possibilities. The Sunday after Dylan's concert in Atlanta, the Beatles made their first appearance on *The Ed Sullivan Show*. They appeared again the day after his Denver concert. And made a final appearance there the day after Berkeley.

Beatles' songs followed Dylan across the country the way "God Bless America" had followed Guthrie. Except Dylan was delighted. "She Loves You" had a peaking melody over a rolling bass and hard drums, and the double-sided "Please, Please Me" and "From Me to You" combined those countrified harmonies with infectious beats— the herk-jerk of "With love / from me / to you"—intercut by a demanding harmonica. In fact, as listener-friendly as it came across, lots of it was demanding: "Come on, come on, come on . . ." "Just call on me . . ." "I wanna hold your. . . ." A call to action.

The new music smelled young and full of the kind of excitement that Little Richard and Elvis had once cooked up. "Rock & roll was real," John Lennon said of his teen years in Liverpool. "Everything else was unreal." It could have been a quote from young Bobby Zimmerman in Hibbing. That early rock & roll had coincided with America's golden age revving up. Ripe with possibility, the sound had traveled overseas as a mix of black and white, immigrant and native born: the mongrel child of a mongrel nation. And it was attacked for that: in 1957, Frank Sinatra had called rock & roll "the most brutal, ugly, degenerate, vicious form of expression." Now the Beatles had brought that sound back to America.

The tradition Dylan had followed rejected that industrial sound, defined itself in opposition to urban dance music, R&B, Motown soul. When folk music celebrated black culture, it was more rural: people like Lead Belly and Reverend Gary Davis, Blind Willie McTell and Elizabeth Cotton. But Beatles music put the spotlight back on Little Richard and Chuck Berry, connecting them to the Marvelettes and Smokey Robinson and the Miracles. One of Pete Seeger's folk protégées would write a song about how rock & roll died the day Buddy Holly's plane crashed in 1959—as if the subsequent soul era of Sam Cooke, Jackie Wilson, James Brown didn't count. The Beatles landed in America as living proof that that was a lie.

By the time Dylan got back to New York in mid-March, the Beatles had three of the nation's Top Ten singles. By early April, it had become the only group ever to have the top five songs on America's pop charts at the same time. The British Invasion that followed—and the American groups that joined in—gleefully jumped categories, combining country-and-western, rhythm-and-blues, folk, and pop. There was no search for a pure Anglo Saxon past but a jubilant present-day mix. "America ought to put statues up to the Beatles," Dylan would insist. "They helped give this country's pride back to it."

That spring, he toured England. There a band called the Animals had what's been called the "first folk-rock hit," supposedly a new species of pop music. They cut a tune that Alan Lomax had collected and everyone from Guthrie to Seeger to Dylan had covered. But this "House of the Rising Sun" began with an electrified strum, then was fleshed out with organ and drums before building to a rock & roll climax.

When Dylan got back to the states, his record label wanted him to record again, and he went right to it. Instead of the deliberate process that had produced *The Times They Are a-Changin'*—six sessions over three months—he cut eleven new tunes in three hours. Ragged, inspired, liberated, *Another Side of Bob Dylan* was mostly original melodies, not Old Songs with New Words—and maybe not even Contemporary Folk.

The new LP announces itself midway through the opening song; the announcement is a giggle. "All I Really Want to Do" could be "I Want to Hold Your Hand" turned inside out, a rhyming list of what the singer *doesn't* want to do. "I don't want to . . . / Analyze you, categorize you / Finalize you or advertise you." Then he giggles. And giggles again, later on. Maybe he's amused by his own wordplay. Or by the high Jimmie Rodgers yodel he uses mid-chorus. Or by the sheer pleasure of letting loose. But instead of re-recording, he leaves the laughter in, and some flubbed lines in other songs. They serve as a declaration: this is not a serious adult record. Not, anyway, like his previous. As he puts it on one cut, "I'm younger than that now."

The arrangements mostly stick to folk guitar and harmonica. But the songs are goofier than *The Times They Are a-Changin'*, hipper, and there's a noticeable lack of overt political protest. In fact, "I Shall Be Free No. 10" asserts it isn't really about anything—and is all about its chord changes and the pleasures of free association. "Motorpsycho

Nightmare" uses Hitchcock's *Psycho* to taunt liberal pieties: the true value of free speech is as a way out of a horror movie. The songs aren't all funny. "Ballad in Plain D" is an eight-minute analysis of a failed love affair; "Spanish Harlem Incident," a two-minute plea to start a love affair—but they're all driven by exuberance: in the music, in the words, in the range and quality of Dylan's voice. The subversive "To Ramona" (one of the few old melodies: a redo of Gene Autry's cowboy waltz "The Last Letter") proclaims that the world is just "A vacuum, a scheme"; you mustn't let it "type you." And the LP ends as it begins, with a list of what the singer doesn't want to be. He won't answer to people's expectations; he won't make promises for life; he won't be "the one." Call it an anti–love song. "It Ain't Me Babe" tries to break free from what Dylan describes elsewhere as the "politics of ancient history."

In some ways, *Another Side* does break free. Except the sound lags behind. Chuck Berry tall tales are still married to a Mother Maybelle Carter strum.

The notes Dylan attached to the record are about confusion or maybe personal freedom: "i know no answers an no truth / . . . there are no morals / an i dream a lot." This came out as his friends in the civil rights movement were helping to initiate a pointedly moral campaign they were calling Freedom Summer. Mississippi, 45 percent black, had less than 5 percent of that population registered to vote, and SNCC's yearlong registration drive—the work Dylan supported by singing in Greenwood—had brought in only a few hundred new registrations. Freedom Summer was an attempt to break that stalemate by inviting Northern college students to the South. A month before 1964's Newport Folk Festival, three of those volunteers—two whites and a black, all in their twenties—disappeared. They were eventually found, beaten and murdered by the Klan. "If white America would not respond to the deaths of our people . . ." as SNCC leader John Lewis put it, "maybe it would react to the deaths of its own children."

"go joshua, go fit your battle" Dylan writes in the notes to

Another Side, "i have t' go t' the woods / for a while / i hope you un-derstand / . . . i will be with you / nex' time around . . ." He arrived at Newport a different kind of star. Peter, Paul and Mary had done a live cover of "The Times They Are a-Changin'." Over on country radio, Johnny Cash had turned "Don't Think Twice, It's All Right" into a twangy croon. Dylan had replaced his workshirt with the ur-ban hip of a black turtleneck and a jacket. The densely written new song he premiered was again about pursuing a sound, about music's "dancing spell" and the singer's need to follow. Never mind protest or anger; in "Mr. Tambourine Man," he wants to dance "with one hand waving free."

The liberated *Another Side of Bob Dylan* didn't sell as well as the previous protest music. Some in the folk community objected to this new direction. The editor of *Sing Out!* called the record too "inner-directed . . . innerprobing, self-conscious." He said Dylan had "lost contact with people," been consumed by the "American Success Machinery," become "a celebrity [with the] awful potential for self-destruction," and then compared him to James Dean. "Any songwriter," the critic concluded, "who tries to deal honestly with reality in this world is bound to write 'protest' songs. How can he help himself?" Because Dylan's new music didn't seem to protest, he wasn't dealing with reality—not honestly, anyway.

The other possibility was that the reality was new and that the best way to deal honestly with it, to report on the COMPLICATED CIRCLE, was with a new, "self-conscious" language. By that fall of 1964, Guthrie's dream of One Big Union had so morphed that orga-nized labor was throwing its weight behind the war president, Lyn-don Johnson. Dylan's new songs responded with a kind of gallows humor. He'd once deceived himself into thinking he had something to protect; now there was "mutiny from stern to bow." Brushing aside these old falsehoods, insisting there's no single truth, it's as if he was fighting to clear some breathing space inside that COMPLI-CATED CIRCLE, some smaller circle where he could see and hear what was really going on.

At his concerts that winter—in Massachusetts and New York, Ohio and Maine, Wisconsin, and California—Dylan mixed the fare. He always opened the show with "The Times They Are a-Changin'," as if setting the terms of the discussion. "My whole concert," he said, "takes off from there . . ." Then he placed so-called love songs next to so-called protest songs and let the boundaries melt. On Halloween, 1964, for example, at New York's Philharmonic Hall, he opened with "Times," followed with his Spanish Harlem love song, then went to politics with a talking blues that mocked the Red Scare. In this case, he was playing to his own, an audience sprinkled with old Greenwich Village friends quick to adjust and hip to his inside jokes.

But the new material that Dylan introduces next challenges even *their* enthusiasm. The songs are long, loaded with words, and often hard to follow, never mind understand. That the crowd even tries is a testament to the power of Dylan as a performer. His singing and playing, his ability to *inhabit* a song, has gotten to the point where he can bring listeners on board almost no matter how difficult the ride. He breaks the long songs down into pieces, his voice rising and falling on each phrase, skewering the melody, making every note count. At the same time, he maintains Guthrie's technique of modesty—that way of putting the music forward while holding himself back. It pulls the listeners like a magnet.

"Gates of Eden" winds over eight minutes, a skein of words stretched across a repeating melody. The singer introduces it at the Philharmonic as a "sacrilegious lullaby in D minor." Then giggles. Then calls it a love song. But it sounds like protest. Carefully enunciating each word, he sketches a world of greed and false pride, of paupers mindlessly exchanging possessions. This isn't Guthrie's "California's a Garden of Eden,"—or the Salvation Army's pie in the sky. Dylan's heaven is defined as *not* being day-to-day reality, because day-to-day reality is defined as brutal verging on meaningless. "Of war and peace," the song begins, "the truth just twists." It goes on in thick, coded language to argue that any promise of paradise has to be false. And ends with a succinct formula: only the singer's words can tell what's true, and "there are no truths outside the Gates of Eden." By that geography, you have to be "innerprobing" to find the truth. There's no Commonism, only an individual search: the solitary prospector.

When the song ends, Dylan tries to reassure the Philharmonic. "Don't let that scare you," he laughs. "It's just Halloween." But the next new song is even longer—eleven and a half minutes—and scarier. Again it's structured as an attack on the hollowness of the modern world, from the lack of anything sacred to the con of advertising, all set to what sounds like an old mountain ballad. The chorus is an edgy, constantly shifting reassurance: "It's alright, Ma, I can make it." "It's alright, Ma, if I can't please him." Echoes of the Elvis tune Dylan tried to cut two years earlier, but where "That's All Right, Mama" is full of confidence—jump beat and slap bass underlining how it's fine "any way you do"—Dylan's "It's Alright Ma (I'm Only Bleeding)" zeroes in on the ways it's *not* fine: the rules of the masters, the old-lady judges, the false gods. And the sound reinforces that: he packs the ballad form with quick rhymes, pouring them out in long breaths as if he were fighting to keep his head above water, above the golden age's great wash of manufactured goods. It's a protest song, but what it's protesting amounts to mid-twentieth-century daily existence: "life and life only."

That life—Dylan's COMPLICATED CIRCLE—grew out of an agreement; call it a consensus about the truth. Instead of protests, instead of slowdowns and walkouts and bombings, certain roles were set. Management would manage, workers would work, and the government would act as go-between—some called it a "broker state"—maintaining stability. Negotiations replaced massacres in a truce where all parties could benefit. Unionized workers would get regular, measured wage increases. That meant they could make payments on cars and suburban homes and into their kids' college funds. And that, in turn, kept the economy spinning. Consumer wages (and debt) fed profit, and big business prospered. By the early sixties, there was as little strike activity as during World War II, when most of organized labor had taken a no-strike pledge. In what has been called "the heyday of American liberalism," the trade union movement had become "tame even when it was powerful."

Meanwhile, the very nature of work was changing. When Agassiz first got to the Upper Peninsula, about half America's workers were farmers, a quarter were in the industrial sector, and a quarter provided services. By 1960, fewer than 10 percent farmed, about a third did heavy industrial work, and 60 percent were part of the service industry. The workforce had become more mobile, less unified, and less unionized. 1956 was the peak of American union membership—and even then only a third of nonagricultural workers belonged. After that, the percentage started to fall. So that labor leader Walter Reuther could declare in 1960, "We are going backward."

The nature of unemployment was changing, too. Back in the thirties, Steinbeck, McWilliams, Guthrie had seen California's government-run migrant camp as an example of how the state could create a collective solution. To big business and large landowners, it was creeping socialism. By Dylan's era, the free market had won the argument, but major aspects of government assistance—housing aid, food stamps, unemployment insurance, healthcare—were all part of President Johnson's Great Society. Major unions called it the "reincarnation of the verve and excitement of the New Deal." Congress passed Johnson's reforms not as attacks on capitalism but as part of the state's now established role: to help the poor and the elderly while maintaining the truce between management and labor.

In this golden arrangement, unions tended to support state policy, including the Vietnam War. The leader of the AFL-CIO, coined the term "silent majority" to describe its law-abiding members: believers in the American way, thankful for prosperity, wanting things to stay as they were. So the CIO, which had once championed integration and equality, refused to support the 1963 March on Washington or the Poor People's March that followed Dr. King's assassination in 1968. As Reuther, dissenting president of the auto-mobile workers union, put it, "[Labor] continues to live with the past. It advances few new ideas . . . [and] is becoming increasingly the comfortable, complacent custodian of the status quo." Was this the times a-changin' that unions had fought for? Was this losers getting to win?

Dylan had another chance to make a political statement in early December 1964. The Free Speech Movement held a rally on the university campus at Berkeley. Its demands for students' rights grew out of SNCC's work in the South and helped set the stage for the antiwar protests to come. Both Dylan and Baez were in the area doing concerts; both had an off-day on their schedules; both were invited to appear at the rally. The chance of them being there may have helped boost the crowd to some six thousand.

"There's a time," student leader Mario Savio told the gathered students, "when the operation of the machine becomes so odious, makes you so sick at heart that you can't take part. . . . And you've got to put your bodies upon the gears and upon the wheels, upon the levers, upon all the apparatus—and you've got to make it stop." It's the language of Joe Hill, of the old labor movement. Except it wasn't.

"Unfortunately," Savio went on, ". . . [there's] no sense of soli-darity at this point between unions and students." Instead, the red flag seemed to have passed from worker to young protester—the emphasis shifting from bread to roses: to counterculture. The Free Speech Movement was Dylan's turf—the fight to "tell it and think and speak it and breathe it"—and that "odious machine" could have come right out of one of his new songs. But when Savio interrupted his speech to introduce "one last person," it was Baez. Who then sang "Blowin' in the Wind." The song's author never showed.

Instead, Dylan went back east to work on yet another LP, his third in less than a year and a half, a recorded output of over thirty original songs. He laid down some of the new material to the usual acoustic guitar and harmonica. But it didn't sound right. One song was a spin-off from Chuck Berry's "Too Much Monkey Business," where Berry's wry voice sprints over a series of hurdles—crummy jobs, fake salesmen, conniving women—and concludes it's all "too much monkey business for me to get involved in." Borrowing the machine-gun delivery and quick rhymes, Dylan updates the picture: "users, cheaters, six-time losers . . . Twenty years of schoolin' / And they put you on the day shift." The result, "Subterranean Homesick Blues," described a frantic world far from the subterranean mellowness of folk music, but this acoustic version didn't sound different. Same for "Love Minus Zero/No Limit," all about a lover who steps away from the odious machine: "She knows there's no success like failure / And that failure's no success at all." Both songs used the language of a new era but sounded like the old, folkie one.

The next day, Dylan came back into the studio with a band: drums, bass, piano, and three guitar players. "Subterranean Homesick Blues" still begins with Dylan's acoustic strum but is now joined by the pinprick of a lead guitar and then the kick of the rhythm section. His advice not to take advice—"Don't follow leaders / Watch the parkin' meters"—becomes exuberant. And the slow roll of "Love Minus Zero" gets added depth, too. But it's a third cut, "Maggie's Farm," that really begins to dig into the possibilities.

For "Maggie's Farm," Dylan started with "Down on Penny's Farm," a 1929 string-band tune and one of the commercial recordings on Harry Smith's folk anthology. Its cheerful melody disguised complaints about tenant farming: "You work all day . . . but you get no pay." Dylan's song outlines the work he won't do and why. "Well, I try my best / To be just like I am / But everybody wants you / To be just like them / They say, 'Sing while you slave,' but I just get bored." The clash of electric guitar and harmonica stir up an industrial noise, the drum fills keep jolting things forward, and the singer's voice rises to the challenge. Dylan's still using some of that Carter Family restraint, but he's figured out a way to convey a new, sardonic anger. When Maggie's brother hands out the week's wages—a nickel and a dime—Dylan extends *dime* just enough to give it an edge, the sound of insult being added to injury.

The music's not only gone electric; it's gone blacker. "Outlaw Blues" sets Guthrie's kind of hero in a tune that sounds like Chuck Berry's "Memphis," and brags like Muddy Waters and Bo Diddley. "Don't ask me nuthin' about nuthin'," the folkie from Hibbing declares, "I just might tell you the truth." The song ends with a confession that redefines outlaw: "I got . . . a brown-skin woman, but I / Love her just the same."

Bringing It All Back Home is Dylan's bluesiest LP since his first. It arrives at rock & roll the way the Delta blues musicians did: taking tradition upriver to the electricity of the big city. Still, the band and Dylan don't quite fit together. The arrangements feel like just that: folk songs arranged for rock & roll instruments. At one point, he gets a couple lines into a verse before realizing the band hasn't joined him; followed by bursts of laughter. If he's trying to bring his sound back home, he hasn't arrived yet.

The day after cutting rock & roll, he returns for a final session that begins electric and ends with him solo, again, and acoustic. The LP's last song, "It's All Over Now, Baby Blue," is set in some end-time when the saints are coming through. A jazzy guitar picks behind an upbeat strum as the singer tells his lover she has to change. Why? Because the world is changing—even the carpet's moving under her. She has—we have—no choice but to move forward, to "strike another match . . . start anew." It's another restless farewell, a love song as protest, balanced between sadness and possibility.

In the notes to the record, Dylan listed people, including Joe Hill and James Dean, that he "would not want to be." The reason? ". . . they are all dead." New times demand new forms of rebellion. As he was finishing *Bringing It All Back Home*, protestors were choking the jails in Selma, Alabama. Breaking some from Dr. King's patient nonviolence, SNCC invited Malcolm X to come down and speak. Angry, direct, he told the young organizers that if America is the master's house, he sees it on fire. And he's praying for a wind to come help feed the flames. Less than three weeks later, he was assassinated. A week after that, the Selma demonstrators attempted to march to the state capitol in Montgomery, only to be turned back by state troopers with clubs and tear gas.

The broker state tried to restore calm. Just before *Bringing It All Back Home* came out, President Johnson put the Voting Rights Act before Congress. "What happened in Selma," he declared in a nationally televised speech, "is part of a far larger movement which reaches into every section and state of America. [I]t is . . . not just Negroes but really it is all of us who must overcome the crippling legacy of bigotry and injustice. And we shall overcome."

But even as he adopted the language of civil rights, Johnson was escalating the Vietnam War. That spring's launching of bomb strikes would result in over three hundred thousand missions, dropping more than six hundred thousand tons of bombs.

When the Selma protestors tried again to march to the capital, Joan Baez was just finishing a tour with Dylan. She did their last two shows in Pittsburgh, then headed to Alabama for a "Stars for Freedom" concert organized by singer Harry Belafonte. Belafonte's calypso tunes were classified as folk music, and he knew the scene, including Dylan, who recorded with him. Baez, Seeger, Peter, Paul and Mary, Odetta all sang for the marchers. Dylan wasn't there.

"I felt he was going through some fantastic emotional things," his SNCC friend, Bernice Johnson Reagon, recalled, "and I didn't want to make any judgment. . . . When he simply drifted away from the movement, it was the whites in SNCC who were resentful. The blacks in SNCC didn't think that. . . ."

Instead of performing at the Selma march, he flew to the West Coast to promote *Bringing It All Back Home*. Interviewed by the *L.A. Free Press*, he dismissed "writing songs on protest subjects. . . . Sure, you can. . . . But who hears them? The people that do hear them are going to be agreeing with you anyway." He was looking for a broader audience and a broader definition of protest, because, he insisted, the problem was broader.

Much of the civil rights movement had focused on black people registering to vote. Dylan told the interviewer, "There's more to it. . . . There's more to it than picketing in Selma, right? There's people living in utter poverty in New York." He was all for getting the right to vote, but "Who they going to vote for? Just politicians; same as the white people put in their politicians." He seems to want a larger change, a more fundamental one. "[The Negro Civil Rights Movement] is proper," he declared. "It's not 'Commie' anymore. . . ."

Before Malcolm X was killed, he'd dismissed voter registration, criticizing "the entire system of democracy." And Martin Luther King's position was evolving: "We shall eliminate slums for Negroes when we destroy ghettoes and build new cities for *all*," he emphasized. "We shall eliminate unemployment for Negroes when we demand full and fair employment for *all*." Speaking to the protestors on the capitol steps in Montgomery, King put segregation into a larger context as a "political stratagem . . . to keep . . . southern labor the cheapest in the land." That left the poor—blacks and whites—as pawns in the game. King maintained the Selma protests were about more than voting rights. "Let us march until no starved man walks the streets of our cities and towns in search of jobs that do not exist."

Dylan's friends in and around SNCC were starting to change strategies. A month before Dylan's *L.A. Free Press* interview, John Lewis had declared that "to be effective . . . the civil rights movement must be black-controlled, dominated, and led." What role did that leave for SNCC's white supporters? "The job of white people who believe in freedom," one would decide, "is to confront white America." If you consider that one of the aims of Dylan's new music, it redefines the idea of bringing it all back home.

The single off the album, "Subterranean Homesick Blues," was his first to make the US charts, peaking at number thirty-nine. Around the same time, the Byrds' rock & roll version of "Mr. Tambourine Man" became a number-one hit in both America and England. If this was confrontation, it was surging into larger arenas.

Dylan's "public famousity" was expanding from songwriter and underground influence to pop star.

He began his last purely acoustic tour that April in England. As documented in D. A. Pennebaker's film, *Don't Look Back*, it's a numbing series of one-nighters. The singer's besieged by interviewers; teenage fans squeal outside his hotel, bang on his limousine. He's still opening his show with "The Times They Are a-Changin'" and playing gorgeous acoustic renditions of his songs. But his new, partly rock & roll LP has begun to hit the airwaves, and he's now dressing the part: sunglasses, turtleneck, tight pants, long hair, his skin even paler, his eyes even sleepier. To repeated questions about who he is and what he believes—attempts to make him a spokesperson for his generation—he often answers in the negative: "I'm not angry." "I don't see anything to believe in." "I'm not a folksinger." He messes with the truth, making up stories about his past, putting reporters on, distancing himself from any and all movements.

Isolated, then, and still only twenty-three, he's feeling his way toward and through fame. At one point, he and a friend jam backstage, trying to remember the songs of Dylan's early idol, Hank Williams. They start in on the haunting "Lost Highway," a lament about going astray that Williams wrote when he was twenty-two. Dylan does a verse about wine, cards, and lies but can't remember the rest. His friend prompts him—"I'm a rolling stone"—and Dylan takes it from there: "I'm a rolling stone, all alone and lost."

STRUGGLE

n early 1941, Woody Guthrie decided he couldn't continue working in a system he didn't believe in. He quit his well-paid radio job in New York City and drove to Los Angeles. There, he stewed: angry, depressed, out of work.

> 4/4/41
> Los Angeles,
> Broke, feel
> natural again,
> but it ain't
> natural to be
> broke, is it?

What rescued him wasn't a new system or a revolution but the federal government. The Department of the Interior was sponsoring a documentary film about the Grand Coulee Dam and needed a singer with the "common touch" to write the score. Alan Lomax recommended Guthrie, and Guthrie, without any guarantee he had the job, put his wife and three kids back in the car and drove to the state of Washington.

The Grand Coulee Dam job was, in essence, to promote FDR's domestic agenda. As Guthrie headed north, the American Communist party had just withdrawn its support of Roosevelt's policies. The president's stated goal was to "protect the system of private property

and free enterprise. . . ." He saw himself as "that kind of conservative . . . that kind of liberal." Things had to change—the Depression made that obvious—but the goal was never radical change. As
the motto for his 1936 reelection campaign put it, "Reform if you
would Preserve;" Later FDR made it clear: "I have not sought, I do
not seek, I repudiate the support of any advocate of Communism
or any other 'ism' which would by fair means or foul change our
American democracy." Guthrie, on the other hand, believed, "The
only New Deal that will ever amount to a damn thing will come
from Trade Unions."

So the job at the Grand Coulee had him working for a government he didn't much believe in, but it was a job. And it was a
job that seemed to side with 'the people' against big business. Local
entrepreneurs thought electrification should be left to the free market: private dams run for profit. They saw the Grand Coulee as an
unconstitutional nationalizing of power. FDR's Bonneville Power
Authority, on the other hand, backed the project as "a purgative of
national despair," one of four giant western dams that would show
what America could achieve. As the depressed economy continued
to falter, here was a chance for government to step in and establish a
planned, centralized "economic democracy."

Like the oil booms of Guthrie's childhood, the dam would destroy streams, wetlands, and wildlife. And his political education
taught him that the main beneficiaries of a capital project would
be capitalists. But the promise of work went beyond just his job.
Whether it was a local hired to run a jackhammer, a migrant pouring concrete, or a farmer able to water his crops, the Grand Coulee
meant food for hungry families. The dam was an improvement (like
the canal in northern Michigan), a way of taming nature and bringing electricity and irrigation to rural outposts. "So that several thousand families of migrating farm workers," as Guthrie put it, "could
move out there and settle down."

The singer's communist involvement made it impossible for him
to get civil service clearance; the best he could do was a temporary

appointment for a month's work. He spent his first week being toured around. "I saw the Columbia River and the big Grand Coulee Dam from just about every cliff, mountain, tree and post from which it can be seen." He met the workers, the administrators, the local farmers. He visited towns full of Okie migrants hoping to get on the project's payroll. "He loved to talk to the people," as his wife, Mary, put it, "get their stories."

Afterward, he settled down to turn his research into music. It was like his study of Okies that produced *Dust Bowl Ballads*, but the process was sped up: in three weeks, he wrote (or in many cases, rewrote) twenty-six songs.

They were documentary songs for a documentary film. The term *documentary* was coined in the twenties, when it was seen as a way to counter "the pessimism that had settled on Liberal theory," the pessimism that "democratic citizenship was . . . impossible." But the approach dated back at least to Mother Bloor's era, when photographer Lewis Hine proclaimed his 1905 portraits of immigrants were ". . . to show things that had to be corrected . . . to show things that had to be appreciated." A documentary approached reality in an apparently straight forward, unemotional way. It served as an antidote to slanted mainstream reporting. As one study put it, the documentary was out to dignify the usual and level the extraordinary. It took a picture of the facts; it told the truth.

Guthrie was hired to document the Grand Coulee Dam. To him, that meant producing more than just an objective record. According to the Marxist *New Masses* magazine, an artist "in the fullest sense of the term" not only raised issues but recommended "an implicit course of action." That's what Guthrie was aiming for. The slogan "Art is a weapon" had become a rallying cry for radical artists. Guthrie took it a step further by slapping an industrial sticker on his guitar: THIS MACHINE KILLS FASCISTS.

He approached the Grand Coulee songs a lot like he had the Dust Bowl ballads: putting new lyrics to old melodies and writing from the point of view of the worker or, of someone looking for work. So

he took a Jimmie Rodgers' tune, "Muleskinner Blues," and shifted
the story to the Pacific Northwest: instead of a mule skinner, Guthrie's narrator is a hard-rock man, looking to run a jackhammer. And
"Jackhammer Blues" is about a man who's managed to get the job,
working "to bring the people some electric light."

Song after song boosts the dam as the dust bowl's happy ending:
"Your power is turning our darkness to dawn." Refugees would end
up with work and a place to raise a family. "Goodbye," he sings, "to
the ol' skid row!" And there was an added benefit: instead of the
river "just a-going to waste," it would "run ten or fifteen cities of
electric currents and run all the factories that was gonna beat Hitler
and Nazism and Fascism." Over 90 percent of the power from the
Grand Coulee would end up going to war production. "I wish we
had," Guthrie sings, "a lot more Grand Coulee Dams."

If Guthrie paints the project as a new kind of industrial Arcadia, he also documents the dark side. "Ramblin' Round," written
to the tune of Lead Belly's "Goodnight, Irene," is the story of an
outcast who's had to leave his family and sweetheart. Though his
mother prays he'll be "a man of some renown," he's ended up "just
a refugee," a peach picker working for a dollar a day. As he stares at
the surplus fruit left to rot, he thinks, "There's a hungry mouth for
every peach." Haunting and all but hopeless, it's a song of waste—of
how the system lives off waste.

And "Pastures of Plenty," also written at Bonneville, redefines
hope. Written to the tune of an old English murder ballad, "Pretty
Polly," it tells the story of drifting migrants, ghostlike reminders of
what doesn't work. "On the edge of your city, you'll see us and then
/ We come with the dust, and we're gone with the wind." Dylan,
quoting that line in "Song to Woody," makes Guthrie seem like
one of those men, and in a way, that's what the Grand Coulee songs
set out to do: to put the listener in that place, to make an unseen
reality real. "A good documentary," as the head of the New Deal's
photography unit declared, "should tell not only what a place or a
thing or a person *looks* like, but it must also tell the audience what

it would *feel* like to be an actual witness to the scene." "Pastures of Plenty" makes the ongoing Depression feel like not only hard times but a battle zone. "Every state in this union us migrants have been / And we'll work in this fight, and we'll fight till we win." While he calls the Grand Coulee Dam "the biggest thing man has ever done," the fight for Commonism—the fight to make the world level—is even bigger.

After a month in Portland, the job was over. Guthrie had created some of his most evocative songs—and been paid a total of $266.66. Now he was back facing the same dilemma: how to make a living in a system he didn't believe in. Five months earlier, when he left *Pipe Smoking Time* and New York City, Pete Seeger was just starting a folk group called the Almanac Singers. The week Guthrie and family arrived at the Bonneville job, the Almanacs were singing at a rally for twenty thousand striking New York transit workers. Since then, they'd cut two albums. Now they invited Guthrie to come east and join them, making music for the union movement.

To Mary Guthrie, it wasn't a real job offer. The Almanacs paid little to nothing. And hadn't they just come from the East? Guthrie later wrote how Mary was "stuck so full of catholic religious notions" that she thought of his union work as "a fibby line." That was part of what he called the "sad mismatch" of their marriage. But she was also tired of chasing the dream: after those first three years in Pampa, she'd spent two years in L.A., a year back in Pampa, a couple months in New York, and four months in L.A. again, and the past month in Washington. Their oldest child was almost school age. She needed what her husband's Grand Coulee songs kept coming back to: a decent income and a place to live.

Woody was different. She saw that he was more "for the downtrodden people . . . [than] for himself, even for his family. . . ." His idea of a decent job was not only feeding his kids but helping to make the world level. The Almanacs offered him a chance to fight for that.

The group formed as a collective, determined "to live cooperatively, share and share alike, setting aside . . . individual ambition." Lee

Hays was the twenty-seven-year-old son of a Methodist minister from Arkansas. He'd been "chief helper" to Claude Williams, a Southern preacher who defied segregation, fought to organize tenant farmers, and embraced Marxism. Hays pulled his roommate into the band, a twenty-two-year-old aspiring writer from New Jersey named Millard Lampell. But the center of the Almanacs was Pete Seeger. Most of the songs on the group's first two albums featured Seeger's eager vocal and his banjo playing; the others tend to act as background chorus.

The Almanacs specialized in catchy tunes meant to rally crowds and motivate action. Their debut album, *Songs for John Doe*, was a Popular Front manifesto, all antidraft and antiwar. Jimmie Rodgers's "T for Texas" was turned into "C for Conscription" (complete with Seeger yodeling), and the old minstrel show standard, "Liza Jane," got revamped to make fun of FDR's policies: "Cut the pay and raise the rents / It's all for national defense." Their second album, *Talking Union*, sounds like Seeger's graduate thesis at the school of Woody Guthrie—from a cover of "Union Maid" to the sign-off on the title cut, "Take it easy but take it," one of Guthrie's trademark phrases. The Almanacs' style was Guthrie's; they were trying to turn his model of a folksinger into, as Seeger said, "a national movement."

Mary encouraged Guthrie to go east. It was his chance to work for the "downtrodden people." "What we've got to do," he wrote the Almanacs, "is to bring American Folk Songs up to date. . . . Our job ain't so much to go way back into history. . . . Our job is the Here & Now. . . . But we've got to try and include a Timeless Element in our songs . . . something that tomorrow will be as true as it is today." That was the job he wanted. He said good-bye to his wife of seven years and their three towheaded young children and started hitchhiking east.

Two weeks later, when Guthrie got to the Almanacs' Lower East Side apartment, the news had come that Germany had invaded Russia. That changed everything. Suddenly, the Communists were potential US allies, and their premier, Josef Stalin, had become "Uncle Joe." The American Communist Party quickly dropped its neutral stance. Just as quickly, the Almanacs dropped their antiwar and anti-FDR songs.

They set out, instead, to define the coming war in Popular Front terms and get American unions involved. Guthrie had no sooner arrived in New York than his new group was getting ready to leave on a national tour. To raise gas money, they quickly cut a dozen songs, almost all traditional and seemingly apolitical. Up-tempo sea chanteys, farm songs, they were the sound of an earlier time when people labored and sang in groups: songs about working together. On the recordings, they divided the leads about equally among Guthrie—at twenty-nine, the senior member of the group—Seeger, and Hays.

Though Guthrie's recordings up till then had been solo, a lot of his performing had been with others: from the cowboy band in Pampa through his success with Lefty Lou to his New York appearances with Lead Belly and others. From the beginning, he'd been developing the sound of a regular guy—and been playing familiar melodies—to make it easy for others to join in. The music was meant to be communal: at a migrant camp or a skid-row bar or on the radio. Now he was part of a group with the same goals.

"Our idea," Guthrie wrote, "is to bring songs and fun and serious entertainment into the union halls so as to make it a better, livelier, peppier, and a lot more sensible place to come to than a pool hall. . . ." They went on the road, singing for workers in Pittsburgh, Cleveland, Detroit, Milwaukee. After stopping in Denver, they pushed on to a performance for Harry Bridges's longshoremen's union in San Francisco. They were underpaid and often exhausted, with long drives between gigs and nights spent on friends' floors. But contrast it to Dylan's rambling cross-country drive two decades later, and it was a trip with an agenda. "We say the most important thing to do is to beat everybody that's like Hitler," Guthrie wrote, "and we say the biggest and just fight in this direction is the Union fight—and the job of the organized to organize the ones that ain't. . . ."

Soon after reaching the West Coast, Hays and Lampell headed

back home. Guthrie met with Mary and the kids in L.A. As Seeger remembered it, he tried to reconcile things, but she wanted to settle down near family, and he wanted to keep organizing, to keep traveling. Leaving his family behind, again, he and Seeger continued, "hitch-hiking on credit" up into Oregon and Washington. They took the northern route back east, stopping to sing for copper miners in Butte, for workers in Duluth (where Robert Zimmerman was four months old), and then on to Michigan's Upper Peninsula where—almost twenty-eight years after the 1913 massacre—the copper miners of Calumet and Hecla still didn't have a union.

Back in New York, Guthrie moved into the Almanacs' communal living space. There he began writing his life story. As he reworked (reinvented?) history, tossing freshly typed sheets of paper all over the floor, he found himself at the center of an emerging folk revival. It was the outgrowth of work done by an earlier generation—John Lomax, Charles Seeger, Carl Sandburg—and some of the elders came by to pass the torch. Mother Bloor, almost eighty now, offered advice, encouragement, and fresh vegetables from her farm. Elizabeth Gurley Flynn brought a suitcase of Joe Hill's papers, and Guthrie pored over them, simultaneously writing his own story and studying the past.

"He walked like somebody who knew something," is how Hays put it, "and indeed he did. He knew a great deal. He read a great deal. He was a well-educated man and he was a principled man." Guthrie's job—his act, the role he played in the fight he cared about—meant he underplayed the learning. To young New York folk singers, Guthrie was, as one remembered, "the authentic thing. For the rest of us, it was more or less something we adopted." Some saw through the act. "[He] pretended," is how one housemate recalled it. ". . . He loved to have people think of him as a real working-class person and not an intellectual." Challenging the Singing Hobo, one singer told him, "You never picked a grape in your life."

Maybe. But what he was working to create was a type, a model. In that way, he shaped *Bound for Glory* into a how-to book: how to fight for change, how to find something to believe in, how to grow up. It emphasized the Lone Wolf, the hobo-as-outlaw-as-hero. And it worked. As one young fan told Hays, "Woody represents freedom, the ability to just pick up and go anywhere you want to, whenever you take a mind to. . . . Absolute freedom." Hays was a little astonished at the idea.

But as Guthrie was creating that legend, he was also committing himself to a group effort, to politics that emphasized the many over the one. "You will see a lot of good in the way the Almanacs do things," he wrote an old friend in Los Angeles: "work, think, argue, raise hell, fight, run, fart, fall, and also march right through the walls of union halls, and win the friendship and many letters of reference and recommendation from the Union Heads . . ."

To Guthrie, singing with a group, with the Almanacs, was a shared way "of saying what's on your mind." Even, he added, "where it ain't too healthy to talk too loud, speak your mind, or even to vote like you want to . . ." Back when Guthrie crossed the Oregon border for the Grand Coulee job, a routine check had turned up "confidential information . . . that subject person is a Communist." Soon FBI Director J. Edgar Hoover was signing a request to investigate Woodrow W. Guthrie under the law that made it illegal for public employees to be "members of subversive organizations" or to "advocate the overthrow of this government."

What the Almanacs were advocating was the defeat of fascism, both overseas and at home. Fascism, Guthrie wrote, "is nothing in the world but greed for profit and greed for the power to hurt and make slaves out of people." They fought it as a group, with everything at hand, including and especially music. Hays wanted the Almanacs to write "that great marching song of belief and hope, which will be our song of battle."

"Art is a weapon," Guthrie reaffirmed, "and as deadly as steel cannons or exploding bombs." He was now using his weapon to get the United States out of its neutrality and into the war effort. In "My Daddy Flies That Ship in the Sky," a group of kids (they might have been his own, now a continent away) talk about how their parents are helping to build planes that will presumably help the Soviet Union stop Germany. In the verses of "The Sinking of the Reuben James"—sung to the tune of the Carter Family's "Wildwood Flower"—Guthrie calls for the US to avenge the loss of one of its convoy ships. To enlist more people in the cause (and to raise rent money), the group started hosting communal sings, which they called hootenannies. "Almanac Singers really doing good work," Guthrie wrote Alan Lomax in December. "Two of them sober this evening."

Then came Pearl Harbor. America entered the war, and that thrust the Almanacs into the political mainstream. Suddenly everyone was fighting fascism. They appeared on *This Is War*, broadcast nationally on all four radio networks to an estimated thirty million listeners. They got an agent at William Morris. They signed a record deal with a major label.

One historian called 1942 "an exhilarating year for American Communists." The war effort pulled together liberals, commies, middle-of-the-roaders, in what was being called the United Front. It looked a lot like the Popular Front. A "Salute to our Russian Ally" rally at New York's Madison Square Garden would draw twenty-two thousand, including New York City's mayor, the governor, and the vice president of the United States. While membership in America's Communist Party was still tiny—forty-five thousand in a nation of 135 million—it was up from fifteen thousand a decade earlier. That spring, as a nod to his new allies, FDR commuted the jail sentence of Earl Browder, the party's general secretary.

The rush of enthusiasm for the United Front carried the Almanacs forward. A couple months after Pearl Harbor, they were asked to audition for a two-week booking at the prestigious Rainbow Room, high above Rockefeller Center. Afterward, they went back to their shared apartment and discussed whether to take the job. The way Seeger recalled it, "We weren't willing to change, and the Rainbow Room and others weren't willing to take us on our own terms." Soon those terms became public, as New York newspapers started outing the Almanacs as Communist sympathizers. United Front or not, times hadn't changed that much. Within weeks, the gigs, the record deal, the agent were gone.

That's not how Guthrie tells it in *Bound for Glory*. In his version, he comes in to the audition alone and is asked to dress up and perform as a hayseed. It's *Pipe Smoking Time* all over again, and he walks out, "glad to be loose from that sentimental and dreamy trash, and gladder . . . to be singing with the people." This solo version fits better in *Bound for Glory*'s narrative—and plays to America's fascination with the Lone Wolf, the solitary hero. That's who Woody Guthrie is turning himself into, even as he's dedicating himself to a collective approach.

He tries to reconcile the contradictions. In a piece he writes around this time about the Carter Family outlaw ballad "John Hardy"—the one he'd turned into "Tom Joad"—he asks,

> What is an outlaw? . . . [T]he outlaw is beat. Beat to start with. The whole world is against him. Reason why is because he's not organized. He's just by his self. Wants to holler, cuss, fight, work to change the world around a little bit better . . . but he's by his self. Bound to lose. . . . Why do people set down and write up great songs and ballads about their outlaws?
>
> Here's why. An outlaw does it wrong. . . . And the Union does it right. . . . [But] an outlaw does one big thing. What? It's easy.
>
> He tries.
>
> Tries his best.
>
> Dies for what he believes in. Goes down shooting.

He focuses on that resistance in one of his songs from this period, "East Texas Red." It's about a brutal railroad brakeman, "the meanest man on the shiny rails." He comes on a couple of hobos huddled around a pot of stew, kicks the stew over, laughs, and sends them packing. The men vow revenge. A year later, they return to the same spot and build another campfire. When Red shows up, they pull a gun. The brakeman drops to his knees and begs forgiveness. Though Guthrie maintained he wasn't for "bloody revolution," in the song, the gun "played the old one two / And Red was dead." Then "the other two men / Set down to eat their stew." End of song. No apology, no sweetening, no compromise. It's an antifascist fable, a celebration of frontier justice, an outlaw ballad about grown-up anger.

After anticommunism broke up the Almanacs, Guthrie found work in New York's extended radical network. The New Dance Group, also a collective, worked under the motto "Dance is a weapon in the class struggle." One of its choreographers, Sophie Maslow, had already made a piece to Guthrie's *Dust Bowl Ballads*; now, she wanted to take some of the Almanacs' tunes, combine them with Carl Sandburg's poetry, and create a square dance–meets–modern art piece called *Folksay*. She asked Earl Robinson and Guthrie to play at the performances and put an assistant, Marjorie Greenblatt Mazia, in charge of the musicians.

Mazia, twenty-four, was the daughter of a socialist-leaning former garment worker and a Yiddish poet. A married woman, she lived in Philadelphia but regularly commuted to New York to dance. Her biggest role so far had been in the Martha Graham Company's groundbreaking *American Document*, a stark, edgy piece that portrayed US history as a still ongoing struggle for freedom.

Mazia's assignment was to explain to Guthrie how music and dance could work together: what he called "the business of organization." As a folksinger, he was used to proceeding "according to my old philosophy of 'inspiration' and 'feeling.'" But that meant, "I sung the wrong counts, paused wrong, got the speed wrong and the time wrong." Meanwhile, the dancers "bumped and tromped on one another." Mazia showed him how to work with the group, and he took it as a larger lesson. "I saw why socialism was the only hope for any of us, because I was singing under the old rules of 'every man for his self' and the dancers was working according to a plan and a hope. (I learned that a planned world is what you need.)" In the process, he fell in love.

Mazia saw Guthrie as an artist, an artist of Martha Graham's caliber. "I have always felt," she'd write him later, "that knowing her and you both so well has been the greatest lesson of my life." He was her "lover and teacher and inspiration." She preserved his drawings and writings, helped organize his autobiographical novel, urged him to write down and keep track of his songs. As Lomax and Seeger had convinced him he was a folksinger, now Mazia encouraged him to think of himself as someone who made art. Soon they were living together, and almost as quickly she was pregnant.

Guthrie's first marriage had begun in the midst of the Depression. Nine years later, the war was finally turning the nation's economy around. US government orders from the private sector had totaled $12 billion in the last six months of 1941; in the following six months—after Pearl Harbor—that leaped to $100 billion. Some seventeen million new jobs were created. Between 1942 and 1945, America would see the highest level of employment in its history.

The war did nationally what the Grand Coulee had done locally. It drew rural workers off the farm to industrial jobs, with nine million Americans changing residences. Soon 10 percent of the population was in the military, leaving openings that almost doubled the number of working women and boosted African Americans to more than a third of the workforce. If the changes suggested what the post-war nation might look like, it also revealed long-simmering tensions. In Los Angeles, mobs of servicemen beat up Negroes and Mexican Americans. In Detroit, thirty-four people died in a three-day uprising, half of them "coloreds" killed by the police.

To people like Guthrie, this was domestic fascism and part of the greater ideological war. The largest corporations' share of manufactured goods produced rose from 30 to 70 percent. At the same time, union membership grew by 40 percent. The government wanted a United Front during wartime, so it appointed a National War Labor

Board to settle wage disputes. Most unions took a no-strike pledge for the duration of the war.

As a still married father of three, Guthrie had a draft deferment. While Seeger, Lomax, and others in the folk scene entered the military, he looked for work. He wanted to form another group. First, he wrote Maxine Crissman, but Lefty Lou was done with show business. Then he proposed a quartet with Lead Belly, Sonny Terry, and Brownie McGhee. Terry, a blind harmonica player, and singer/guitarist McGhee had come up from North Carolina and played in folk circles, sometimes appearing as part of the Almanacs. The way Guthrie saw it, the new quartet—he wanted to call them the Headline Singers—would comment on current events from the point of view of an integrated, predominantly black group.

It was a long way from "Run, Nigger, Run." The group never happened, but Guthrie would go on to cut songs with Terry and McGhee, and they helped change his sound. Their Piedmont blues style reversed the old Carter Family scratch, with McGhee playing melody on the guitar's high strings. That left the low ones for syncopated bass lines—like the left-hand of a ragtime piano player—and Terry's harmonica underlined the rhythm. Compare Guthrie's prewar recordings to what he did from the midforties on, and you can hear him moving more toward this bluesy style, toward black dance music. He described "the honor and the privilege of studying under the one and only Lead Belly." As his thinking and his musical collaborators changed, so did his sound: it integrated the way he hoped the country would.

Guthrie's and Mazia's daughter, Cathy, was born in early February 1943. Both parents were still married to other people. In March, *Bound for Glory* came out to enthusiastic reviews, and Guthrie was offered a deal for three more books. He might actually have a paying career as an author. Then, as the allies began bombing runs that prepared the way for the invasion of Europe, Guthrie got his divorce from Mary—and lost his deferment. If drafted, he was likely to fall under the army policy of assigning "potentially subversive personnel" to units where there was "a minimum opportunity for damage." It's how many of his friends were being kept out of the action.

Instead, Guthrie decided to join the Merchant Marines, whose members were represented by the National Maritime Union. Founded a few years earlier by Spanish Civil War veterans, the NMU was one of the country's most radical and the first union to include in its standard contract a non-discrimination agreement: it was open to and provided equal pay for Negroes. Guthrie's friend and sometime singing partner Gilbert "Cisco" Houston, was already a merchant marine. Their shared politics—they'd met in California through Will Geer—meshed with the NMU's. As Guthrie wrote, "Really why we're fighting this war . . . [is to] bring an end to the imitation world and to build up one that we can look at and sing about, and say, 'It's ours. Mine. Yours.'"

That was the grand fight: to end the imitation world. "I'm a union man from head to toe," he sang in his "Talking Merchant Marine," "I'm U.S.A. and C.I.O. / Fightin' out here on the waters / To win some freedom on the land." The dangers were real. The NMU was on the leading edge of the European war effort, helping to transport men and goods to the front. By the time Guthrie joined, some six thousand of its members had been killed; by the end of the war, it would be the branch of the military with the highest percentage of dead, almost double the army's.

On his first trip, as they slowly crossed the Atlantic, Guthrie read Marx and Engels and Darwin. "Our ships are manned by men of all tongues and colors," he'd write later, "and I saw the whole world there before my eyes while I sang to the men a dozen spells a day, between working hours washing dishes." A week out, his convoy was attacked and one of the cargo ships torpedoed and sunk. It was in the quiet afterward that he told Houston and another shipmate he didn't expect to live that long, anyway. He told them about his mother's long, faraway look and how he sometimes "felt woozy." Whatever had taken her, he told his shipmates, "I'm beginning to suspect that I have it, too."

He wrote a song called "Union's My Religion." Building on the idea of Jesus as an outlaw and a workingman, it ends with a declaration of faith: "When I seen my union vision / Then I made my quick decision / Yes, that union's my religion / That I know." Walt Whitman had a poem about "some strange musician / . . . an ecstatic ghost" whose music could "renew . . . languishing faith and hope." Mother Bloor liked to quote it; the war reinforced Guthrie's conviction to be that ghost.

Off Palermo, Italy, his ship caught a torpedo. He made it home safely, then re-upped for another tour of duty. He kept hoping the Grand Alliance of Russia, England, and the US was becoming more than just a temporary coalition. In November 1943, the Allied leaders met in Tehran. "Joe Stalin! Churchill! And Franklin D!" Guthrie sang. "And our new union world was born on that spot." American Communists saw Russia becoming a "permanent member of the family of nations," working toward a "people's democratic revolution." In early 1944, they reconfigured as the Communist Political Association and vowed to work within America's two-party system. The emphasis shifted even further from class struggle to cooperation. By the spring of the year, that position helped boost Communist membership back up to its 1938 peak of some eighty thousand.

When Guthrie returned from his second tour of duty, he heard about a new record label in the city. Its tiny studio was run by Moe Asch, who had a history of recording jazz and folk; he'd already cut some sides with Lead Belly and Seeger. As Asch tells the story, Guthrie arrived one day, sat down on the floor, and announced, "I'm a communist, y'know." Himself a subscriber to the *Daily Worker*, Asch was unfazed. He had Guthrie cut a couple of trial tunes, then extended an open invitation: come in and record whenever and whatever he wanted.

Three days later, Guthrie returned with Cisco Houston and cut an astonishing sixty-two songs in a single session. The marathon of ballads, commercial tunes, and Guthrie's own songs amounted to a crosssection of the repertoire he'd built up over the past decade—

with a special emphasis on the old songs, the folk songs. As Guthrie put it, "We tried hilltop and sunny mountain harmonies and wilder yells and whoops of the dead sea deserts, and all of the swampy southland and buggy mud bottom sounds that we could make." So, he'd jump from the traditional "John Henry" and "Hammer Ring" to Jimmie Rodgers's "Muleskinner Blues" to his own pro-war, anti-fascist "What Are We Waiting On?" Or he'd go from his version of "House of the Rising Sun" to the Wobbly-influenced "Hobo's Lullaby."

But that was just the beginning. The next day, Guthrie cut fifteen more, took a few days off, then recorded forty-nine songs over two days before returning the next week and laying down thirty-five more. He'd never had free rein in a recording studio before, and the "ecstatic ghost" ran with it. He played guitar, harmonica, fiddle, and mandolin. He brought in Houston, Seeger, Sonny Terry, Bess Lomax. As he dredged up old work to cut, he revamped his answer to "God Bless America," now calling it "This Land Is Your Land." Soon he'd be back on the North Atlantic, dodging torpedoes. And he could feel the first whispers of his mother's disease in his blood. This was his chance to lay down what he'd learned. Altogether, it was an outpouring of some hundred fifty songs.

This three-week binge accounts for a high percentage of all the Guthrie recordings that exist. Listened to together, they reveal not the outlaw or the Okie dust bowler, but the performer. Not the sensitive solo artist cast in the somber black-and-white of a Dorothea Lange photo, but a collaborator in full color. He's still doing a kind of journalism, still changing "So Long, It's Been Good to Know Ya" into a song about a solider enlisting in the army—and shifting the point of "The Biggest Thing Man Has Ever Done" from praising the Grand Coulee Dam to fighting the "Axis rattlesnakes." But a lot of the songs he and his friends cranked out were party songs: Guthrie playing fiddle on the instrumental "Hen Cackle" or trading guitar licks on "I Ain't Got Nobody." For the old square dance number "Ida Red," he, Houston, Terry, and Lomax form a string band with

Guthrie calling the verses: "Ida Red, big and plump / Eighty-four inches around the rump." At one point, Woody jumps to his highest range and shouts, "Don't give a damn if I do die / Dance till the break of day!"

The wartime shortage of shellac made it unlikely any of this would be released anytime soon, but at least it was being recorded: a way of preserving—or maybe fighting—history. Less than two weeks later, Guthrie was back at sea. This time he was part of a huge invasion designed to end the European war. At one point, under submarine attack, he, Houston and a friend went below deck to sing for the skittish soldiers. Though the NMU was integrated, the army still wasn't, and the radical trio had to insist that the black troops got to harmonize with the white.

Their ship eventually delivered some three thousand infantry to Omaha Beach. On the way back out, it hit a mine: "She is twisted and hurt and she shakes like she is nervous. . . ." The crew managed to make it to shore, where there's a brief leave in London (Guthrie found time to record for the BBC), and then it was home. When he tried to re-up, he found his seaman's papers had been voided. A fellow marine would tell the FBI that Guthrie was "very pro-Russian and advocated racial intermarriage;" the FBI categorized him as a subversive. "I thank my God in heaven," he eventually wrote, "that I'm on these black lists. If my name wasn't on these lists, . . . I don't guess I could enjoy a decent night's sleep." Alan Lomax had already been cited; Seeger and others would soon be. Beneath the nation's newfound prosperity, beneath the wartime United Front, ran the constant threat of backlash.

For nine months, Guthrie was home with Mazia and their infant daughter. He started work on a second novel, joined the Communist-organized "Roosevelt Bandwagon" for the 1944 election, wrote songs, and performed when he could. A New York radio station gave him a fifteen-minute program, and he worked up a statement of belief for the first show. Like "This Land Is Your Land," it was in reaction to a pop hit of the day.

"Born to Lose" had a jazzy big-band melody led by a bouncy steel guitar, what people were calling Western swing. Written and performed by Ted Daffan and his Texans, it begins, "I've lived my life in vain," then proceeds through a series of disappointments capped by "Now I'm losing you." But it doesn't sound particularly sad. There's a jaunty accordion break, and when Daffan concludes "There's no use to dream of happiness," it's to the same good-timey hillbilly beat. If this is despair, it's despair you can dance to, and crowds across the country did just that. "Born to Lose" sold a million copies in 1943. In booming, wartime California and up at the Grand Coulee, once-displaced and unemployed Okies spent Saturday nights whirling their partners around big halls, two-stepping to this celebration of loss.

Guthrie had heard it over the loudspeaker system on his merchant marine vessel. The song's smugness, its acceptance of the status quo, got to him. "I couldn't rest easy till I run out and grabbed my pencil." He scribbled down his statement of belief:

> I hate a song that makes you think you're not any good. I hate a song that makes you think you are just born to lose. Bound to lose. No good to nobody. No good for nothing. Because you are either too old or too young or too fat or too slim or too ugly or too this or too that . . . Songs that run you down or songs that poke fun at you on account of your bad luck or hard traveling.
>
> I am out to fight those kinds of songs to my very last breath of air and my last drop of blood.

He starts with what he hates so he can jump to what he's fighting for:

> I am out to sing songs that will prove to you that this is your world and that if it has hit you pretty hard and knocked you down or rolled over you, no matter what color, what size

you are, how you are built, I am out to sing the songs that make you take pride in yourself and in your work.

It's a declaration—maybe a definition—of one man's grown-up anger. "All the songs that I sing are made up for the most part by all sorts of folks just about like you," he adds. That's the capper: his songs are communal; "we" make them together.

Not long afterward, Asch released a compilation album that included a few cuts from Guthrie's marathon session. Guthrie declared in the liner notes, "Every band on the radio sounds exactly alike. . . . Do the big bands and the orgasm gals sing a word about our real fighting history? Not a croak." He took his anger and decided to do something more about that.

He told Asch he wanted to cut a series of records with the working title American Documentary. As Asch recalled it, Guthrie planned to have them focus on "the struggle of working people in bringing to light their fight for a place in the America that they envisioned." The idea was for Guthrie to write about current events: A one-man Headline Singer composing "a kind of musical newspaper." It wasn't far from a theater project Lomax's roommate, Nicholas Ray, had worked on before the war. Along with director Elia Kazan, Ray had created *The Living Newspaper*: the day's headlines turned into what they called "dramatic documentary."

Guthrie didn't have much time. Though the war was winding down, the draft was still on, and being single, his seaman's papers voided, Guthrie was eligible. He got his notice early in 1945, passed his physical in April—three days before the death of President Roosevelt—and was inducted May 7, the day the Nazis surrendered. On May 24, just before he was sent off to basic training in Texas, he went into Asch's studio and cut five songs as a kind of dry run for the American Documentary series.

The result, *Documentary #1 STRUGGLE*, is less musical newspaper than history book. Instead of reporting on contemporary events, Guthrie goes back in time, composing songs "based word for word," he wrote, "in the truth of bloody trade union history." But he tells the stories *as if* they were current events, putting himself into the situations, singing from the point of view of an eyewitness.

The first tune he cut, "Mean Talking Blues," didn't make the final album, but it helps show what he wanted *STRUGGLE* to document: the fight workers faced trying to create One Big Union. "Mean Talking Blues" frames it as a battle between good and evil—with Guthrie narrating as Lucifer, the fallen angel, a cheater and a scab. "If I ever done a good deed, I'm sorry of it," he proclaims. "God likes unions, and I hate God."

The next two cuts come back down to earth, pulling their facts from Mother Bloor's autobiography, published five years earlier. There's the tune he's calling "Miner's Christmas" and its companion piece, "Ludlow Massacre." The latter, set in 1914, is sung in the voice of a Colorado striker "worried bad about my children." When the National Guard opens fire on the strikers' camp, thirteen kids are killed. In retaliation, the union manages to get hold of some weapons "and the red-neck miners mowed down them troopers." The song ends with the kids' burial and then the line Dylan would borrow: "I hung my head and cried." Like "East Texas Red," "Ludlow Massacre" is about violence, revenge, loss.

The next tune, "Buffalo Skinners," deepens that mood. It's a minor-key variation on a turn-of-the-century tune John and Alan Lomax had collected. A bunch of out-of-work cowboys sign up to hunt buffalo, but at the end of the season, their boss refuses to pay. The cowboys get together and kill him. In the Lomax version, there's a final, somewhat soothing stanza where the buffalo skinners head back home. Guthrie's ballad simply ends: "So we left that drover's bones to bleach / On the plains of the buffalo."

The final song Guthrie cuts that day is an original ballad long enough to take up two sides of a 78. "Harriet Tubman" may be the apex of his reeducation on race. Like "Tom Joad," it's structured in two parts: the first taking us from when five-year-old Tubman is sold into slavery up to her escape, the second covering her fight to free others. Guthrie sings all the songs on *STRUGGLE* in the first person, but this is the nerviest, his Okie accent taking on the role of the black female freedom-fighter. Again the song includes a call for armed resistance, as Tubman argues that if President Lincoln would "give the black man [in the Union Army] guns and . . . powder . . ." it would "cripple . . . this snake of slavery." Then Guthrie-as-Tubman calls out, "We've got to fight to kill him dead."

The way Guthrie envisioned *STRUGGLE*, it was going to describe the battle against all kinds of oppression, from slavery through the exploitation of cowboys in the 1870s to attacks on miners in the early twentieth century. He saw it as one connected story: the real fighting history that never made it onto the radio.

Before being sent to basic training, Guthrie fiddled with song selection. Planning on eight songs in all—a four-record album with two sides per 78—he pointed out to Asch that with "Harriet Tubman" filling both sides of one record and the Bloor songs another, they could pair his earlier "East Texas Red" with either "Buffalo Skinners" or his take on the outlaw-as-hero, "Pretty Boy Floyd." For the fourth record in the album, he was working on another long ballad to be called "Worker's Life."

The title hints that the melody might have been a variation on the Southern textile workers song, "Weaver's Life." But it also echoes a book called *Pages from a Worker's Life* by William Z. Foster, published five years earlier. Like Mother Bloor's book, Foster's autobiography tells a radical history of the American labor movement. Foster was a Wobbly and eventually joined the Communist Party. By the time Guthrie was recording *STRUGGLE*, he was a prominent advocate for a more hard-line, confrontational brand of communism. With the Soviet Union declaring its intention to install a Communist government in Poland, the wartime Grand Alliance was already starting to come apart. Instead of cooperation, Stalin and the Kremlin were returning to the idea that capitalism and communism had nothing in common. Party theorists had begun to attack the Popular Front as a "notorious revision of Marxism." In mid-June 1945, when

America's Communist Party shifted course to take this new, more militant line, the man it elected to lead them was William Z. Foster.

Guthrie shifted with the party. In a July letter to Asch, he recalled the prewar CPUSA as "the one organization I could stand up and feel proud of. . . . I used to feel that I could tell you just exactly why you should go down and join your Communist Party." That may have been what he wanted "Worker's Life" to convey: a culmination of the other cuts' fierceness. Instead, he left for basic training and never seems to have finished the song.

In August, Japan surrendered, but Guthrie wouldn't be released from active duty until the end of December—and then only because he finally married Mazia and qualified for a discharge. In the meantime, *STRUGGLE* was released.

It wasn't the album Guthrie had outlined. For one thing, Asch decided to put out only three 78s instead of four. It still had both Bloor songs and "Buffalo Skinners," but "Pretty Boy Floyd" replaced "East Texas Red." And "Harriet Tubman" was gone. Instead, there was "Union Burying Ground," a graveyard blues about labor martyrs, and "Lost John," a traditional, up-tempo song with Sonny Terry providing the whoops of an escapee from a chain gang. Overall, the result was more cheerful than Guthrie's original concept, less unified, and slightly more commercial. Still, it added up to an unflinching look at labor history, and Guthrie called it his "pet album . . . six songs and ballads . . . I've always been proudest of. They sound to me like I hope I sound to other folks."

If this is the sound he's been aiming for, it's more open than his earlier records, more blues influenced, with less Carter Family restraint. And it includes a deep vein of anger.

To Moe Asch, it had to do with postwar despair. He described Guthrie and his friends as "so disillusioned. They thought they were fighting for a better world. But when they saw what the peace treaty did, when they saw the League of Nations fighting among themselves, when they saw the capitalistic movement taking over, Woody lost hope and disintegrated."

Maybe. Guthrie admitted to wondering, around this time, "if it wouldn't be better to just haul off and quit hoping." But he concluded "about all a human being is, anyway, is just a hoping machine." After his discharge, the thirty-three-year-old promptly joined another collaborative Seeger was organizing, People's Songs. "It was a bunch of people," Guthrie wrote, "working together in a field where they had all worked more or less alone, . . ." an attempt "to organize all of us that write songs for the labor movement." Guthrie called the collective "the best sounding Democracy I've heard so far" and swore he could see "our new world just around the next bend." He doesn't sound like a hopeless man.

As America's postwar boom kicked into gear, Guthrie had his greatest commercial success. In the summer of 1945, Jack Guthrie's version of "Oklahoma Hills" became the number-one song in a category Billboard was now calling Most Played Juke Box Folk Records; Gene Autry was on the same chart. And Woody would soon begin receiving royalties from the Maddox Brothers and Rose's cover of "The Philadelphia Lawyer." In early 1946, he'd go on to record some of his finest work: children's songs he'd written for his daughter Cathy, performed in an open, emotional style he described as "bubbly." Later he'd compose the beautiful "Plane Wreck at Los Gatos (Deportee)," about martyred immigrant workers, and the haunting "I've Got to Know," with its Cold War landscape: "Hungry lips ask me wherever I go / . . . What makes your boats haul death to my people? / . . . Why can't my two hands get a good-pay job?"

Guthrie never seems to have lost hope, but *STRUGGLE* shows that he began to see the fight differently. The war hadn't given birth to One Big Union; the battle against fascism continued. To Guthrie and his friends, the postwar golden age of American capitalism signaled the return of the imitation world. The United Front began to look like a fluke: a brief interruption between the Palmer Raids that followed World War I and the blacklisting that followed World War II. By 1946, the Grand Alliance had dissolved. Stalin was characterizing the war as "the inevitable result of . . . monopoly capitalism," and Churchill was talking about Communism's "iron curtain," behind which "[p]olice governments are prevailing in nearly every case, and . . . there is no democracy."

The end of the war also ended US labor's no-strike pledge. Two million workers walked out in early 1946; it would be five million by the end of the year: some of the most intense labor strife in the nation's history. But the CIO's Operation Dixie, a push to unionize the South, failed. And the 1946 elections brought a conservative Republican sweep. The new Congress would pass the Taft-Hartley Act, limiting strikes, opening the way for right-to-work states, requiring union officials to sign anti-communist affidavits. Unions began to purge reds and suspected reds. Guthrie soon decided that President Harry Truman "don't like my trade unions, don't like organized labor, don't like the Communist Party, don't like the human race."

Guthrie's peak years of creativity coincided with the Popular Front: the decade that started in California in the late thirties and ended in postwar New York City. Early in 1947, four-year-old Cathy Guthrie was burned in a freak electrical fire. She died the next day. Guthrie described "an empty spot . . . a spot lots emptier than I ever felt it before, a spot so sinking and so empty that I reach round a thousand times a day . . . to fill up this hungry and thirsty empty place." At the same time, his Huntington's chorea symptoms got worse. "Just dizzy," is how he described it. "Woozy. Blubberdy. And scrubberdy and rustlety, tastley . . . the soberest drunk I ever got on."

He'd make another concept album for Asch, this one about the executed radicals Sacco and Vanzetti, but it ended up draggy and repetitive. More and more, he wasn't physically able to produce the sound he wanted.

Not many people heard his pet album, *STRUGGLE*. His reputation would be built on *Dust Bowl Ballads* and songs like "This Land Is Your Land" and "So Long, It's Been Good to Know You." But *STRUGGLE* was his last, best reflection on the fight for a level world. It argues that even if he and his friends had failed, if his vision of Commonism only appealed, finally, to a fraction of American citizens, that didn't mean the fight was wrong. Or over. On the album he was proudest of, you hear the sound of an adult calculating the cost of change, trying to tell one man's truth about what it's like to "go down shooting."

At the beginning of the end of the Popular Front, on New Year's Eve 1945, Seeger, Hays, Lomax, Earl Robinson, and others gathered in a New York City basement to launch People's Songs. They were trying to reinvent the movement, to survive the emerging Cold War, to preserve their hopes and ideals. The meeting soon turned into a hootenanny where everyone sang. When it was Guthrie's turn, he could've launched into the punchy "Union Maid" or "Roll On, Columbia," songs of confidence and optimism. Instead he sang a cautionary tune, that slow ballad about the miners' Christmas that he was now calling "1913 Massacre."

TAKE A TRIP
WITH ME IN 1913

The strike had been broken. The mines were back running with a shorter, eight-hour day, a new grievance procedure had been put in place, and C&H was rehiring workers—except union supporters. Left out in the cold were mostly immigrant families: Croatians, Italians, Finns. It was for their children that WFM's women's auxiliary organized a Christmas party.

They held it in Italian Hall. Big Annie Clemenc had raised a little under sixty dollars to buy the kids "mittens, stocking, toys and candies." The parents and children gathered on the afternoon of Christmas Eve, milling about in the crowded room, excited about getting their presents. Holiday songs were sung, and they'd gotten to the part of the program where a thirteen-year-old Finnish girl was going to play the piano. Then, in Mother Bloor's version of events, a man pushed open the door and yelled, "Fire!"

Annie Clemenc tries to keep everyone calm; she tells the Finnish girl to keep playing. There's piano music and, beyond the walls, down the stairs, the distant sound of people running, pushing, yelling.

The first body is carried in five minutes later. Then another. And another.

As the bodies, packed on top of one another, are extracted from the stairwell, Catholic priests arrive to perform last rites. The church has been antistrike, and Annie Clemenc yells at the crowd, "Don't let those scab priests touch these children!" She's arrested.

By that night, in a town Mother Bloor calls "paralyzed with grief," a funeral fund has been started and some $1,500 raised. But most of the donors are members of the anti-union Citizen's Alliance, and the strikers won't accept the help. Bloor recalls a grieving Finnish mother saying, "I love my children like my soul, but I would put them in the ground naked before I'd touch a penny of your blood money!"

A delegation then takes the donations to the hotel room of Charles Moyer, president of the Western Federation of Miners. He also refuses it. "We have clothed our naked, we have fed our hungry, and we will bury our dead."

Moments after he's slammed the door, a mob pushes its way back in, beats him up, and, according to Bloor, shoots him in the back before dragging him to the railroad station. There, James MacNaughton helps toss the bleeding Moyer on a train for Chicago, telling him to go away and stay away.

The funerals are the next Sunday, three days after Christmas. Bloor describes a trainload of iron miners arriving to provide security for the mourners. Big Annie leads the procession, "carrying a red flag." They march through town, then out into the snow-covered country. "Never as long as I live," Bloor writes, "can I forget that procession winding through the hills and woods with the seventy-three little white coffins—coffins of children killed by capitalist brutality and greed."

Bloor goes on to talk about the investigative committee set up by President Wilson. And the speaking tour she went on with Big Annie in a not very successful attempt to raise money for the union. In the end, Bloor says, the Calumet strikers "were finally starved out. . . . Many of the miners' demands, including the eight-hour day, had been granted, but they did not get union recognition."

All told, her description of what happened in Calumet takes up a dozen pages in her three-hundred-page autobiography. It doesn't pretend to be objective. Mother Bloor's dedicated her life to a workers revolution, and she makes the 1913 massacre part of it. Like Joe Hill, the children in Calumet died for a cause: for One Big Union. They were martyrs.

Newspaper articles, local investigations, Congressional reports have other versions of what happened and why.

Italian Hall was a two-story brick structure built just five years before the tragedy. It was located in the town of Red Jacket, population 4,200. (It wasn't officially called Calumet till 1929.) The hall was both a business venture and a gathering place. A sign across the top, in gilt capitals, read, SOCIETÁ MUTUA BENEFICENZA ITALIANA. The street floor was divided in two: on one side was an A&P—its awning proclaimed THE GREAT ATLANTIC & PACIFIC TEA CO.; the other side was a saloon named for the Italian family that ran it: VAIRO.

On the second story, the meeting hall was seventy-eight by thirty-eight feet with eighteen-foot ceilings. It was reached by a stairway six feet wide. You climbed twenty-three steps to a ticket office, took a right on the landing, and passed through swinging doors into the hall. For the Christmas party, rows of folding wooden chairs had been set up facing the platform at one end: the piano was up there, along with two Christmas trees. Starting at two in the afternoon, the room filled with some 500 children and 175 adults, almost all of them "foreigners."

For the first hour, someone watched the door to make sure only pro-union families entered. But soon the place was packed, and once the festivities began, no one seemed to have paid much attention to who came and went. Some of the children had rehearsed a Mother Goose play, but it was canceled; the room was too noisy, the kids too restless.

A woman announced—in English and then again in Finnish—that they'd now begin handing out presents. The young ones formed an eager line next to the stage, hurried up to get their gifts, then hurried down to show what they'd got. "Well, Peter," one parent told another, "this day ain't so bad for the children. The children will remember today for a hundred years."

According to a number of witnesses, around four thirty, at the height of the party, a stout man in a long coat and a fur cap burst into the hall and cried, "Fire, fire!" More than a half dozen people testified that he was wearing the distinctive white lapel pin of the Citizens Alliance. Others heard the cry but couldn't tell who made it. And a few claimed that no one shouted "Fire," that the crowd simply panicked.

In the din of the hall, partygoers began to shove toward the one known exit: the six-foot-wide stairs. Mary Lantto and her baby were knocked off the stage: "I went on my knees near that heater. Got up from there as fast as I could and tried to hold my baby with one hand and the heater with the other so the crowd would not bring me down with them." Farther from the stage, all Andrew Saari could see was "the people were going out so fast . . ." He decided, "there must be some kind of trouble . . ."

It was too many for the stairwell to handle. As the pressure from above (and below?) increased, people were jammed against the walls, barely able to breathe. Some fell. That, in turn, tripped others. In the narrow space, bodies were forced on top of bodies.

Parents tried to hold their children above the crush. John Aho rushed over to try to help, but "it was all filled up. . . . They were all laying against each other's back, and just as soon as you could take them away some would fall down. . . . Most of those that I carried were children."

It became, as one report put it, "one solid mass from which no one could emerge."

Over seventy people died in less than three minutes.

Up in the hall, many were unaware. Photographs taken afterward show folding chairs still neatly lined up. Outside, an alarm sounded, and friends and relatives started running to the site. The fire department arrived. Its log entry would note: "Disaster. No Fire . . . Fire call and a stampead [sic] following down stairways."

Outside, deputies kept relatives from entering. Meanwhile, rescuers climbed in the second-floor windows and worked their way down the stairs. There, they found bodies so twisted together, they were hard to untangle and remove. "It was full up," one witness testified, "to the top of the door."

Many had suffocated. Some had internal injuries. Most showed no wounds or marks of any kind. The official count was seventy-four dead. Sixty of those were between the ages of two and sixteen. Almost fifty of those were from Finnish families, but most were young enough to have been born in America.

Many of the dead were carried down the block to Village Hall. There's a photograph of children, arms crossed over chests, their bodies covered in white sheets, dirty feet sticking out below and, above, their quiet faces: mouths partly open, eyes carefully closed.

It was the worst tragedy in Keweenaw history, more than double the number that had ever died in a mining accident.

Charges and countercharges began immediately. Christmas morning, Charles Moyer issued a statement: "My information is to the effect that no striker or anyone in sympathy with the strike brought about this catastrophe. There are many who testify that a man from the outside came up the stairs and yelled 'Fire!'"

A pro-company newspaper headlined Moyer's statement: USES CHILDREN'S DEATHS TO BENEFIT HIS STRIKE. It added that Moyer was also saying, unofficially, that the man responsible wore a Citizens Alliance pin. That was untrue, the paper declared, because "it is generally known" that only identified members of the WFM could enter the hall. The union, it concluded, was trying "to capitalize on the terrible tragedy of Christmas eve."

Another local paper traced the suggestion that the Citizens Alliance had been responsible to Annie Clemenc, "the woman who became notorious through her connection with violence during the strike."

In the version that appeared in the *New York Times*, "an intoxicated man staggered to the door of the little hall and shouted 'Fire!'" It didn't mention whether he was pro- or anti-union.

The local Finnish paper reported that the man who cried fire had been wearing a Citizens Alliance pin. This pro-strike paper added that the deputies downstairs held the exit door closed and laughed when people tried to escape. "From all we have seen," it concluded, "we learn that it was a put up job by the Citizens Alliance." The local sheriff promptly closed the Finnish paper, charging it with "publishing material to incite a riot."

Reports differ on how much the Citizens Alliance raised for the funeral fund, but some put it as high as $25,000. Led by the sheriff, a delegation of mine managers and leading citizens offered the money to Moyer in his hotel room on the evening of December 26. When he refused it, that group left and another returned—apparently without the sheriff—and started to rough him up.

According to Moyer, someone hit him in the head with a revolver, "the revolver exploded and the bullet entered my shoulder and my back." Then he was dragged out of the hotel in Hancock, down the hill, and across a five-hundred-foot-long bridge to the railroad station in Houghton. There, Moyer testified, James Mac-Naughton grabbed him by the throat: "If you ever come back to this district again we will hang you." MacNaughton later denied saying that or even being at the scene, or for that matter, that he was anywhere in the vicinity, and Moyer later retracted that part of his testimony.

The next day, Saturday, four of the victims were buried. On Sunday, December 28, there were church services for most of the others. Photographs show the small coffins laid out in crescents along the fronts of the altars.

Five thousand people made their way from downtown out to the Lakeview Cemetery: a procession two miles long. Mourners in black coats marched on new white snow. Many of the coffins were small enough for one person to shoulder.

As the funeral parade moved slowly past blocks of company housing, some twenty thousand watched in silence. Annie Clemenc led the procession, but the photographs show her not with Mother Bloor's red socialist flag, but the huge American flag that had been cut by bayonets—and was now edged in black crepe. Singers chanted "Rock of Ages" and "Nearer, My God, to Thee."

At the cemetery, out-of-work miners had dug long trenches in the frozen ground. More than sixty coffins were laid there in unmarked, common graves.

Brief eulogies were delivered in English, Finnish, Austrian, and Croatian. The WFM had invited Clarence Darrow to speak, but he was worried that—like Moyer—he might be beaten or kidnapped. An attorney who did speak declared, "It is not charity we want, it is justice."

To Mother Bloor, the deaths were a deliberate act, a mass murder. Opponents of the strike—supporters of Calumet & Hecla, deputies, vigilante thugs—had been threatening to shut down the party. That's who shouted "Fire!" and that's who held the exit doors shut from the outside.

But the coroner's inquiry didn't rule on that. It limited itself to the cause of death—suffocation—adding only "the stampede was caused by some person or persons within the hall. . . ." The grand jury that was convened brought no indictments. And a congressional investigation proved inconclusive. Keweenaw was left with two contradictory versions: their children died in a horrible accident; their children were murdered.

The tragedy revitalized the strike. Moyer returned to Keweenaw the first week in January, and two thousand gathered to hear him. Calumet's workers, he declared, deserved the support of a national walkout. "The cause of the striking miners is just and they will win." The deaths at Italian Hall drew widespread attention and enough donations to refill the union's treasury.

But when Moyer turned to the AF of L for steady funding, America's largest labor organization refused. Its investigators reported "too many Socialists have been dabbling in strike difficulties." Trying to distance itself from radical politics, the AF of L refused to provide any more money. In a speech to United Mine Workers in late January, Moyer lashed out:

I am going to say to you and I am going to repeat it more forc-
ibly in the future, if God gives me breath to speak, that if this
fight of the copper miners is lost in the state of Michigan, the
loss of that strike will be charged directly by me to the inac-
tivity of the Executive Council of the American Federation of
Labor.

In other words, if it had really been One Big Union, the miners
could still have won.

By now, the number of paying union members in Keweenaw had
dropped below 2,500. Local backlash against the WFM extended
even to some Finns, who organized an Anti-Socialist League, declaring Moyer and his organizers "human jackals and hyenas." The
mining companies, meanwhile, continued to refuse to negotiate.

In March 1914, three months after Italian Hall, the WFM
blinked. The union would end the action, Moyer announced, "if
the men themselves want to do it." By the beginning of April, the
WFM had spent some $800,000 on the strike, half of it raised by
mandatory assessments on distant locals. All but bankrupt, it cut
strike benefits to $4 a week for a family of four. "While we still be-
lieve your *cause* is just," Moyer emphasized, "we cannot be expected
to do the impossible."

On Easter Sunday 1914, Keweenaw's remaining WFM members
took a vote. More than two-thirds opted to end the action. Nine
months after it began, the strike was over.

So, in many ways, was the Western Federation of Miners. The
action in Michigan left the national organization and many of its
locals deep in debt. The WFM had failed, again, to establish itself
in the Copper Empire and was alienated, again, from the AF of L.
Two years later, it dissolved. It would reorganize as the International
Union of Mine, Mill and Smelter Workers, but it was never again as
active or as radical.

Over the course of the nine-month walkout, some 2,500 workers abandoned Keweenaw for good. Many couldn't survive on the union's strike benefits; others feared for their families' safety; others found better jobs. Western mines continued to pay higher wages. And just days after the Italian Hall tragedy, Henry Ford announced his car company in Detroit was offering an unprecedented five dollars a day: almost double what most Michigan miners were getting. In the twenty years between 1910 and 1930, Houghton County's population would drop by 20 percent.

Those who stayed watched an industry in decline decline further. Technology—including the one-man drill—upped production but meant fewer jobs. A couple of months after the strike ended, when the First World War broke out, the disruption of international trade led to lower copper prices. In response, C&H cut both wages and hours. Prices climbed back up, but only for the duration of the war. By 1920, there were a third fewer copper mines in Michigan—and a total of only eight thousand men working them. The next year, prices crashed, and they stayed low through the decade, driven down by increased competition from not just Western mines but Canadian, African, South American. By the midtwenties, Michigan was producing just 10 percent of America's copper—and the Great Depression would halve that percentage again.

In 1933, C&H turned off its pumps, and water started to rise in the shafts below Calumet. The company scavenged the last ore remaining in the columns of rock left to stabilize the tunnels. In 1939, C&H sealed off the last entrance into the vein that Edwin Hulbert (and some pigs?) had discovered. The lode had produced a total of more than three billion pounds of copper. That same year, the National Labor Relations Board ordered Keweenaw's copper mines to let their workers vote on bringing in a union. One company after another was organized until, in the winter of 1942, the workers finally got a union at the region's last corporate holdout, C&H.

Guthrie's *STRUGGLE* was issued three years later, in 1945. Its cover was a lithograph of mourners, some holding rifles, gathered

around an open grave. The record included the original version of
"1913 Massacre."

The song opens with a repeated guitar phrase picked out on the
high strings. It sounds like a slightly up-tempo lullaby. Then Guthrie's voice enters, pitched in the high middle of his range, warm,
inviting: "Take a trip with me in 1913."

Following the narrative of Mother Bloor's book, Guthrie guides
us up the stairs of Italian Hall and into the Christmas party. He acts
as our host, telling the story in an everyman's voice, putting himself
in the scene and pulling us in, too. He shows us the Christmas tree,
the little girl playing piano, the dancing and singing. He introduces
us to the partygoers: "I'll let you shake hands with the people you
see." He tells us what Bloor told him: that the miners are "risking
their lives," earning less than a dollar a day. But he never mentions
the strike. All he says is that the party is a chance for the miners'
families to have some "fun." And us, too: "Before you know it,
you're friends with us all / And you're dancing around and around
in the hall."

It's as friends, then, that we get the first hint that something's
wrong. The tune doesn't change: the guitar repeats the same,
lullaby-like pattern. But it begins to sound a little mechanical; it
starts to have an edge. Our host tells us the "copper boss thug men
are milling outside." He doesn't mention why, only that the dancing, the fun, is threatened.

It's here, halfway through the song, that he switches from the
present tense: suddenly the story becomes history.

> *The copper boss thugs stuck their heads in the door.*
> *One of them yelled and screamed, "There's a fire!"*

Guthrie borrows Mother Bloor's description of Annie Clemenc
trying to calm the crowd, reassuring them that there's no fire; it's
just "the thugs and the scabs." But when a man grabbed his daughter
and ran out, "a hundred or more followed."

Downstairs, Guthrie reports,

The gun thugs they laughed at their murderous joke
While the children were smothered on the stairs by the door.

For the couplet to rhyme, it should end "smothered on the stairs by the smoke." But there is none. The killer isn't fire; it's fear. That's the murderous joke.

Guthrie's version of the events is Mother Bloor's. Her "I can hardly tell about it or think about it" becomes "Such a terrible sight, I never did see." As he sings the phrase, his voice doesn't appear to change, but you notice a sadness, a starkness, and wonder if it's been there all along. Then in an almost detached, reportorial style—*STRUGGLE* was, after all, meant to be a musical newspaper, a documentary—he lists the final death toll: Bloor's count of seventy-three.

In the last stanza, after the bodies of the children have been carried back upstairs, the Finnish girl continues to play piano. Guthrie turns the music into a memorial. "The piano played a slow funeral tune." And the melody of "1913 Massacre" begins to sound like it might be that tune: less a lullaby now than a dirge.

Guthrie pulls back from the scene to show the town lit up by a Christmas moon. And then adds the final couplet:

The parents they cried, and the miners, they moaned
See what your greed for money has done.

"1913 Massacre" lasts about three and a half minutes. Guthrie tells the story in his neutral voice and is gone, back into silence. It's deliberately sparse: no Almanac Singers, no Sonny Terry harmonica, none of the collaborative sound he's been working on. It's just his voice and guitar. And he keeps the story sparse, too: no profile of Annie Clemenc or James MacNaughton, no funeral march through the snow, no red socialist flag, no debate about who's to blame or why.

When the song came out, the tragedy was more than thirty years in the past. But Keweenaw was still divided about what happened, still saw different truths. The majority of those who'd remained in copper country—company management, local businesspeople, a lot of the "native-born" population, those workers who'd been rehired by the mines, most of the local media—maintained that the incident had been an accident. Nobody murdered anybody. To call the deaths at Italian Hall a massacre was to buy into a radical, left-wing version of history.

As time passed, the key issue became how the exit doors opened. Never mind if someone had shouted "Fire!" or who that someone might have been. Union supporters—socialists, foreigners—claimed the doors at the foot of the stairs opened out and had been held closed by thugs. But company supporters maintained that couldn't be true because the doors opened inward. It was more likely that the first few people rushing down the stairs had fallen, blocking the doors and jamming the exit. Those who followed fought to get out, but there was no way. It hadn't been the Citizens' Alliance or the deputies or some vigilante mob that had killed the kids. The dead and dying had closed off their own passage to freedom.

By the time Guthrie wrote his song, this had become the official version. It was printed in local and national newspapers, repeated by historians, taught in school (to the degree the incident at Italian Hall was taught at all). The man wearing a Citizens Alliance pin and shouting "Fire!" was dismissed as legend. The idea of the exit doors being held closed by "conspiratorial deputies" was just that: a conspiracy theory. Forty years after "1913 Massacre" came out, in 1987, the state of Michigan erected a plaque at Italian Hall; it declared: "Although there was no fire, seventy-three persons died while attempting to escape down a stairwell with doors that opened inward."

The bronze historical marker confirmed that though an awful thing had happened, no one was at fault. And because that was the truth, the region could mourn together, could heal without blame or anger.

In that context, Guthrie's song was propaganda: heartfelt and moving, maybe, but propaganda. Sixty years after the strike, a local was still calling it a "lousy miserable song . . . so full of lies it makes me mad. . . ."

Guthrie had followed Bloor's narrative and accepted her conclusion: that what happened at Italian Hall was deliberate, was part of a larger worldwide battle. In her autobiography, the chapter that precedes "Massacre of the Innocents" is about her trip to Europe in 1912, where she can see how "capitalism inevitably leads to war." And the chapter that follows her description of Calumet is about America's "post-war repression." In her version of history, then, the rebellion in Keweenaw was tied into the World War I years, when the rebellion was hot and the annual number of strikes in America doubling. That led to the government's crackdown—"witch-hunting campaigns" as Bloor called them—that threw hundreds of Wobblies into prison. Eugene Debs was arrested; Big Bill Haywood fled to Russia.

Then in November 1917, the Bolshevik Revolution, as Bloor put it, "flashed its message of hope to the world. . . ." Suddenly, "The land and all its resources, the factories, the mines, the railroads, the banks, belonged to the people." The long-dreamed-of revolution had arrived. In one part of the world, anyway, the workers owned the machines, and the movement would spread, inevitably, from country to country.

That included the United States. In the summer of 1919, Ella Reeve Bloor—the woman who'd ridden a ferry with Walt Whitman and marched with suffragettes—climaxed her radical history by cofounding America's first Communist Party. In her eyes, this is what the 1913 copper strike had been leading to; this was the greater good its child martyrs had died for.

Most of the songs Guthrie wrote for *STRUGGLE* supported that. They're tales of resistance, of militancy in the face of defeat: Joe Hill's moral, "Don't Mourn. Organize." Or as Guthrie explained it to Moe Asch: "I believe that the real folk history of this country finds its center and its hub in the fight of union members against the hired gun thugs of the big owners." Wasn't that why Alan Lomax, the Seegers, and others had invented this thing called folk music, to isolate and focus on this hidden vein of American history? Guthrie's STRUGGLE had been conceived to bring that story out in the open and to continue the fight.

Even in the companion piece to "1913 Massacre," the sorrowful "Ludlow Massacre," though the grieving father hangs his head and cries, he can see the goal ahead: "God Bless," he calls out, "the mine workers' union!" Not God bless America, but God bless the WFM, the workers' cause, One Big Union. That's the victory Guthrie sees in the distance. "I am out to sing songs that prove to you that this is your world. . . ."

But "1913 Massacre" doesn't do that. It's a different kind of song. While it follows Bloor down to the smallest detail, it doesn't mention socialism. Or even the strike. Guthrie blames the copper bosses' thugs, but in his version, it's a massacre without a clear motive or a breath of hope. "I hate a song that makes you think you were just born to lose." Well, isn't this that song?

Over Guthrie's repeating guitar phrase, the story feels inevitable. Where people gather to have fun, where they're trying to help each other through hard times, evil always waits outside. And Guthrie sings it like that—with a restrained, personal moan as if it was one of his mother's old ballads. If this is the sound he hopes to be remembered by, it's the sound of unavoidable loss.

In his version of his family's history, the Guthries' string of bad luck began when the Okemah house caught fire. Then his older sister died of burns. And they finally broke apart after another fire sent his father to a hospital and his mother to a mental asylum. As he was writing "1913 Massacre," he had no way of knowing that his daughter, Cathy, would also die from burns, but he'd already gotten "the murderous joke." It's a song not about fire but about fear—the fear of fire—and how fear can lead to the death of innocents.

"1913 Massacre" has a no-exit feel. There's no revolution coming, and God doesn't bless anything. If its dead are martyrs, they're martyrs to a defeated cause. Part of that may be the history Guthrie knows from Bloor. By the time Italian Hall happens, the strike is all but over; management has won. The tragedy only ends up prolonging a doomed cause. There was that moment when the workers were chanting, "We are the bosses," but by the Christmas party, that was long gone. And the WFM never thought of the strike in those terms. It wasn't trying to change the basic system; it had conceded that the earth—what was dug from the earth—was already bought and owned. It just wanted the workers to get more of a share, to be partners in the business.

Guthrie wrote "1913 Massacre" at the end of the Second World War. His hope—that it had been a war against fascism and would continue at home—was fading. The House of Representatives had reauthorized a special committee on un-American activities. Blacklisting of communists would follow, just as attacks against Wobblies and socialists followed World War I. And unions were already starting to make the concessions that would lead to the golden age of capitalism. Seen in that light, the 1913 strike becomes a kind of precursor. The compromised demands of the miners—how they're outmanned and outmaneuvered by the company—anticipate what will become of the modern labor movement.

Guthrie's song divides the world into good and evil. He walks us up the stairs into Italian Hall so we can meet the good. And then he shows us how evil wins, what it feels like when fear takes over and hope is gone. Instead of revolutionary propaganda, "1913 Massacre" ends up something darker, more complicated: a version of "Pastures of Plenty" that asks what happens when you work in this fight, and you fight till you lose.

That Dylan in 1960 even knew of "1913 Massacre" is a testament to how comprehensive a Guthrie fan he was. STRUGGLE had sold poorly and quickly gone out of print. Maybe, as he later claimed, Dylan heard it when a redheaded transcendentalist played him a 78 in Dinkytown, or maybe he heard Jack Elliott's version. But he was soon playing "1913 Massacre" in Minneapolis coffeehouses and even appropriated the melody to serenade an early girlfriend: "Hey, hey Bonny, I wrote you a song."

Then he reaches New York and meets the ailing Guthrie. When he needs to talk about his shattered idol, he comes back to the tune and finds something else. The melody Dylan appropriates has already been used to convey the sound of loss. If his "Song to Woody" is a memorial to an older generation's "hard travelin'," so was Guthrie's "1913 Massacre." The failure of the 1913 strike was like the failure of Oklahoma's socialists, the failure of California's farmworkers strike, the failure of the Almanac Singers and the Popular Front. That long struggle is Guthrie's subject. It drives this grown-up, complicated sound he's after. "I am just now," he noted around the time he was making *STRUGGLE*, "learning really the kind of songs I want to write, how to write them."

Though "1913 Massacre" leaves out Mother Bloor's flashing message of hope, it still follows her version of the truth. And, so, contradicts the agreed-upon history. Guthrie's song is the story of how the American system kills its own. It describes a deliberate act: dozens of children are smothered to death because a small group of people own the wealth of the earth—and they'd rather kill than share. To Guthrie, those were documented facts. To the state of Michigan and official history, his "lousy, miserable song" was just repeating an old conspiracy theory, part of the Left's version of the truth, the losers' version, long since proven wrong.

Except on the key fact, Guthrie turns out to be right.

If you go back and look at blueprints, photographs, newspaper accounts, they show that Italian Hall was built to the most up-to-date safety guidelines of the early twentieth century. And that included exit doors that opened out, not in.

Locals knew. When the coroner and the grand jury and the feds investigated, Italian Hall was right there. Anybody could see how the doors opened. But over the years, the community wrote a different version of history. Call it a willful act of forgetting; call it an un-truth. The bronzed declaration that the doors opened inward reassured people that what happened couldn't have been murder.

It wasn't until a hundred years after the deaths that a new generation acknowledged the facts. Maybe enough time had gone by. Maybe the ashes of the ghost fire were finally cold. The state reviewed the evidence and altered the historical marker. It now reads: "As the children filed to the stage to receive presents, someone yelled 'Fire!' People panicked and rushed toward the exit. There was no fire. Many were trampled on the stairs." All mention of the doors— and which way they opened—was removed.

But just because it's been established that the doors could have been held closed, does it mean they were? Was it a murder, a massacre? Bloor states point-blank it was, but there's some question whether she was even at the Christmas party—or just put herself there. And by her own description, she never got downstairs where she could have seen if the deputies were blocking the exit. That the dead were mostly found in the stairwell, not by the door, suggests the crush happened higher up, on the too narrow stairs.

But finally, the question of murder doesn't hang on any of that. If someone deliberately shouted "Fire!" and set off the panic—and all the inquiries seem to agree that's what happened—that person was liable for the death of sixty-three children and eleven adults. The majority of the witnesses testified that the man who shouted was wearing a Citizens Alliance pin, but there was no thorough follow-up, no real attempt to find out who that someone was.

That was the true conspiracy around Italian Hall. And over the years, the official story only deepened it.

Guthrie breaks the silence. He not only reasserts that it was mass murder, but in the last line of his song, he solves the mystery: he names the murderer.

The lullaby-like guitar figure doesn't waver. The timbre of his voice doesn't change. "The parents they cried, the miners they moaned / See wha—" And he holds the hard *a*, holds it a long time till it becomes not a letter or part of a word but pure sound: a harsh, sustained wail, announcing an arrival. "See wha-a-a-a-a-t . . . your greed for money has done."

Maybe Bloor helped lead him here. Her book, after all, talks about "children killed by capitalist brutality and greed." But Guthrie had already reached this conclusion. Three years before he recorded "1913 Massacre," he was defining fascism as "nothing in the world but greed for profit and greed for the power to hurt and make slaves out of people." *STRUGGLE* argues that the history of America is the history of that greed winning.

But who is he naming exactly? Whose greed caused the mass murder in Italian Hall?

It depends on how we hear the accusation. It depends, more specifically, on who we think is making it. Is the last line of the song what the parents cry and the miners moan—the final thought our new friends leave us with before 1913 and the trip to the copper country fade back into the past? If so, "your greed for money" is aimed at the capitalist bosses: at MacNaughton and Shaw and Agassiz. It's their money; they're responsible. They, in effect, yelled "Fire!"

But the way it's sung, the last line could also be from our narrator. It could be Guthrie stepping out of history to explain the story he's just told, to draw a conclusion. And if it's Guthrie, then he's talking to whoever's listening to the song. He's talking to his audience, to us. "See what your greed for money has done." And, he implies, is still doing.

It's both, of course. "1913 Massacre" is simultaneously about the past and the present—and how the one keeps determining the other. Guthrie's song, his search, keeps jumping back and forth in time, comparing one era to another, hunting for the truth. And as it does—maybe because it does—something else rises from "1913 Massacre," rises from beneath the loss and sadness. It's the sound of what's been covered up but refuses to stay that way, refuses to leave the past alone: the sound of anger.

HOW DOES IT FEEL?

You could say the silence started in Calumet in 1913. Word spread that the doors opened inward, that no one was to blame. What followed was a great quiet, a hundred years of agreed-upon untruth.

Or you could say it began just afterward, during the patriotic rush of the First World War and the Palmer Raids that followed. The Wobblies were crushed, the call for a workers' alternative stilled.

Or you could say it began after the Second World War. If you see the two global conflicts as a single long realignment of power, then after America emerged as a superpower, its centurylong Red Scare kicked back in with a vengeance. That's how Elizabeth Gurley Flynn saw it. She traced the "hysterical and fear laden" atmosphere of the late 1940s back to when she was a union maid visiting Joe Hill in prison. "Now," she said, "it is part of the American tradition." In other words, once the nation of immigrants had defined itself, had determined an American Way, it also established the opposite: an Un-American Way.

In 1918, it was the U.S. Senate's Overman Committee investigating Bolsheviks. In 1930, the Fish Committee looked into William Z. Foster and other communist influences. Eight years later, it was the establishment of the House Committee on Un-American Activities, which continued to operate through the fifties. "The real issue," as HUAC's first chairman, Martin Dies, put it, was "between Americanism on the one hand and alienism on the other."

No one did more to define the Un-American than J. Edgar Hoover. His career began in 1917 jailing "disloyal aliens" as part of President Woodrow Wilson's Justice Department. Soon Hoover was in charge of carrying out the Palmer Raids. By 1924, he was head of the nation's Federal Bureau of Investigation. When he appeared before the Senate Internal Security Committee in 1948, he testified to "some thirty-five years of infiltration of an alien way of life in what we have been proud to call our constitutional republic." That math put the beginning of the infiltration—and the silence—in 1913.

Hoover testified as the Popular Front was making one last national effort. Henry Wallace, former vice president under FDR, had mounted a third-party run for the presidency. Seeing little difference between Democrat Harry Truman and Republican Thomas Dewey, Wallace vowed to establish "the century of the common man." That included expanded health care, the nationalization of the energy industry, and cooperation with Russia instead of Cold War. Attacking what he called the Red Scare "witch hunt," Wallace proclaimed, "those who fear communism lack faith in democracy."

What was left of the Popular Front rallied around him. Alan Lomax headed up a "musical desk" and brought in Guthrie, Seeger, Hays, and others. People's Songs churned out tunes, including a fiddle-and-guitar blues by Guthrie: "The road is rocky, but it won't be rocky long / Gonna vote for Wallace: he can righten all our wrongs."

It was a final electoral test of their progressive ideas, a last chance to present their case to the people. But liberals decided Wallace was "an apologist for Stalin." And those attacks were supported by America's labor leaders, who united to denounce Wallace as a dupe "being used by the Communists." Crowds jeered him when he toured Indiana, Iowa, Missouri. When he campaigned in the South—with Pete Seeger, among others—Wallace refused to sleep at segregated hotels, eat at segregated restaurants, speak to segregated audiences.

The locals responded by pelting him with tomatoes and eggs and shouting "nigger lover." On election day, his Progressive Party was crushed, getting less than 3 percent of the vote. As one folksinger put it, ". . . all the hopes and dreams of the brave new postwar world came crashing down at the end of the Wallace campaign."

That same year, Whittaker Chambers fingered Alger Hiss as part of a Communist spy ring within the US government. Richard Nixon began his rise as a young anti-Communist Republican. It was the year the California's Un-American Activities Committee cited People's Songs as a Communist front—and included as a "following Communist" a suspect the FBI would refer to as "Woodroe" Wilson Guthrie.

Guthrie stayed defiant, continuing to appear at Communist rallies and write for the *Daily Worker*. His FBI file described him as five foot five, 135 pounds, with reddish-brown, close-cropped hair, blue eyes. Under the category of Peculiarities, it noted, "Weather-beaten face." He was thirty-six years old, the father—with two wives—of five children, and Mazia was pregnant with a sixth. His disease was more and more obvious, his most productive years behind him.

On Labor Day 1949, Guthrie drove up the Hudson River to Peekskill, New York, to a concert by Paul Robeson. The Negro actor/singer/activist had tried to appear a few days earlier, but the local papers had declared him a "subversive," and an anticommunist crowd had blocked the entrance to the show, attacked the audience, burnt a cross on a nearby hill. "Our objective was to prevent the Paul Robeson concert," the head of the local American Legion declared, "and I think our objective was reached."

Determined not to be silenced, Robeson returned, and twenty thousand people gathered to hear him. Pete Seeger opened, singing with a new, as yet unnamed quartet. Meanwhile, an estimated eight thousand protestors ringed the outdoor venue, shouting, "Go back to Russia!" "Kikes!" "Nigger-lovers!" When Robeson appeared, he set his deep, operatic voice to a mix of classical pieces, spirituals like "No More Auction Block" and political songs like "Joe Hill," which he'd helped popularize a few years earlier. He designed his program as a reminder of a progressive tradition that stretched back into American history.

When the show ended, the performers and the audience retrieved their cars and started to exit out a narrow roadway. Lee Hays, riding with Guthrie, called it a "gauntlet . . . A tunnel lined on both sides with the enemy. And docks, boards, bottles, rocks." Police offered no protection. Instead, Hays reports, they "slowed down vehicles so the hoodlums could get better aim." Cars were overturned, windshields smashed, passengers pulled out and beaten. It was like the vigilante men in California, like the Citizens Council in Calumet. "I've seen a lot," Hays heard Guthrie mutter, "but this is the worse." On both sides of the gauntlet, anticommunists waved signs saying, WAKE UP, AMERICA. PEEKSKILL DID!

America did, too. Early in 1950, Wisconsin senator Joseph McCarthy started publicizing lists of supposed communists working for the federal government. Less than three weeks after Peekskill, Russia tested its own atomic bomb. A week later, China officially became a Communist country. In June, President Truman put US troops on the ground in Korea in response to what he called "unprovoked aggression" by Communist forces.

That same month, a group called Counterattack published *Red Channels*, a "Report of Communist Influence in Radio and Television." It featured indexes of people and organizations that were allegedly out to "infiltrate every phase of our life." Included along with Leonard Bernstein, Aaron Copland, Lena Horne, Arthur Miller, and many others were Will Geer, Burl Ives, Millard Lampell, Alan Lomax, Earl Robinson, Pete Seeger. Guthrie wasn't named, but *Red Channels* included as Communist fronts both the American Labor Party, to which he and his wife were registered, and People's Songs.

In the midst of this, Seeger launched the Weavers, the quartet he'd previewed at Peekskill. It was like the Almanacs but with a sweeter, more presentable sound. Its objective was to "beat the blacklist," as member Lee Hays put it, not by attacking it directly but by being "as commercial and successful as possible."

The Weavers began playing a Greenwich Village club just as hill-billy music was gaining new popularity. Leading that revival was another Jimmie Rodgers fan, the twenty-five-year-old Hank Williams. His first hit, "Move It On Over," had borrowed the melody of Charlie Patton's delta jug band blues, "Going to Move to Alabama," smoothed it with a country swing arrangement, and sweetened it with his rich, warm vocal. Williams was popularizing the folk sound in a way that so-called folk musicians were missing out on. "[We'd] gotten into such a box," is how Seeger put it, after the Wallace campaign, "that we were just singing to our old friends in New York." The Weavers—Seeger, Hays, the young Fred Hellerman, and Ronnie Gilbert—were determined to break out of that box. The sound they were after was a "great synthesis" of styles from black gospel to hillbilly to international music.

Guthrie had been one of the driving spirits of the Almanacs; eight years later, he was noticeably absent from the Weavers. He wasn't too old; Hays was only a couple years younger. And though Guthrie was famously scruffy, the rest of the Weavers needed some cleaning up, too. It may have been that his stiletto voice had no place in the group's more commercial harmonies. Or that his disease had already taken too much of a toll. It didn't help that he was, according to Seeger, "always an unreliable performer." And maybe he wasn't willing to make the political adjustment. The Weavers' first recording was "The Peekskill Story, Pts. 1–2," but they quickly decided to temper their radical politics. "We felt," as Ronnie Gilbert put it, "if we sang hard enough and strong enough and hopefully enough, somehow it would make a difference."

It worked, at least in part. Between 1950 and 1952, the group had a string of hits: Lead Belly's "Goodnight, Irene," a sing-along "On Top of Old Smokey," the South African "Wimoweh," and the lilting, hummable "Kisses Sweeter Than Wine." They success-fully brought folk music into the Top Forty. Or folk songs, anyway.

Because on record, their jovial, uplifting sound was often cushioned in masses of horns and strings: "Almost the opposite," Seeger later claimed, "of how we wanted to sound." But he also admitted he was tired of "congratulating myself on not 'going commercial.'" To break out, they entered into what Hellerman called "a certain kind of self-censoring as much aesthetic as political."

As a result, the Weavers got to play nightclubs in New York, Miami, Las Vegas. The men dressed in matching green corduroy jackets or tuxedoes, Ronnie Gilbert in an evening dress. Guthrie "really didn't approve," according to Seeger: ". . . we got a little too fancy for his tastes." But Hays wrote Earl Robinson, "I am so wrapped up in the problem of what to say to this big new audience of ours that I am not in the least ashamed that the old audience is gone. . . ." In live performances, depending on the venue, the Weavers might make reference to a new and better world, or sing the Hays/Seeger tune "If I Had a Hammer," their coded message opposing the Red Scare. But even "Hammer" was a little too much for radio and wouldn't become a hit until a dozen years later, when the teenage Mary Travers heard the Weavers do it in concert and brought the tune to her own well-dressed folk group: Peter, Paul and Mary.

The Weavers' politics were still radical, but their sound was genial: audience-friendly harmonies non-threatening songs that went with a clean-cut, middle-class image. Guthrie, in his own way, went with the trend. He rewrote "So Long, It's Been Good to Know Ya" for the Weavers, turning it into a kind of benign romantic comedy, and was soon collecting an advance check for $10,000. The Weavers' label, Decca, went on to offer him a recording contract. His circle of friends might still have the "utmost contempt" for commercial music, but that's what they were now making. The Weavers became part of the soundtrack for the postwar golden age, the sound of consensus.

But singing "Wimoweh" in tuxedoes couldn't last. "The only question really," Hellerman emphasized, "was *when* we would get our subpoenas." The same month *Red Channels* came out, the Los

Angeles office of the FBI accused Guthrie of being part of a political group whose "ultimate purpose . . . is sabotage against the United States during war with Russia." An immediate investigation was ordered. In August, the agency declared the best way to find Guthrie would be through one "Allan Lomack." Lomax would soon escape to England, his trip partly financed by royalties from the Weavers' version of "Goodnight, Irene."

Guthrie could still joke about it. In a song he wrote about the FBI, he declared, "I *will* point a gun for my country / But I won't guarantee you which way." In March 1951, the Bureau made him the subject of a Communist Index Card, raising his category of threat. That spring, Will Geer was called before HUAC. "I love America," he testified. "I love it enough to want to make it better." He refused to name other communists. As a result, he wouldn't get regular acting work for two decades (when he landed the job of the patriarch on TV's *The Waltons*). In the summer of 1951, a Weavers appearance on NBC was canceled, as was a booking at the Ohio State Fair. When Mother Ella Reeve Bloor died, age eighty-nine, the group made a collective decision not to attend her funeral, out of fear it would further incriminate them as Reds.

Both the Weavers and Guthrie were cited as communists at a HUAC meeting in early 1952. Decca Records dropped them both. That spring, his marriage falling apart, Guthrie was temporarily committed to Bellevue Hospital. He showed a baffling array of symptoms: staggering, slurring of speech, threats of violence and suicide. Six months later, doctors diagnosed Huntington's chorea.

At the hospital, doctors noted that Guthrie was "ranting about the 'Hoover gang,'" but his conspiracy theories turned out to be based in reality. The FBI had been trailing him and continued to after his release, eventually designating him for Detcom and Comsab status, categories reserved for national security threats subject to high-priority arrest in the event of war. The folk revival's symbol of "absolute freedom" began to wander compulsively. In the summer of 1954, informers in Tulsa, Oklahoma, described him as "beat up" with "gray hair." In early 1955, an FBI agent made a "pretext phone call" to his now ex-wife, Marjorie, and learned that Guthrie had entered Brooklyn State Hospital and was likely to be hospitalized from then on. Given his "fairly well advanced . . . deteriorating disease," the bureau recommended to Hoover that Guthrie be taken off the Security Index. His brain was mostly fine, his loyalty still to "the only people that I love on this earth, my union hearted army," but "chorea," as he wrote, "gets worser and dizzier. . . ."

In the summer of 1955, as Guthrie sat in the hospital "halfways knocked out," Hays and Seeger were called to appear before HUAC. They shared the same lawyer, but when asked if they were now or ever had been Communists, Hays cited the Fifth Amendment, refusing to incriminate himself, where Seeger stuck to the First Amendment that granted him free speech—or silence. Asked if he'd sung for the Communist Party, Seeger answered, "I have sung in hobo jungles, and I have sung for the Rockefellers, and I am proud that I have never refused to sing for anybody. That is the only answer I can give along that line." The Weavers tried to struggle on, but there were almost no bookings. Seeger soon resorted to his "guerilla tactics," cobbling together a living via appearances on college campuses and at summer camps.

The Red Scare was more than a scare—one of its victims called it the American Inquisition—and it was larger than folk music. "Our own field," as Ronnie Gilbert noted, "was the smallest part of it." It ran through academia, the government, organized labor. After the merger of the AFL and the CIO in 1955, the combined organization launched a concerted effort to deny communist influence. That included purging not only suspected members but any vestiges of the party, which apparently included music itself. Asked to sponsor a new union songbook, an AFL-CIO secretary responded, "What are you trying to do, make fools of us? . . . They don't sing at union meetings. . . . I've never heard of anything so ridiculous in my life."

Meanwhile, revelations about Stalin's dictatorship shook party loyalists. The world's primary example of functioning socialism now admitted its government had been behind widespread censorship, purges, death camps. Membership in America's Communist Party had already fallen to twenty thousand; as the details of Stalin's dictatorship were revealed, it plummeted to three thousand. Meanwhile, the threat of communism fed the US military: its budget went from 5 percent of the gross national product in 1950 to 13.5 percent three years later. As military spending had helped shock the nation out of the Great Depression, now it helped stimulate the golden age.

Between 1950 and 1970, the real gross national product rose by $350 billion. Basic wages for production, which had gone up by 45 percent in the late forties, rose by 56 percent in the fifties and another 44 percent in the sixties. It was the opposite of the Great Depression: now, capitalism flourished, and socialist countries looked gray, poor, repressive.

America's economic boom was a corporate one. Between 1945 and 1960, the assets of US corporations almost tripled. It was a little like Calumet and Hecla in the copper empire, with profits going primarily to stockholders. While the golden age saw this marked increase in wealth, how it was distributed didn't change much. The rich got richer; the percentage that went to the middle-class held even; and the poor ended up with a smaller share. Where inequality dropped in Europe after World War II, and as one economist put it, "people felt that capitalism had been overcome"—in the United States, the golden age pushed inequality past even where it had been in the early nineteenth century, the era of the Boston Associates.

The same way C&H tried to keep the economic peace by incorporating progressive ideas, American corporations in the golden age expanded health care, pensions, disability insurance. But what seemed to disappear was the idea of any alternative to capitalism. Earl Robinson called the midfifties McCarthy period "the silent generation thing."

Beneath that silence, the folk revival still existed. In 1955, when Seeger gave a concert at a junior high school in Palo Alto, California, thirteen-year-old Joan Baez discovered who she wanted to be.

In the same audience was Dave Guard, an undergraduate at Stanford University, who went on to form a Weavers-like group that turned into the Kingston Trio. Meanwhile, in San Francisco that fall, Allen Ginsberg read his poem "Howl," and an alternative literary movement, the Beats, began, connected to what he called "a recovery of . . . folk wisdom and folk energy and folk exuberance and folk suffering. . . ." In December, Rosa Parks, having studied nonviolent protest at the Highlander Folk School, refused to move to the back of a Montgomery, Alabama, bus.

If it wasn't revolution, it was some kind of rebellion—a breaking of the silence—and pop culture soon got wind of it. Guthrie and Lomax's old roommate, Nicholas Ray, had moved to Hollywood in the midforties to be director Elia Kazan's assistant. There, like Kazan, he "abandoned his radical activism of more than a decade with surprising ease." In the face of the Inquisition, both managed to keep their careers going: Kazan gave HUAC the names of alleged Hollywood Communists, and according to some, Ray also cooperated.

Both men's next projects tried to capture what was stirring beneath the American silence. Kazan made *On the Waterfront*, the story of a corrupt longshoremen's union that gets busted when a young worker sees the light and names names. It read as anti-Communist, anti-union, and, at the same time, pro-rebellion. Its star, Marlon Brando, became a teen idol. As Kazan wrote in his autobiography, "When Brando, at the end, yells at the mob boss, 'I'm glad what I done—you hear me?—glad what I done!' that was me saying, with identical heat, that I was glad I'd testified as I had."

As Kazan's movie premiered, Ray started shooting his project. Declaring, "[I've] done my share of films about the depressed areas of society," he focused instead on middle-class adolescent rebellion: consulting psychiatrists who worked with juvenile delinquents, trailing Los Angeles cops who dealt with youth problems, hanging with a "real" gang from Hollywood High. Ray came to see juvenile delinquency as a specific anger: anger at the era's "insidious social conformity," at the consensus that had helped produce the golden age. He took his film's title from a book-length clinical study of a psychopath, *Rebel Without a Cause.*

For an ex-Commie, it was a pointed phrase. It identified the film's hero by what he wasn't. He wasn't a radical or an organizer or even an activist. That was the point: he didn't have a cause. This new kind of teen rebel was angry at everything and nothing, at the status quo, at the silence. For his lead, Ray picked the twenty-four-year-old James Dean, fresh from shooting Kazan's adaptation of Steinbeck's *East of Eden.* Already being hailed as the next Brando, Dean seemed to personify this new rebel—wary, romantic, confused, solitary, and apolitical. In Hibbing, Bobby Zimmerman papered his bedroom with pictures of Dean and studied the actor's detached cool, his boyish giggle, his hipster phrasing the way Guthrie had studied Will Rogers.

It was a new trend, a new demographic. Hollywood had first gotten wind of it that spring of 1955, when a B-movie with a hackneyed plot and so-so cast did better than expected at the box office. *Blackboard Jungle* also featured teen rebels, but it was noteworthy for this weird phenomenon: during the opening credits, kids in America and Europe went wild for the song playing in the background. Its melody borrowed heavily from Hank Williams's "Move It On Over," but "Rock Around the Clock" was raunchier, its spirit more defiant. People were already beginning to create a new category for it: rock & roll.

As Ray began shooting *Rebel,* Mother Maybelle Carter was on tour with country star Hank Snow and a twenty-year-old regional sensation being marketed as "one of the newest though most exciting personalities in the Hillbilly field," Elvis Presley. Born more than twenty years after Guthrie, the "hillbilly cat" was also a Carter Family fan and covered their songs in some of his first recording sessions. But his idea was to mix hillbilly with blues and gospel. On his first single, he'd taken Arthur Crudup's up-tempo blues, "That's All Right," and added a sly backcountry vocal. The flip side was a hopped-up version of Bill Monroe's hillbilly waltz, "Blue Moon of Kentucky." These mutations were even more explicit in his live shows. As Mother Maybelle maintained her careful modesty, he'd appear in a chartreuse jacket with his hair slicked back, legs jiggling madly in flowing pants. "I can't overemphasize how shocking he looked and seemed to me," recalled Roy Orbison, who at nineteen saw Presley open for the Carters. "There was just no reference point in the culture to compare it." Or there were many references, commingled and rearranged.

Early in 1956, on the night Presley was making his second national TV appearance from a studio in Midtown Manhattan, up in Harlem, Seeger and others had organized a musical revue to raise money for Woody Guthrie's family. The old guard came out: Lee Hays and Earl Robinson were narrators. Seeger, Reverend Gary Davis, and others performed Guthrie's songs. Millard Lampell of the Almanacs tied them together with a narrative based on Guthrie's writings. The script had more to do with Guthrie as artist/philosopher/hobo than with his politics. The scare, after all, was on, and the "Red" organizers had had a hard time even finding a hall that would house the event. After a final singing of "This Land Is Your Land," Seeger, with tears streaming down his face, pointed up to a mezzanine seat. Guthrie rose, gaunt and shaky from his disease, and lifted a clenched fist: a forty-three-year-old rebel too sick to fight for his cause. One biographer called it "the beginning of Woody Guthrie's canonization."

His legend would grow without him. He couldn't perform anymore, and his records were hard to find. On the other hand, his illness meant he wasn't dragged before Congress like his friends. As he told them when they visited the hospital, "You don't have to worry about me. I'm worried about how *you* boys are doing. Out there if you guys say you're communists, they'll put you in jail. But in here, I can get up there and say I'm a communist and all they say is, 'Ah, he's crazy.' You know," he concluded, sense of humor intact, "this is the last free place in America."

He became a sort of martyr. As Clarence Darrow had said of Big Bill Haywood, "He will die, but . . . a million men will grab up the banner. . . ." In Guthrie's case, he didn't have to die. Young folk singers like Bob Zimmerman took up the banner, but it wasn't the red flag of socialism. In the midst of the Inquisition, Seeger and others spread the word about their friend: a great songwriter, a man of the people in the tradition of Whitman. What they tended to leave out was his Commonism; it got sheared away by the silence of the times.

A decade passed, a decade Guthrie spent in the hospital. It began with the murder of Emmett Till and ended with the murder of Malcolm X. Under presidents Eisenhower, Kennedy, Johnson, the Cold War heated up and became Vietnam. In the roar of the market's golden age, manufacturing began to shift out of America; a service economy emerged. It was the decade of the so-called second folk revival that began with the Guthrie tribute concert, the decade of the Kingston Trio and Peter, Paul and Mary, the decade Dylan went from junior high school to the verge of pop stardom.

By 1965, exhausted from his British tour and the constant press attention, Dylan had begun inventing an even wilder, less believable past. "Actually the first record I made was in 1935," he told a British interviewer. "John Hammond came and recorded me. Discovered me in 1935, sitting on a farm." He seemed frustrated and bored by his own live set. "I knew what was going to happen all the time," he told a reporter, ". . . which songs they were gonna clap on loudest." He'd later claim he wrote the material for his next record "after I had *quit*. I'd literally quit, singing and playing. . . ."

Maybe.

But if he's telling the truth, it was a short retirement. His British tour ended on May 10; he took a few weeks vacationing with his wife-to-be (and turned twenty-four). By June 15, he was in the studio cutting a new record.

His producer, Tom Wilson, was a black man. A Harvard graduate with a degree in economics, Wilson had produced jazz, gospel, a Pete Seeger record, and the three previous Dylan albums. He was knowledgeable about various kinds of music, responsive to what artists wanted, and willing to let musicians stretch out. Given that Dylan didn't have a band—he had, instead, a sound he wanted—Wilson brought in studio musicians. The guitarist, piano player, and rhythm section were the same he'd used on the electric cuts from "Bringing It All Back Home" six months earlier. They were professionals, a little older than the singer, with a track record of working on pop hits. Bass player Joe Mack, for example, had created the groove on a string of hits for Chubby Checker, Bobby Rydell, the Orlons. The musicians weren't there to produce anything too radical, but they had ears for the commercial sound that both Wilson and his star were after.

To this mix Dylan added a wild card. He'd met twenty-two-year-old guitarist Michael Bloomfield in Chicago, where Bloomfield was a devoted student of the blues. He admired the earlier generation of country players, like Son House. But where House insisted, "The real old blues don't go for jumping," Bloomfield liked the jump, the electrified city blues. He modeled his playing on men like B. B. King, Hubert Sumlin, and the wild Pat Hare who helped create the urban grit of Muddy Waters and James Cotton. Rehearsing with Dylan just before the recording session, Bloomfield recalls, "I figured he wanted blues, string bending, because that's what I do. He said, 'Hey, man, I don't want any of that B. B. King stuff.' So, OK, I really fell apart. What the heck does he want?"

It wasn't clear. As Bloomfield recalled their first day in the studio, "No one knew what the music was supposed to sound like." They started with eleven takes of a conventionally structured up-tempo blues. "Well, I ride on a mail train, baby," it begins, assuming an old-timey sound and perspective: more songs from an invented freight. Except by the third verse, the words start to swerve off track and head for that COMPLICATED CIRCLE. People talk but can't connect; "your train gets lost." Instead of creating a sound that incorporates that swerve, the band keeps pumping straight ahead, the organist underlining the beat, the drummer staying in a narrow groove, as if there were no such thing as losing your way.

Next they try six takes on another urban blues, "Sitting on a Barbed-Wire Fence." But for all its edgy, funny imagery, the tune comes across as tired. "She's turning me into an old man," Dylan sings, "and, man, I'm not even twenty-five." He sounds it, and Bloomfield's overextended guitar solos don't help.

By the time they start work on a third number, the band has settled into its role: precise, competent, slightly predictable. Dylan pulls out some words he's scribbled during his "retirement" and is now calling "Like a Rolling Stone." That may be a nod to the Hank Williams line from "Lost Highway" or to Muddy Waters's "Rollin' Stone," a blues standard about a displaced, powerful drifter, or it may refer back to the original proverb. Joe Hill, on the eve of his execution, handed a poem through the bars to his guard: "My will is easy to decide / For there is nothing to divide. / My kind don't need to fuss and moan—/ 'Moss does not cling to a rolling stone.'"

Dylan's lyrics are a rush of images, but the band sounds almost sleepy, playing something close to waltz time behind the singer's country-smooth vocal. Take after take follows with no hint of urgency or anger.

The session ends without coming up with anything usable. The band's been playing variations on the blues, but it isn't, finally a blues band. That's not what the studio musicians are good at. Bloomfield is, but he's been asked not to bend notes. It's as if they've been requested to re-create history and, instead, ended up mired in old forms. If Dylan's looking backward—and he'll eventually call the LP *Highway 61 Revisited*—it's not just to revisit the old South-to-North blues route. He wants to see what's changed. And he wants to change it. He wants the truth of history, updated.

When the musicians reassemble for a second day of recording, another wild card's been added. Or rather, has added himself. Twenty-one-year-old Al Kooper, a session guitarist and friend of Tom Wilson's, is there to watch but suddenly decides to sit in on organ. It's not his instrument, and when the producer sees him behind the keyboards, they both laugh. The band tries a few takes of this "Like a Rolling Stone" song, with Kooper's organ staying slightly behind the beat, holding notes the way Dylan does in his vocals, prolonging them, straining against the groove.

Enter the third and final wild card: Dylan as rhythm guitarist. He may have written the melody to "Like a Rolling Stone" on piano; that's how it was first shown to the band, anyway. And he's not known as an electric guitar player, not since Hibbing High. But now he straps one on and helps kick off the song by playing a scratchy rhythm figure: two beats, then a faster strum, then again. On electric guitar, with the band joining in, it sounds like dance music: a funky little slither, the shadow of James Brown, whose "I Got You (I Feel Good)" is all over the 1965 soul and pop charts.

The net effect, when the musicians finally hop aboard, is an odd mix. There's still the lope of hillbilly music—the steady one-two, one-two striding across the song's landscape—but inside that is this tight dance beat. Meanwhile, Kooper's organ is underlining and then smearing the pattern, while Bloomfield's playing this intricate, steady guitar pick from the country blues. Below all that, the rhythm section's churning out big pop sounds that you might hear on a Phil Spector girl-group record.

A big pop sound is the point: they're out to make a hit. And it works.

Leave them there, in the studio, a minute and skip forward. Once they get a finished version of the number, there will be a month's delay. Supposedly the label balks at the song's six-minute length (about the same as Guthrie's "Tom Joad"). But when it finally does come out, it'll immediately take off. Five days after its release, the crowd at the Newport Folk Festival already knows it. As traditional singers give "workshops" and concerts—the Reverend Gary Davis introducing his last song by saying, "This is the truth"—Dylan will appear in leather jacket and tight black pants. One of the festival's board members will call Dylan's electric set "[an] explosion of lights, sound, and anger." Seeger and others will complain about that explosion—about the volume, or maybe it's the look. Or how short Dylan's set is. Or how he's betrayed the Guthrie tradition, dropped the cherished banner. Or how his voice is wailing over and inside the song. But within a week, the single will be at number two in America, topped only by the Beatles' "Help."

It's a hit, a Top Ten song. Over the next forty years of his career, Dylan will only have three others, and none will chart higher. "I think 'Like A Rolling Stone,'" he'll say, six months into its success, "is definitely the thing which I do. After writing that I wasn't interested in writing a novel, or a play. I just had too much, I want to write *songs*."

But all that's in the future. It wasn't a hit or even a song till he and the musicians found it.

Back in the studio, they do fifteen takes. On some, Dylan screws up the words; others have technical difficulties; and often, as Wilson points out, "Something's wrong time-wise." They're not improvising exactly, but the producer and singer have deliberately set up a situation where nobody quite knows what they're doing. It has some of the spontaneous feel of a Lomax field recording or one of Guthrie's marathon Asch sessions. That's part of the truth as Dylan understands it, that it has to sound fresh, that neither the musicians nor the listeners can know what's coming.

On the take they'll finally use, the drums' opening smack seems to surprise the band. "Here we go! Where are we going?" The organ hits and holds, sounding churchlike, and then there's that dancey rhythm guitar figure.

"Once upon a time," the singer begins. He's said it a little tentatively in other tries, but now he's sure: we're going down into the past, hold on tight. His voice is a little rushed, slurring the lyrics, almost as if they don't really matter. But there's that confidence, that authority: he knows what he's hunting for.

The song's aimed at a woman, but maybe more important, at someone who's made it. Or had it made. The singer talks directly to her, his voice calm at first, the musicians working beside him as he starts to list the things she's done, the life she's led. It's almost a formal accusation, a grievance letter like the one the copper miners sent to management. When the singer asks her to confirm—you did do these things, "didn't you?"—his voice gets its first hint of anger.

The way the melody works, each verse doubles back on itself—rising as if to crescendo, then returning—and that suits the story line. The singer lists what the woman's done and then comes back to point out how things have changed. You used to dress fine, now you're scrounging. The tune keeps doing this, descending as it repeats, till—led by the organ's sustained chords, it has the potential to turn into a harangue, a litany of failure. Except Bloomfield's guitar is stirring, and a tambourine's banging away, and when the verse ends by explaining what she's been scrounging for, it's on a high, held note: "your next me-eee-al!"

The singer's been studying for this moment, studying—among others—Woody Guthrie's stiletto. It's this sound, this held note, that signals the beginning of the truth.

Dylan's used the approach and the structure before. "Like a Rolling Stone" is another restless farewell, another repeating pattern he can break and bump against. But as he rides the held note out of the verse and into the chorus, something else happens. "It's a whole way of doing things," Dylan will say, a year after the session. "I'm not talking about words. It's a certain feeling, and it's been on every single record I've ever made. That has not changed."

How does it feel?

That question, at the start of the chorus, switches the song into suddenly more than a harangue, something more open-ended than that—directed not just at her but at us. And it's a question in form only. The music, the release, the last of the singer's escaping breath gives the answer.

How does it feel? It feels good. It feels great.

What does? Well, being alone, having no destination, discovering that you're a stranger. He could be describing the classic Woody

Guthrie outlaw, except this isn't a song about a rambling hero. He's not asking about her "hard travelin.'" No, the question here is how it feels to have been prosperous, to have had it made, and then to see it all come crashing down. And the answer the music gives is that it feels great.

There's the squib of a harmonica that abruptly stops. No time for that now; we're still gaining momentum.

The second verse is fiercer, both lyrically and in how it's delivered. As soon as the past is laid out—her time attending "the finest school"—the ground is cut out from under: "But you only used to get juiced in it." The loss is immediate, followed (as the verse doubles back) by the consequence: the sudden and unavoidable need to make a "de-eee-al!" It's that high held note again, and the chorus is already nearly familiar enough for us to sing along. It now has the magnetism of a hit, something anybody in a bar or driving or walking home from school can chime in on, knowing the question, knowing the answer. Great! It feels great.

Again, the squib of a harmonica; still no time for it.

"Awww!" the singer yells as he enters the third verse. He's plainly angry now, even lecturing a little. You never cared, he says; you thought you were above it; "You shouldn't"—a noticeable pause to underline the words—"let other people get your"—another pause—"kicks for you."

This isn't labor history; the song has nothing to do with labor history. But the piano's quick boogie-woogie shake is pissed at one class of people doing and the other just riding along, observing. As the verse does its double-back, the consequences grow. The consensus that's been struck—this golden age, this prosperous status quo—has taken everything from you it could—the held note—"ste-ee-al."

On the third go-round of the chorus, the singer blows a lyric and just leaves it that way. Screw it; the sound is what matters. And the sound is a howl that should be the end of the song. We've all had to compromise; we're all paying the price; we've all lost on the deal. What else is there to say?

This time, the harmonica squibs a little longer, like it's trying to shake free.

But instead of fading out, the band cranks up another notch. Somehow the rhythm section finds the strength to go on not only longer, but harder, higher.

The storyteller returns to once upon a time, to that mythical past when there was a "princess on a steeple." She spent her days "Exchanging all precious gifts," amused at how the mighty had fallen. When the verse doubles back, the singer tells her—tells us—that's over. And in this new era, we'd better go back to those who've fallen—we've got to go back—because we've ended up with nothing. And that brings on the final exhilarating news: "You're invisible now, you've got no secrets to conce-ee-al. . . ."

That's where this history brings us: to a new start. Not a fresh start; there's been too much past for that. But each circular, spinning verse has drilled through another layer of lies.

Now there's a last roll of drums before the final chorus. The singer asks the familiar question as if it has new mysteries to reveal. He sounds, if anything, more confident that we'll find what we're after. The idea of traveling with no destination—of dropping old assumptions, of living like a rolling stone—has become a kind of promise and threat.

What the anger's revealed, down beneath the silence, is something more precious than exchanging all precious gifts. It's revealed that there *is* something more precious. Anger has found its way to hope. Asked about his songwriting a few months after "Like a Rolling Stone" was released, Dylan says, "Every song tails off with 'Good luck . . . I hope you make it.'"

The harmonica finally gets to break loose, and it jigs off toward the future, fading as it goes.

UNDERGROUND

t's a month shy of a hundred years since the 1913 massacre. It's almost fifty years since "Like a Rolling Stone" first came over the radio.

To take a trip to Calumet, Michigan, you can catch a small plane out of Chicago and watch the Midwest landscape pass below: squared-off farms where there was once prairie, some of the farms broken up into smaller suburban parcels, those bisected by cul-de-sacs and driveways, all connecting eventually to the interstates that crisscross the country. Every acre seems to be parceled out, lived on, worked. This land is clearly somebody's.

Once you get to the northernmost part of Michigan's Upper Peninsula, the view is emptier, more remote. It feels like you can look back down over the decades, as if the continent and its history are laid out before you.

Houghton County has a small, rural airport a half dozen miles outside the town of Houghton itself. In between is low open country, tundralike, cut with marshland, evergreens, tamaracks, white birch.

At the peak of a hill that descends into Hancock and Houghton sits the Quincy Mine. It's named for its financiers' hometown of Quincy, Massachusetts. Over a century and a half, Quincy produced 1.5 billion pounds of copper and paid stockholders some $30 million in dividends. Its number 2 shaft house is a massive sheet-metal structure, a set of triangles perched on rectangles, built in 1908. The slant of its roof matches the incline of the main shaft, seven thousand feet below.

At the entrance to one of the outbuildings, a sign reads: PLEASE RESPECT THE PAST. Next to it, another says, HISTORIC PLACES HOLD CLUES TO WHAT LIFE WAS LIKE HERE NOT SO LONG AGO. Step inside, and the walls are streaked with graffiti. Nearby is a brick hoist house dating back to the 1800s, a big boiler room that's now roofless and in ruins, drainage canals filled with weed and broken brick. A billboard promises guided tours: you and your family can ride a tram car to the mine entrance and then down seven levels beneath the earth. The tour's closed for winter.

Just past the mine, Hancock and Houghton face each other across a finger of Portage Lake. Combined, they have a population of about fifteen thousand. Hancock, this side of the bridge, looks tired: the wide main street empty, the few businesses struggling. This was where the mob beat up WFM president Charles Moyer, pulled him from his hotel, then dragged him across the bridge to the train station in Houghton.

Houghton is home to Michigan Technological University. Founded in 1885, Mich Tech started with twenty-three students studying to become engineers for the local copper companies. It now has a student population of about seven thousand. Half the graduate program comes from overseas: twenty-first-century immigrants looking for advanced degrees in geology, business administration, environmental engineering.

In the basement of Mich Tech's glassy modern library are bound ledgers from the offices of Calumet and Hecla. You can read the scrawled letters from that first difficult summer: Agassiz reporting to Shaw how "Mr. John Hulbert on his return home yesterday made no attempt to interfere in any way. . . ." Or telegrams from after the Italian Hall disaster: MacNaughton writing Shaw Jr., "Moyer is trying to make capital out of this frightful accident to further his own selfish ends." There are boxes and boxes of memos, invoices, bills paid: the history of a corporation.

At dusk, with the sun low over the cold landscape, the drive north goes back past the Quincy Mine and the airport. After a few miles of empty highway, you come to Calumet. There's no reason for the town to be here except what's beneath it. The city grew up around the indentation where Edwin Hulbert found a man-size boulder of almost pure native copper. Housing and streets and stores grew up around the mine entrance.

Today, Calumet has the half empty look of a lot of American towns. The big municipal structures—library, police station, auditorium—are all from the nineteenth century, the heyday of the industrial age. They're surrounded by small shuttered houses, empty lots, corner groceries with signs saying WE ACCEPT FOOD STAMPS. A couple of Calumet's central streets are being restored to attract tourists. Antique shops sell rusty mining tools and Finnish grammar books. A candy store plays a constant loop of old-timey parlor music. In a preserved 1890s saloon, stained glass glows over a dark oak bar.

Italian Hall is beyond restoration. Its site is now a small park, but the seventy-five-year-old building was condemned and torn down in 1984. The official reason was that it had become a safety hazard, but some think it had more to do with the past: the old building stood as a daily reminder of how history continued to divide the town. All that's left of it now is a single brick archway next to a historical marker. On the arch, the labor council of the northwest Upper Peninsula AFL-CIO has put up a small bronze plaque with a quote attributed to Mother Jones: MOURN THE DEAD; FIGHT FOR THE LIVING.

Nearby, the neighborhood's empty. There's nothing much except someone's asbestos-sided house, a camper top that's been left at the end of the driveway.

The next day, in the thin northern light, you can follow Route 203, Veterans Memorial Highway, out of town. That's the route that was taken by the procession of little white coffins—the one Mother Bloor swore she'd never forget. After a couple of miles, you come to Lakeview Cemetery. If there's a lake view, it's from on top of the hill where the more prosperous families are buried, many above ground in big mausoleums. The graves of those who died at Italian Hall are down in the low sections to each side.

There, past rows of carefully laid out gravestones, you come to a small bare area. It looks unused—as if it was being held for the future, as if there was nothing beneath the surface. But a recently erected marble marker explains: 42 PROTESTANT VICTIMS OF THE ITALIAN HALL DISASTER WERE INTERRED IN THIS SECTION IN DECEMBER OF 1913.

There are only a few gravestones. One plain four-foot rectangle has MOTHER ELIINA 1887–1913 carved on top and, below, SON WESLEY 1909–1913. To its left, a newer-looking ground marker reads, SAITA M. RAJA 1903–1913. Eliina was twenty-six when she died. She was born in Kankajoki, Finland, and her parents—the Rajas— came to America when she was thirteen or fourteen. She married Herman Manni, a Finnish miner, when she was twenty-one; he was twenty-three. Wesley was born a couple months later. Another son arrived two years after that, and another was seven months old during the Christmas season of 1913. Eliina, pregnant with her fourth child, went to the party with her little sister, Saita, ten, and her oldest son, four-year-old Wesley. They were late getting there and were up at the top of the stairs when the panic started. All three were found in the stairwell. Eliina and Wesley were buried in the same casket. By the spring of 1915, a year and a half after the tragedy, husband and father Herman Manni was back working for the mining companies.

Ten miles southeast of the cemetery is Torch Lake. Torch Lake connects to Torch Bay, which is an arm of Portage Lake, which opens onto Lake Superior. Torch Lake is where C&H located its stamping mills and smelter. After miners had cut stamp rock loose from the shaft wall, after trammers shoveled it into skip cars, it would emerge on the surface and then be hauled by steam locomotives along the now vanished Hecla and Torch Railroad. At the mills, the rock was crushed and the copper washed free of the waste under a steady stream of water; a giant pump pulled sixty-five million gallons a day out of Torch Lake. The pump and the mill are gone; all that remains, on one raised section of ground, are a set of fifty-foot-diameter concrete outlines. They look like ancient religious symbols.

The site's been developed as a tourist attraction. Scattered around are pieces of old iron equipment: a snowplow, a handcart to load copper ingot, a coal stove. In the summer, a narrow-gauge train carries visitors past a one-room schoolhouse and a Congregational church, now a historical museum. Municipal docks jut out where the ore boats used to dock. A sign reads NO SWIMMING . . . UNDERWATER OBSTRUCTIONS. Within a few feet of the shore, Torch Lake goes from iron-red to black.

During the heyday of the mines, two hundred million tons of milling by-product—stamp sands—were dumped into Torch Lake. Starting in the 1920s, the sands were dredged out, chemically reprocessed to recover any missed copper, then dumped back in. An estimated 20 percent of the lake is filled by sediments up to seventy feet deep. In the 1980s, the US Environmental Protection Agency named Torch Lake an Area of Concern, citing "fish tumors of unknown origin." It was subsequently declared an environmental Superfund site.

Drive farther north, and you pass Centennial number 6, another sheet-metal shaft house. This one still has a conveyor belt and some railroad tracks that look like they were active not that long ago. The ground is covered with rubble: by-products of the search that went on some three thousand feet underground. Farther up the road, former mining settlements remain: Ahmeek, Michigan, population 146. Delaware, Phoenix, Mandan are ghost towns: a few gray shacks and foundations.

The whole region is dotted with remains. If you go down First Street in the town of South Range, you'll find a 50-by-150-foot building on a red sandstone foundation. The cornerstone reads A.D. 1913. It was the Socialist Meeting Hall; now it's a storage building with two garage doors cut into the front.

Farther south, Seeberville is where WFM's first martyrs fell: the two striking miners killed by deputies firing into a boardinghouse. Seeberville is a dozen small buildings on two small streets, all overshadowed by a huge slag heap. The hoist for Champion number 4 is boarded up. What looks like its old processing plant now holds a scrap metal business. The little storage building to one side still has hand-painted signs on its brick walls: MINERS PUT YOUR LAMPS OUT.

At the A. E. Seaman Mineral Museum, part of Mich Tech, there's a display on the history of the Copper Country. It begins by describing Native American mines, then outlines the boom of industrialism led by Calumet and Hecla, and then goes on to tell how Keweenaw's population dropped by half—from ninety thousand to forty-five thousand—after the 1913 strike. By the time World War II broke out, 37 percent of Houghton County was on public assistance.

The war briefly improved the local economy, but the population continued to fall through the fifties and sixties. The year before "Like a Rolling Stone" came out, C&H announced that its tubing and processing equipment was using more copper than its mines produced. The final shutdown began not long afterward.

The Mineral Museum displays all kinds of underground wonders: geometric stacks of pink crystals, tulip-shaped limonite, pyrite that looks like fungus, calcite in light red diamonds. You can imagine a man swinging a pick in the dark, lifting his head, and having his miner's lamp pick up these strange shapes and colors. And then putting his head down and swinging his pick again, because what he was after was copper.

The museum illustrates how the Calumet lode was mostly sand and red igneous rock: rhyolite. It was shot through with copper: small cubes of it, sprays like gold-green ferns, dark chunks, fans, bunches like red grapes, narrow green hips, and large outgrowths like pieces of coral reef. Its uses changed over the years—from copper buttons to electric wire to circuit boards—but the basic economics remained the same. The companies that laid claim to the land paid workers to go down and bring back what was valuable. Valuable because it was useful: it could be turned into something else. And even more valuable because it was scarce and hard to get to.

By the 1970s, America's golden age had begun to fade, and the peak of union membership had passed. As manufacturing jobs went overseas—as companies insisted on non-union payrolls in right-to-work states—as automation (like the one-man drill) created a smaller workforce—productivity rose, but wages didn't. Dylan released a song called "Union Sundown" in 1983. "Democracy don't rule the world. . . ." he sang, now age forty-one. "This world is ruled by violence." In the chorus, he explained how union "Sure was a good idea / 'Til greed got in the way."

By the early eighties, America's industrial Midwest slowed, stopped, and became known as the Rust Belt. Real hourly income was on a decline that would leave it lower in 1995 than it had been in 1973. Less than a quarter of the nation's nonagricultural workers belonged to unions. Unemployment in the Upper Peninsula hit nearly 19 percent.

If you go up from the Protestant section of Lakeview Cemetery—up over the hill with its mausoleums, then down the other side—you come to the Catholic section. There's a bare area here, also, with a marker that says this mass grave holds "22 CATHOLIC VICTIMS."

Three small identical monuments read, KRISTIAN KLARIC 1901–1913, MARIA KLARIC 1903–13, KATARINA KLARIC 1905–1913. The twelve- and ten-year-old girls were students in Calumet's Grant School; they took their little sister to the Italian Hall party. Their father and mother, both from Lokve, Croatia, and a baby brother stayed home. After the strike, Frank Klaric returned to work for C&H as a timberman, retiring after putting in fifty years.

Through the 1990s, the percentage of the nation's wealth that went to workers continued to decline, shifting instead to owners and investors. At the start of that decade, America's twenty largest financial institutions controlled 12 percent of the country's total financial assets; by 2009, they held 70 percent. At the same time, unions continued to shrink: from 15 percent of the workforce in 1996 to 13 percent in 2003. The last sustained national rise in wages came in 1970. The country's real growth rate has dropped every decade since then, and what new jobs have been created have mostly been in the relatively low-paying service sector.

Drive along the strip malls outside Houghton, and you see corporate chains: a Pizza Hut, Taco Bell, McDonald's. There's a Quick Change oil, a Napa auto parts. Farther out, you find car sales, plumbing supplies, the Salvation Army. A gravel operation still makes money by digging in the earth; it's called Pebbles, Inc. Out in the woods are some small lumbering companies.

By the end of the twentieth century, the United States was the most unequal in terms of income distribution—the least level—of all developed nations. And the one where it was hardest to climb out of poverty.

If the golden age's promise of pie-in-the-sky never came true, neither did Mother Bloor's dream of a socialist alternative. In the Soviet Union, its centralized five-year plans couldn't both pay for the Cold War and feed its people. The final collapse came at the end of the eighties: from August through December 1989, Communist systems failed in Poland, Czechoslovakia, Hungary, Romania, and East Germany, with Yugoslavia and Albania soon to follow. The Soviet Union officially dissolved in 1991.

Nicholas Cvetkovich's marker gives only his name and dates: 1883–1913. He was born in Croatia and immigrated to Calumet when he was twenty-four. He worked as a trammer and was described as "very vocal in the union." At age thirty, he took his seven-year-old son, Nick Jr., to the Christmas party at Italian Hall. The boy survived. His father was found dead in a corner with a jacket thrown over him. "The story which came through the family was that he was probably silenced. . . ."

In the A. E. Seaman Mineral Museum, a display declares that the Copper Country's mining era is probably over; any future profit from underground will most likely come from "heritage tours." During the economic downslide of the seventies, locals began lobbying to create a historic district to bring in tourist dollars. In 1989, Calumet's downtown and the Quincy Mine complex received national historic landmark status. Three years later, Congress passed and President George Herbert Bush signed an act creating the Keweenaw National Historical Park.

Unlike most national parks, Keweenaw isn't a single nature preserve, but dozens of "heritage sites" spread out over a hundred miles. They've been chosen to tell the story of copper mining and its "large scale corporate paternalism." Or as the congressional act put it, to "interpret the historic synergism between the geological, aboriginal, sociological, cultural, technological, and corporate forces . . ." Sites include various settlements and mines, the Finnish American Center in Hancock, and a forty-five room mansion built by a mine owner in Laurium in 1908. Now a hotel, its ad reads: "Come live the Copper Baron lifestyle for yourself. . . ."

Back in 1913, America's richest 1 percent—families like the Agassizs and the Shaws—controlled about 18 percent of the country's wealth. That number had dropped to 16 percent by the time Guthrie rode his freight into California. When Dylan cut "Like a Rolling Stone"—in the golden age—it was down to 12 percent. But if you then jump to 2000, the richest people in America held over 20 percent of the wealth. And five years later, that approached 25 percent.

As wealth concentrated among a relative few, overall debt grew. Just before the so-called Great Recession began in 2007, total family and business debt was almost three times the gross domestic product. One quarter of all the households in the United States either had zero net worth, or owed more than they had. When the housing market collapsed, and that credit was called, the golden age began to look less like a model of how the system should work and more like a fluke.

Leading economists began to wonder if the United States "may be an economy that needs bubbles just to achieve something near full employment." Put in Guthrie's terms, the only way modern global capitalism seemed able to produce enough "jobs with honest pay" was through the equivalent of a land or copper rush: a boom economy pursued by boomchasers. The prospector's dream.

Down in the Catholic section of Lakeview Cemetery, across an access road from a marshy patch of birch and scrub pine, there's a marker for Victoria Burcar. Victoria was seven at the time of the Christmas party. She went with her six-year-old brother, Carl. Their father and mother were both from Croatia. Though his sister died, Carl managed to escape the crush on the stairs and told his parents that he'd seen the man who yelled "Fire!" With their child a witness to murder, "the family was concerned for his safety." They moved out west to Red Lodge, Montana, a coal mining town. By the 1920s, the Burcars were in Tacoma, Washington, where their two sons grew up to work in local smelters. Carl Burcar married and by 1940 had two children under three and was working as a foreman at a wholesale grocer's warehouse. The man who had seen the man who yelled "Fire!" died in 1983.

Between 2009, when the Great Recession officially ended, and 2013, America's wealthiest 1 percent accounted for 95 percent of the total growth in income. Meanwhile, average family income for 90 percent of American families dropped by more than 10 percent. And if you compare 2011 to 1973, the drop was nearly 15 percent. Four years after the housing bubble burst, there were five and a half million fewer full-time jobs. Over a third of the new jobs that did emerge were part-time. By June 2013, the nation reached a historic high of 2.7 million temp workers: jobs without benefits, the kind Joe Hill and the Wobblies were protesting a century earlier.

The year Dylan cut "Like a Rolling Stone," a typical male worker's income was about $34,000. Almost five decades later, the comparative figure was $33,000. By 2013, 15 percent of the nation lived below the poverty level. Nearly 40 percent of American children were growing up in poverty or near-poverty. A record number of Americans received food stamps. Long-term unemployment was the worst it'd been since the Dust Bowl.

Michigan had already lost half its auto-manufacturing jobs before the Great Recession. In 2007, it had the highest unemployment rate in the country at 7.4 percent; that was 9.3 percent by 2012. At the end of that year, with its percentage of unionized workers dropping, the so-called "birthplace of the American labor movement" passed a right-to-work law, the twenty-fourth state in the nation to do so.

Right-to-work made it harder for unions to organize, but labor's declining influence and the lack of strikes were already obvious. By 2012, union membership in America had dropped to 11 percent of the workforce, the lowest since World War II. Take out government jobs and look only at the private sector, and fewer than 7 percent of employees belonged to a union: the lowest level in a century. The lowest level, that is, since 1913.

The landscape of Keweenaw—its sandstone shores and low, tree-covered hills—looks permanent. But beneath the surface is a history of change: caverns and pockets where molten rock once flowed, fault lines where whole sections of the continent slid and shifted. It's that change that brought wealth: the gray is lead; the yellow sulfide, the gold we call gold; and the reddish-green is copper. This mix of elements goes down three to five miles: the earth's crust. On it, our lives are lived; in it, we plant our crops, bury our dead. This crust floats on what's known as the earth's mantle: a huge, rocky shell eighteen hundred miles thick. And inside the world's shell is a molten core, a kind of rage.

You could start there.

Chapter I: Once Upon a Time

1 iron and other minerals: Kiril Spiroff, "Geological History of
Michigan," 1964, www.michigan.gov/documents/deq/GIMDL
-GGGHM_302331_7.pdf.

1 veins of copper settled: Larry Lankton, *Cradle to Grave: Life, Work
and Death at the Lake Superior Copper Mines* (New York: Oxford
University Press, 1991), 5–6.

1 seven thousand years ago: Robb Gillespie, William B.
Harrison III, and G. Michael Grammer, "Geology of
Michigan and the Great Lakes," Michigan Geological
Repository for Research and Education, Western Michigan
University, 2008.

2 "drew out of a sack": Lankton, *Cradle to Grave*, 6.

4 "I do not find it easy": President Lyndon B. Johnson, "Why We
Are in Viet-Nam," press conference, July 28, 1965, www
.presidency.ucsb.edu/ws/?pid=27116.

4 "clearly racist": Stokely Carmichael, "Black Power Address," UC
Berkeley, Oct. 1966, www.americanrhetoric.com/speeches
/stokelycarmichaelblackpower.html.

7 nearly 90 percent: Patricia E. Benson and Michael F. Bryan, "The
Emerging Service Economy," Economic Commentary, Federal
Reserve Bank of Cleveland, June 15, 1986, https://www
.clevelandfed.org/en/newsroom-and-events/publications
/economic-commentary/economic-commentary-archives/1986
-economic-commentaries/ec-19860615-the-emerging-service
-economy.aspx.

8   over forty thousand: "The History Place Presents the Vietnam
War," historyplace.com/unitedstates/Vietnam/index.

8   one to three million: Charles Hirschman, Samuel Preston, and
Vu Manh Loi, "Vietnamese Casualties During the American
War: A New Estimate," *Population and Development Review* 21, no.
4 (Dec. 1995): 783–812, https://csde.washington.edu/~glynn/c
/pubs/VietnameseCasualtiesDuringAmerican.pdf.

8   "free of domination": Lyndon Baines Johnson, "On Vietnam and
Not Seeking Reelection," Mar. 31, 1968, www.americanrhetoric
.com/speeches/lbjvietman.htm.

9   Jefferson Airplane, *Volunteers* (RCA Victor, 1969).

10   Dylan, *Nashville Skyline* (Columbia Records, Apr. 1969).

10   Bobby Seale, *Seize the Day: The Story of the Black Panther Party and
Huey P. Newton* (Baltimore: Black Classic Press, 1991), 183–86.

11   staged drama: John Berger, "The Nature of Mass
Demonstrations," *New Society* 11 (1968): 754–55.

12   over four million students: see Kent May 4 Center, www.may4
.org/bestkentstate1970info.html.

12   "[Kent State] marked a turning point": H. R. Haldeman,
The Ends of Power, cited in "Kent and Jackson State: 1970–
1990," *Vietnam Generation* 2, no. 2, article 1 (1995), http://
digitalcommons.lasalle.edu/vietnamgeneration/vol2/iss2/1.

13   "The four years passed": Henry Adams, *The Education of Henry
Adams: An Autobiography* (Boston: Houghton Mifflin, 1918), 59.

13   250,000 bird specimens: "About the Exhibition," Elizabeth Hall
and Max Hall, Museum of Comparative Zoology, (Boston:
Harvard University, 1964, 1975, 1985).

17   the difference between: Nelson Lichtenstein, *State of the Union: A
Century of American Labor* (Princeton, NJ: Princeton University
Press, 2002), 213; and Michael B. Katz and Mark J. Stern,
"Poverty in Twentieth Century America," America at the
Millenium Project, Working Paper 7, Nov. 2001, www.sp2
.upenn.edu/america2000/wp7all.pdf.

Chapter 2: True Stories About Real Events

19   "If you told the truth": Bob Dylan, *Chronicles, Volume One* (New York: Simon & Schuster, 2005), 35.

19   grocery store: Robert Shelton, *No Direction Home: The Life and Music of Bob Dylan* (New York: Da Capo Press, 1997), 25.

19   "I ran away from it": Bob Dylan, "My Life in a Stolen Moment," concert notes, New York Town Hall, 1963, see https://beatpatrol .wordpress.com/2010/03/05/bob-dylan-my-life-in-a-stolen -moment-1962.

19   Dylan denied: Shelton, 24.

19   "my youth was spent wildly": Letter to the Emergency Civil Liberties Committee, "Bob Dylan and the NECLC," www .corliss-lamont.org/dylan.htm.

20   Standard Oil: Shelton, 30.

20   B'nai B'rith: Howard Sounes, *Down the Highway: The Life of Bob Dylan* (New York: Grove Press, 2001) www.nytimes.com/books /first/s/sounes-01highway.html.

20   "it was not a rich town": Bob Dylan, "11 Outlined Epitaphs" sleeve note to *The Times They Are a-Changin'*, 1963, https:// beatpatrol.wordpress.com/2010/04/05/bob-dylan-11-outlined -epitaphs-1963.

20   "the biggest open pit": Dylan, "My Life in a Stolen Moment."

20   all but mined out: Marvin G. Lamppa, *Minnesota Iron Country: Rich Ore, Rich Lives* (Duluth: Lake Superior Port Cities, 2004), 223.

20   "local depression": Lamppa, 225; and Shelton, 27.

20   "iron depletion": John Bucklen, from interview on "I Was So Much Younger Then," Dylan Bootleg Series, vol. 1, disc 1.

20   "Where I lived": Shelton, 46.

21   "Bobby always went": Shelton, 43.

21   "the right side of the tracks": Anthony Scaduto, *Bob Dylan* (New York: Signet, 1973), 20.

21   "the only / job": Bob Dylan, *Tarantula* (New York: Scribner, 1966), 108–9.

21   "If I could have": quoted in Daniel Dalton, *James Dean: The Mutant King* (San Francisco: Straight Arrow Books, 1974), 238.

21   home tape: Bucklen interview.

21   first idol: liner notes to *Joan Baez in Concert, Part 2* (Vanguard, 1963).

21   could pick up: Toby Thompson, *Positively Main Street: Bob Dylan's Minnesota* (Minneapolis: University of Minnesota Press, 2008), 65.

21   "Late at night": Dylan, interview by Kurt Loder, *Rolling Stone*, June 21, 1984, www.rollingstone.com/music/features/the-rolling-stone-interview-bob-dylan-19840621.

21   "Maybelline": Thompson, 65.

22   "loved their music so much": Thompson, 71.

22   "dreadful tragedy": "The Death of Emmett Till," recorded on *Folksinger's Choice* radio show, 1962, released under artist name Blind Boy Grunt on *Broadside Ballads*, vol. 6, *Broadside Reunion*, 1972. https://en.wikipedia.org/wiki/The_Bootleg_Series_Vol._9_%E2%80%93_The_Witmark_Demos:_1962%E2%80%931964.

22   "a blues sound": Thompson, 68.

22   "something you can't quite": Bucklen tape.

22   "To join the band": Shelton, 39.

22   "I didn't run away": Dylan, interview by Nat Hentoff, *Playboy*, Feb. 1966.

22   "Right then and there": Dylan interview with Ron Rosenbaum, *Playboy*, March 1978. www.interferenza.com/bcs/interw/play78.htm.

23   Jack Benny: Kingston Trio, "Tijuana Jail," *The Jack Benny Show*, www.youtube.com/watch?v=zUZDBQ2zrU0&feature=related.

23   sung in coffeehouses: Robert Cantwell, *When We Were Good: The Folk Revival* (Cambridge, MA: Harvard University Press, 1996), 4.

23 categories: see liner notes to Kingston Trio, *The Folk Era*, http://
aln2.albumlinernotes.com/The_Folk_Era.html.

24 "uncontaminated": Georgina Boyle, *The Imagined Village: Culture,
Ideology, and the English Folk Revival* (Manchester, UK: Manchester
University Press, 1993), 4.

24 "the utmost contempt": Will Kaufman, *Woody Guthrie: American
Radical* (Champaign, IL: University of Illinois Press, 2011), 120.

24 "A folk song tells a story": Woody Guthrie, *Pastures of Plenty: A
Self-Portrait*, ed. Dave Marsh and Harold Leventhal (New York:
HarperCollins, 1990), 209 [hereafter PofP].

24 "Folksingers, jazz artists": Dylan, *Chronicles*, 34.

25 beatnik cafés: Ronald D. Cohen, *Rainbow Quest: The Folk
Music Revival and American Society, 1940–1970* (Amherst, MA:
University of Massachusetts Press, 2002), 123; and Cantwell, 272.

25 "The Beats tolerated": Dylan, *Chronicles*, 48.

25 "home base": Cantwell, 272.

25 three and a half million: William Ruhlmann, "Peter, Paul and
Mary: A Song to Sing All Over This Land," 1996, http://www
.peterpaulandmary.com/history/f-ruhlmann1.htm.

25 Joan Baez: Cantwell, 297.

25 "An unspoken feeling": George Wein, *Myself Among Others: A
Life in Music* (New York: Da Capo Press, 2004), 314.

26 half a century: "The Kingston Trio Overview," www.lyricsinfo
.org/artist_the_kingston_trio-about-988.html.

26 number nine: Ruhlman

26 liked the sound: Dylan, *Chronicles*, 32–33.

26 "out of date": Dylan, *Chronicles*, 238–39, 236.

26 "the old weird America": Greil Marcus, *The Old, Weird America:
The World of Bob Dylan's Basement Tapes* (New York: MacMillan/
Picador, 2011).

27 "so real": Dylan, *Chronicles*, 236.

27 if not special: see recordings and interview made May 1960
by Karen Wallace on "I Was So Much Younger Then," Dylan
Bootleg Series, vol. 1, disc 2.

27 "like the record player": Dylan, *Chronicles*, 244.

27 "went in two weeks": Shelton, 73.

27 "It was his voice": Robert Hillburn, "Rock's Enigmatic Poet Opens a Long-Private Door," *Los Angeles Times*, Apr. 4, 2004, http://articles.latimes.com/2004/apr/04/entertainment/ca -dylan04.

27 "When your head gets twisted": "Last Thoughts on Woody Guthrie," read at New York's Town Hall, Apr. 12, 1963, www .woodyguthrie.de/lastth.html.

28 "You could listen to his songs": "A Tribute to Woody Guthrie," from *A Vision Shared: A Tribute to Woody Guthrie and Leadbelly*, Columbia Records, 1988.

28 "I rode freight trains": Dylan, "My Life in a Stolen Moment."

28 from the Southwest: Richard Fariña, "Prologue: Baez and Dylan: A Generation Singing Out!" in *Younger Than That Now: The Collected Interviews with Bob Dylan* (New York: Thunder's Mouth Press, 2004).

28 Gallup: Scaduto, 106.

28 "I skipped": Bob Dylan, interview by Cynthia Gooding, WBAI-FM, Mar. 11, 62, http://expectingrain.com/dok/int/ gooding.html.

28 "I don't like": Dylan, "11 Outlined Epitaphs."

28 "pure hokum": Dylan, *Chronicles*, 7–8.

28 "my own depression": Dylan, "11 Outlined Epitaphs."

28 covering Guthrie originals: see mention of the Minnesota Party Tape, Sept. 1960, at www.mnartists.org/article.do?rid=139827.

29 "juke-box stuff": Ed Cray, *Ramblin' Man: The Life and Times of Woody Guthrie* (New York: Norton, 2004), 419n.

29 "making pretend": Dylan, interview by Gooding.

29 "Ramblin' outa": from "Talkin' New York."

29 gotten a lift: Michael Pollak, "Bob Dylan's Quiet Debut in New York City," *New York Times*, July 3, 2015.

29 "[We] made an arrangement": Walter Eldot, "My Son the Folknik," *Duluth News Tribune*, Oct. 20, 1963.

29   "sobering and psychologically draining": *Chronicles*, 99.

29   "I know Woody": Joe Klein, *Woody Guthrie: A Life* (New York: Knopf, 1980), 425.

29   "Woody Guthrie was my last idol": "11 Outlined Epigraphs."

30   "hungry thirties": Dylan, "11 Outlined Epitaphs."

30   "where is our party?": Dylan, "11 Outlined Epitaphs."

30   "I needed to write that song": From *No Direction Home: Bob Dylan*, Martin Scorsese, director (Paramount Pictures, 2005).

31   "any substantial importance": *Chronicles*, 54.

Chapter 3: A Little Bad Luck

33   "autobiographical novel": Cray, 255.

33   "another one of those little towns": Woody Guthrie, *Bound for Glory* (New York: Dutton/Signet, 1943), 37 [hereafter BfG].

33   "I ain't nothing much": Woody Guthrie, *California to the New York Island* (New York: Oak Publications, 1958), 26.

33   eleven thousand years: W. David Baird and Danney Goble, *Oklahoma: A History* (Norman: University of Oklahoma Press, 2008), 28–30.

34   fifty thousand Indians: Ibid., 126.

34   "mine" the soil: Edwin Tunis, *Colonial Living* (Baltimore: Johns Hopkins University Press, 1999), 104.

35   about two million: Ernest Ludlow Bogart, *Economic History of the American People* (New York: Longmans, Green, 1937), 495–96.

35   east of the Rockies: Klein, 6.

35   tens of thousands: Baird and Goble, 144, 156.

35   traded cattle: Klein, 7.

35   from Kansas: Klein, 5.

35   thirty-seven thousand: Baird and Goble, 126.

35   250 percent: Nigel Anthony Sellars, *Oil, Wheat and Wobblies: The Industrial Workers of the World in Oklahoma* (Norman: University of Oklahoma Press, 2012), 79.

35   "grafters": Baird and Goble, 161.

36   "Because he was able to speak": Klein, 14.

36   "a man of brimstone": PofP, 2.

36   "I might not stop": BfG, 45.

36   "all the prettiest": Ibid., 39–40.

36   "Nigger! Nigger!": Klein, 9.

37   sharecropping: Nick Salvatore, *Eugene V. Debs: Citizen and Socialist* (Urbana: University of Illinois Press, 1982), 234.

37   "parasites": Baird and Goble, 180; Bogart, 505.

37   Democratic sweep: Baird and Goble, 175.

37   started construction: Klein, 9.

37   "I wasn't much more": BfG, 38.

37   "[N]obody ever knew": BfG, 40–41.

37   three years before: BfG, 49; and Klein, 12.

37   "because she hated": Cray, 20.

37   "Mama didn't answer": BfG, 56.

38   No state: Baird and Goble, 179–81.

38   "reverse the corporate revolution": Salvatore, 124.

38   "tyranny and degradation": Salvatore, 127.

38   "right versus wrong": Salvatore, 161, 165.

38   "Kumrids": Klein, 15.

38   sold postcards: Klein, 13.

38   "enthusiastic member": Klein, 25.

38   "one of those ol' hard-hittin'": Woody Guthrie, *Library of Congress Recordings* (Rounder Records, 1992) [hereafter LC].

39   "altogether inadvisable": Gary Gerstle, "Race and Nation in the Thought and Politics of Woodrow Wilson," in John Milton Cooper Jr., ed., *Reconsidering Woodrow Wilson: Progressivism, Internationalism, War, and Peace* (Princeton/Baltimore: Woodrow Wilson Center Press/Johns Hopkins University Press, 2008), 93–124.

39   almost a third: Cray, 15.

39   Three years later: Cray, 17.

39   "My Dad": Woody Guthrie, *The Live Wire* (Rounder Records, 2011).

39   "just worried and worried": BfG, 81.

39   "awful scared, nervous kind of woman": *Live Wire.*

39   "I was a little bit different": LC.

40   "either set herself afire": LC.

40   "She would be all right": BfG, 136.

40   "She commenced to sing": PofP, 4.

40   Wells had been coming in: Baird and Goble, 197; and BfG, 40.

40   "[You] just wake up one morning": *Live Wire.*

40   "Pretty soon the creeks": BfG, 93–94.

40   "The whole country": BfG, 96.

40   more in a month: Baird and Goble, 210.

40   "oil slickers, oil fakers": BfG, 40.

40   "My dad told me": Kaufman, 8.

41   "He went down fighting": BfG, 138.

41   "it all to come back": BfG, 136, 145.

41   shipped his little brother: BfG, 145.

41   "that look": BfG, 157.

41   "I always will think": LC.

41   Houston and Galveston: Woody Guthrie, *American Folksong,* ed. Moses Asch (New York: DISC Company of America, 1947), 3.

41   "alley rat": Klein, 28.

41   a drought began: Marc Reisner, *Cadillac Desert: The American West and Its Disappearing Water* (New York: Penguin, 1993), 156.

42   "had a little bad luck": LC.

42   "dirty, bed-buggy": BfG, 168.

42   a clean-faced kid: Darryl Holter and William Deverell, *Woody Guthrie: L.A. 1937 to 1941* (Santa Monica, CA: Angel City Press, 2015), 14.

42   "I walked the streets": BfG, 174.

42   a public confession of sins: Stephen D. Eckstein, *History of the Churches of Christ in Texas* (Lubbock, TX: Bible Publications, 1992), viii.

43   eliminated any church hierarchy: Ibid.

43   "Will Rogers and Jesus": Klein, 125.

43   "my best doctor": Klein, 407–8.

43   Bristol, Tennessee: Mark Zwonitzer and Charles Hirshberg, *Will You Miss Me When I'm Gone? The Carter Family and Their Legacy in American Music* (New York: Simon & Schuster, 2004), 77.

44   "his tape recorder": Zwonitzer and Hirshberg, 128.

44   the Carter scratch: Zwonitzer, 71–75.

44   "in reserve": John Szwed, *Alan Lomax: The Man Who Recorded the World* (New York: Penguin, 2010), 183.

44   "We played for rodeos": PofP, 5.

45   "The difference between our rich and poor": Will Rogers Memorial Museums, www.willrogers.com/quotes.

45   "[E]very kid in the Southwest": Lee Hays, *"Sing Out, Warning! Sing Out, Love!": The Writings of Lee Hays*, ed. Robert S. Koppleman (Amherst: University of Massachusetts Press, 2003), 153.

45   a fifty-town good-will tour: Zwonitzer, 115; Ben Yagoda, *Will Rogers: A Biography* (Norman: University of Oklahoma Press, 2003), 278.

45   "If I was President Roosevelt": Woody Guthrie, *Alonzo Zilch's Own Collection of Original Songs and Ballads* (Pampa, TX: self-published, 1935); and Cray, 86.

45   about four dollars a week: Cray, 66–67.

46   soon Mary: Cray, 56.

46   still fierce: Reisner, 155.

46   "the most important thing": *Live Wire*.

46   "Any disaster": Zwonitzer, 91.

46   Guthrie remembered how: BfG, 88.

47   first hundred days: Quizlet, https://quizlet.com/21460401/ch24 -flash-cards.

47   "look around for a place": PofP, 6.

47   "mixed-up bunch": BfG, 318.

48   "colors so bright": BfG, 223.

48   "the lonesome whip": BfG, 227.

48   "millions of things": BfG, 228.

48   "singing with the people": BfG, 299.

48   "peppery and friendly": Woody Guthrie, *Woody Sez* (New York: Grosset and Dunlap, 1975), 46.

Chapter 4: Some Vision of the Future

49   "Any event which": Woody Guthrie, "How to Make Up a Ballad Song and Get Away with It," in *Born to Win*, ed. Robert Shelton (New York: Collier Books, 1965), 72 [hereafter BtW].

49   "Nightingale": "1913 Massacre," www.fresnostate.edu/folklore /ballads/FSWB306A.html.

49   "a good old, family style tune": Cray, 419n.

50   Walt Whitman: Ella Reeve Bloor, *We Are Many* (New York: International Publishers, 1940), 21.

50   "I see the enslaved": Bloor, 23–24, quoting from "The Mystic Trumpeter."

50   "earnestly trying": Bloor, 28.

50   "just as radical": Bloor, 30.

50   Debs: Bloor, 50.

50   "like an evangelist": Bloor, 53.

50   "his analysis of the evils": Bloor, 54.

50   Oklahoma's tenant farmers: Lichtenstein, 11.

50   "*To unite and organize*": Bloor, 46.

50   Upton Sinclair: Bloor, 78–95.

51   897,000 socialist votes: Bloor, 96.

51   a socialist mayor: Bloor, 118–9.

51   "owned little enough clothing": Bloor, 121.

51   America's future: Eugene Debs, Open letter to the American Railway Union, *Chicago Railway Times*, Jan. 1, 1897.

51   "new courage and inspiration": Bloor, 141.

52   They then formed: Bloor, 121.

52   "under a dollar a day": Bloor, 121.

52   "widow makers": Bloor, 121.

52   Annie Clemenc: Bloor, 121. In *We Are Many*, its "Clemence" but this is what seems to be the more commonly used spelling.

52   "I have one": Bloor, 122.

52   "a big room": Bloor, 123.

52   "There was no fire": Bloor, 123.

53   "an air-tight coffin": Bloor, 123–24.

53   "the marks of children's nails": Bloor, 123–24.

53   "based word for word": Kaufman, 118.

53   four thousand years: Thomas Avery, *Copper Country—God's Country* (Au Train, MI: Avery Color Studios, 1973), 14; and Charles K. Hyde, *Copper for America: The United States Copper Industry from Colonial Times to the 1990s* (Tucson: University of Arizona Press, 1998), 31.

54   "a great island": Avery, 10.

54   "The entire region": see Arthur W. Thurner, *Calumet Copper and People: History of a Michigan Mining Community, 1864–1970* (Privately printed, 1974).

54   "sterile region": Avery, 22.

54   "rich and abundant ores": Avery, 25; and Hyde, 29.

54   "I cannot fail": Ellis W. Courter, "Michigan's Copper Country," Michigan Geology 1992, www.michigan.gov/documents/deq /CMG92_301731_7.pdf, 16.

54   "bullets, rum, and treaties": Randall Schaetzl, "Indian Cessions," http://geo.msu.edu/extra/geogmich/Indian_cessions.html.

54   Chippewa ceded: Arthur W. Thurner, *Rebels on the Range: The Michigan Copper Miners' Strike of 1913–1914* (Lake Linden, MI: John H. Forster Press, 1984), 12.

54   "The Indians residing": *Indian Affairs: Laws and Treaties*, vol. 2, *Treaties*, ed. Charles J. Kappler (Washington: Government Printing Office, 1904).

54   thirty-two square miles: Schaetzl, "Indian Cessions."

55   overlapping claims: Thurner, *Rebels,* 13.

55   UP copper: Hyde, 43.

55 To split a chunk: Larry Lankton, *Keweenaw National Historical Park Historic Resource Guide* (National Park Service, US Department of the Interior, 2005), www.wuppdr.com/pdf/KNHPHisRes.pdf, 25 [hereafter Lankton, *Guide*].

55 a tallow candle: Lankton, *Guide*, 34.

55 drill a blasting hole: Hyde, 44.

56 "rock house": Lankton, *Guide*, 47.

56 the copper was melted down: William B. Gates Jr., *Michigan Copper and Boston Dollars: An Economic History of the Michigan Copper Industry* (Cambridge, MA: Harvard University Press, 1951).

56 over 70 percent: Lankton, *Guide*.

56 only a few: Hyde, 34.

56 forty-niners: J. R. Van Pelt, "Boston and Keweenaw—an Etching in Copper," in Robert W. Kelley, ed., *Our Rock Riches: A Selected Collection of Reprinted Articles on Michigan's Mineral Resources by Various Authors*, Geological Survey, Bulletin 1 (Lansing, MI: 1964).

56 "swamp and overflowed lands": Northern Prairie Wildlife Research Center, "Wetland of the United States, Their Extent and Their Value to Waterfowl and Other Life: A Century of Wetland Exploitation," https://www.fws.gov/wetlands /documents/Wetlands-of-the-United-States-Their-Extent-and -Their-Value-to-Waterfowl-and-Other-Wildlife.pdf.

57 population rose: Thurner, *Rebels*, 15.

57 the corporation became: US Supreme Court, *Chandler v. Calumet and Hecla Mining Co.*, 149 U.S. 79 (1893).

57 born in the UP: Courter, 59.

57 a summer prospecting: Courter, 60.

57 "swarthy man": Courter, 60.

57 "to attain": Van Pelt.

57 evidence of: Ibid.

57 St. Marys: Courter, 60; and Horace J. Stevens, *The Copper Handbook: A Manual of the Copper Industry of the United State and Foreign Countries* (Houghton, M: Stevens, 1902), 252.

57 "held my discovery": Courter, 60.

58 he bankrolled: Ibid., 61.

58 "Everyone supposed": Gates, 15.

58 prices rose: Courter, 51.

58 eighty-six of ninety-four: Charles K. Hyde, *An Economic and Business History of the Quincy Mining Company*, Historic American Engineering Record (Washington, DC: National Park Service, Library of Congress, 1978).

58 Minesota: Larry Lankton, *Cradle to Grave*, 9 and 17.

58 healthy dividends: Thurner, *Rebels*, 14.

58 "immigrant elite": "An Interior Ellis Island: Ethnic Diversity and the Peopling of Michigan's Copper Country," Michigan Technological University Archives, MS-002, Calumet and Hecla Mining Companies Collection [hereafter MTU Archives].

59 Swedes, Norwegians: Lankton, *Cradle to Grave*, 60.

59 a monthly fee: Courter, 52.

59 scrip: Ibid., 52.

59 "defiantly": Ibid.

59 brother, John: Ibid., 63.

59 stashed it here: "The Founding of the Calumet and Hecla Mine: 1866–1916." www.billcarney.com/coppercountry/c_and_h/c_and_h_at_50.htm.

59 double the richness: Courter, 62; and Lankton, *Cradle*, 20.

60 a fall: Hyde, 50.

60 dollar a share: Courter, 65.

60 "delivering angel": Courter, 63.

60 Samuel Parkman: *Lives of American Merchants*, vol. 2 (New York: Freeman Hunt, Derry and Jackson, 1858), 58; and Hugh Thomas, *The Slave Trade: The Story of the American Slave Trade, 1440–1870*, (New York: Simon & Schuster, 1997), 330.

60 Robert Cabot Lowell: Robert F. Dalzell Jr., *Enterprising Elite: The Boston Associates and the World They Made* (New York: Norton, 1987), 26.

60 first organized industrial system: Dalzell, 3.

60 By 1825: Dalzell, 38 and 67.

61 began to glut: see Dalzell, especially 26–34.

61 already put: Courter, 63; and Gates, 41.

61 a deal: Courter, 63.

61 hard-pressed: Courter, 64–65.

61 the Hulberts continued to focus: Alexander Agassiz, *Letters and Recollections of Alexander Agassiz*, ed. G. R. Agassiz (Boston: Houghton Mifflin, 1913), 56.

62 which had failed: Sir John Murray, "Alexander Agassiz: His Life and Scientific Work," *Bulletin of the Museum of Comparative Zoology at Harvard College* 54, no. 3 (Mar. 1911).

62 a month in the wilderness: David Dobbs, *Reef Madness: Charles Darwin, Alexander Agassiz, and the Meaning of Coral* (New York: Pantheon, 2005), 65.

62 raise the stock assessment: Courter, 64.

62 priced out: Agassiz, *Letters*, 61.

62 "lost his head": Agassiz, *Letters*, 56.

62 "suicidal course": Courter, 65; and Agassiz *Letters*, 64.

62 Shaw fired Hulbert: Courter, 65.

62 "not activated by principles": Courter, 67.

62 a monograph: Mary P. Winsor, *Reading the Shape of Nature: Comparative Zoology at the Agassiz Museum* (Chicago: University of Chicago Press, 1991), 59.

62 "I am going to Michigan": Agassiz, *Letters*, 61.

63 refused to salute: Louise Hall Tharp, *Adventurous Alliance: The Story of the Agassiz Family of Boston* (Boston: Little, Brown, 1959), 81.

63 a grant: Dobbs, 46.

63 "taken the Boston Brahmins": Stephen Jay Gould, *The Panda's Thumb: More Reflections on Natural History* (New York: Norton, 1980), 174.

63 "fat and plenteous": Dobbs, 12.

63 "humbug": Tharp, 7.

63 the largest donation: Dalzell, 149.

63 "very remarkable circumstance": Louis Agassiz and J. Elliot Cabot, *Lake Superior: Its Physical Character, Vegetation and Animals, Compared with Those of Other Similar Regions* (Boston: Gould, Kendall and Lincoln, 1850), 427.

63 "quiet, steady": Dobbs, 58.

63 By the time they got to America: Dobbs, 51.

64 as much as $50,000: Dalzell, 62.

64 "had never indulged": Tharp, 15.

64 the Cabots: Dalzell, 58; Tharp, 3.

64 the Careys: Tharp, 12 and 155.

64 "a prominent textile merchant": Dobbs, 65. That Alex refused to fund his science with his wife's family money was a sign of his principles—and his determination not to be like his father.

64 Lyman's sister: Winsor, 136.

64 his personal collection: Winsor, 29; and Dobbs, 55.

64 "as complete a library": Tharp, 134.

64 That November: Winsor, 37.

65 "convulsing society": Adams, 224.

65 "categories of thought": Winsor, 27.

65 "intelligent and intelligible": Ibid., 11.

65 implications: Dobbs, 74.

65 "truly monstrous": Madeleine Schwartz, "The MCZ at 150," *Harvard*, Nov. 13, 2009, http://harvardmagazine.com/breaking -news/harvard-museum-of-comparative-zoology-at-150.

65 "brain of the Negro": Louis Menand, "Morton, Agassiz, and the Origins of Scientific Racism in the United States," *Journal of Blacks in Higher Education*, no. 34 (Winter 2001–2): 110–13.

65 "the different races": Gould, 172.

65 He saw interbreeding: Menand; and Gould, 174.

66 determined: Dalzell, 140; Winsor, 9.

66 "misguided": Christoph Irmscher, *Louis Agassiz: Creator of American Science* (Boston: Houghton Mifflin, 2013), 222.

66 "cripple the advance": Tharp, 152.

66 "lords of the loom": Dalzell, 202.

66 "no voice": Ralph Waldo Emerson, "The Celebration of Intellect," address to the students of Tufts College, July 10, 1861, *Complete Works* (1904), vol. 12, www.bartleby.com/90/1204.html.

66 "Free negro labor": Tharp, 192.

66 "I am ashamed": Tharp, 159.

66 "rather a store-house": Christoph Irmscher, *Louis Agassiz: Creator of American Science*, (Boston: Houghton Mifflin, 2013), 116.

66 some twenty thousand: Winsor, 63 and 88.

67 house and library: Irmscher, 297; and Dobbs, 102.

67 "was helpless without": Adams, 347.

67 "the unknown primeval": Agassiz, *Letters*, 54.

Chapter 5: Men Possessed by Anger

69 "This wasn't what": BfG, 243.

69 Jack Guthrie: Cray, 95–96.

69 a spangled Western suit: Ibid., 99.

70 "the mecca": Bill C. Malone and Jocelyn R. Neal, *Country Music U.S.A.: A Fifty-Year History* (Austin: University of Texas Press, 1968), 154.

70 hillbilly: Malone and Neal, 145.

70 Orven Grover Autry: Holly George-Warren, *Public Cowboy #1: The Life and Times of Gene Autry* (New York: Oxford University Press, 2007), 22–24.

70 outselling: Mark Zwonitzer with Charles Hirshberg, *Will You Miss Me When I'm Gone? The Carter Family and Their Legacy in American Music* (New York: Simon & Schuster, 2002), 113.

70 yodeling: Lynn Abbott and Doug Seroff, "America's Blues Yodel," *Musical Traditions* 11 (1993).

71 "bright talk": George-Warren, 80–81.

71 "a friend is a friend": lyrics from various Autry songs.

72 learned to yodel: Cray, 96.

72 sidekick: Ibid., 103.

72 five hundred miles: Peter La Chapelle, *Proud to Be an Okie: Cultural Politics, Country Music, and Migrations to Southern California* (Oakland, CA.: University of California Press, 2007), 51.

73 1945: Cray, 111.

73 a newspaper clipping: notes to *The Asch Recordings*, vol. 1, p. 4 (Smithsonian Folkways, 1999); and *Woody at 100: The Woody Guthrie Centennial Collection* (Smithsonian Folkways, 2012).

73 twelve hundred to fifteen hundred: "Farm Labor in the 1930s," *Rural Migration News* 9, no. 4 (Oct. 2003), https://migration .ucdavis.edu/rmn/more.php?id=788.

73 1.3 million: "Farm Labor in the 1930s."

73 "one of the greatest": Carey McWilliams, *Factories in the Field: The Story of Migratory Farm Labor in California* (Santa Barbara, CA: Peregrine Publishers, 1935, 1971), 309.

74 anti-Okie law: La Chapelle, 27–28.

74 "We must stop this": Ibid., 22.

74 "white trash": Ibid., 22–36.

74 American Legion: Ibid., 31.

74 "rough and husky": PofP, 7.

74 "crossnote trademark", La Chapelle, 53.

74 "exactly like": Cray, 109.

75 "workingman's lingo": La Chapelle, 68.

75 *Old Time Hill Country Songs*: Edward Robbin, *Woody Guthrie and Me* (Berkeley, CA: Lancaster-Miller Publishers, 1979), 53.

75 familiar tunes: La Chapelle, 57.

75 birthday cakes: Cray, 127.

75 his father talked: Crissman says he always used nigger, never Negro. Holter and Deverell, 59.

75 "a young Negro": Cray, 109.

76 he argued: Upton Sinclair, "End Poverty in California: The EPIC Movement," *Literary Digest*, Oct. 13, 1934, www.sfmuseum.org /hist1/sinclair.html.

76 a thousand pieces: Cray, 119–21.

76 mixed songs: notes to *Asch Recordings*.

76   the Singing Bum: Goebel Reeves biography, www.oldies.com
/artist-biography/Goebel-Reeves.html.

76   McClintock: Harry "Haywire Mac" McClintock—biography,
www.bluegrassmessengers.com/harry-%E2%80%9Chaywire
-mac%E2%80%9D-mcclintock—1928-.aspx.

77   "Reason why": *Woody at 100*, 107.

78   "Th' Dustiest of Th' Dustbowlers": Holter and Deverell, 12.

78   "good money": Ibid., 25.

78   campaign manager: Guthrie, *American Folksong*, 4.

78   *Light*: La Chapelle, 54; and Anne Loftis, *Witnesses to the Struggle:
Imaging the 1930s California Labor Movement* (Reno: University of
Nevada Press, 1998), 169.

78   dropping in on: Cray, 126–27.

79   conference: "The Evian Conference," https://www.ushmm.org
/outreach/en/article.php?ModuleId=10007698.

79   "without precedent": McWilliams, 211.

79   National Industrial Recovery Act: Loftis, 10.

79   the strike that followed: Ibid., 7.

79   affecting crops: Michael Denning, *The Cultural Front: The
Laboring of American Culture in the Twentieth Century* (New York:
Verso, 1997), xiii.

79   DISARM THE RICH: Loftis, 12.

79   "Communist Party conspiracy": McWilliams, 220.

79   "Whenever a strike": Ibid., 214.

80   "assumed the appearance": Frank Spector, "The Story of Imperial
Valley," undated pamphlet, in *Highlight of a Fighting History: 60
Years of the Communist Party USA*, ed. Phillip Bart (New York:
International Publishers, 1979), 87–89.

80   "It's anger": John Steinbeck, *In Dubious Battle* (New York:
Viking, 1938), 48.

80   "My whole family": Ibid., 4.

80   investigating: Loftis, 150.

80   Henry George: *Our Land and Land Policy*, quoted in McWilliams,
19.

80   A large peach orchard: John Steinbeck, "The Harvest Gypsies," *San Francisco News*, Oct. 5–12, 1936.

80   Marx: in a letter to Friedrich Sorge, Nov. 5, 1880, https://www .marxists.org/archive/marx/works/1880/letters/80_11_05.htm.

81   "dust-bowl refugees": McWilliams, 306.

81   sided with: Loftis, 41.

81   two hundred thousand: McWilliams, 9.

81   fifty cents: Ibid., 317.

81   fifty babies: Ibid., 317.

82   second largest: Loftis, 13.

82   "showing us the way": Harvey Klehr, *The Heyday of American Communism: The Depression Decade* (New York: Basic Books, 1984), 272.

82   National Guard: McWilliams, 227.

82   vigilante groups: Ibid., 256.

82   "But of course": Ibid., 237.

82   "fascist control": Loftis, 86.

82   "largely irrelevant": Klein, 118–19.

82   father of a school friend: Cray, 358.

82   "collective agriculture": Loftis, 167.

82   a quarter: "Why Stagnation?" Paul M. Sweezy, *Monthly Review*, June 1982.

82   "Next to war": Eric Hobsbawm, *The Age of Extremes: A History of the World, 1914–1991* (New York: Vintage, 1994), 94.

83   production tripled: Ibid., 96.

83   "Women folk": Woody Guthrie, "My Constitution and Me," *Daily Worker*, June 19, 1949, as cited in FBI report; see http:// web.ncf.ca/fl512/woody_guthrie/april_10_1951.html.

83   "little ten cent blue book": Ibid.

84   "not welcomed": Cray, 322.

84   "Woody never was": Ibid., 151.

84   "a convinced socialist": Ibid., 151.

84   "Throw out the cops": John Steinbeck, *The Grapes of Wrath* (New York: Viking, 1939), 571.

84 "I was interested": Loftis, 74.

84 "The old methods": Steinbeck, "Harvest Gypsies."

84 "men possessed": Loftis, 191.

84 "The old Lone Wolf": Hays, 166.

84 "I never heard": Holter and Deverell, 35.

85 he'd just become: Robbin, 23–24.

85 "Left wing": Klein, 122; and Robbin, 33.

85 three dollars a week: McWilliams, 270.

86 "nothing but a slave": *Woody at 100*, 1939 tape.

86 banned: Loftis, 163.

86 "a feller that knew": Denning, 272.

86 shut it down: Scott Miller, "Inside 'The Cradle Will Rock,'" www.newlinetheatre.com/cradle.htm.

86 Geer and Guthrie: Klein, 128–29.

86 "the songs of a people": *Asch Recordings*.

86 "[A] policeman will": *Woody Sez*, 15–17.

86 "You might say": *Woody Sez*, 34.

87 "Stalin stepped in": Klein, 129–31.

87 "Communist Joe Hill": Cantwell, 90.

87 "[He] wasn't Joe Hill": Shelton, 158.

87 "What d you think": Liner notes to *Another Side of Bob Dylan* (Columbia, 1964).

Chapter 6: No Martyr Is Among Ye Now

89 "nightingale sound": Notes to *Joan Baez in Concert: Part 2* (Vanguard, 1963).

90 "campfire program": Earl Robinson liner notes for "Alive and Well," (Aspen Records APN 30101), 1986 http://www .folkarchive.de/joehill.html.

90 liked the idea: Cray, 246.

91 "preachy": Dylan, *Chronicles*, 54.

91 "real and important": Ibid., 52.

91 "a Messianic figure": Ibid.

91 Hill was born: William M. Adler, *The Man Who Never Died: The Life, Times, and Legacy of Joe Hill, American Labor Icon* (New York: Bloomsbury, 2011), 97, 110.

91 "the capital of money": Vernon H. Jensen, *Heritage of Conflict: Labor Relations in the Nonferrous Metals Industry up to 1930* (New York: Greenwood Press, 1950), 47.

92 deputized residents: Ibid., 19–53.

92 "education, organization": Ibid., 55.

92 "a fair day's wages" and "without action": Jensen, 61; and Adler, 10.

92 "egotistical": J. Anthony Lukas, *Big Trouble: A Murder in a Small Western Town Sets Off a Struggle for the Soul of America* (New York, Simon & Schuster, 1997), 211.

92 "most militant": see George G. Suggs Jr., *Colorado's War on Militant Unionism* (Detroit: Wayne State University Press, 1972).

92 "the only salvation": Proclamation at 1901 WFM convention.

92 thirty-five thousand: Lukas, 221–26; and Jensen, 55.

93 bankrolled: Patrick Renshaw, *The Wobblies: The Story of Syndicalism in the United States* (New York: Anchor, 1967), 23.

93 "nothing in common": IWW constitution, www.iww.org /culture/official/preamble.shtml.

93 "take possession": Philip S. Foner, *History of the Labor Movement in the United States*, vol. 4, *The Industrial Workers of the World, 1905–1917* (New York, International Publishers, 1965), 4, 15.

93 wasn't through voting: Renshaw, 56.

93 "Political action": Ibid., 52.

94 "Wherever men": Jensen, 213.

94 "A fella": Steinbeck, *Grapes of Wrath*, 571.

94 bicker: Adler, 123.

94 "Get it": Jensen, 215.

94 "straight-forward": Ibid., 194.

94 splinter group: Adler, 123 and 121.

94 A decade of rising prices: Bogart, 693–94.

95 "We will have songs": Adler, 128, quoting Richard Brazier.

95   Some credit him: Ibid., 130.

95   "a few cold": Ibid., 12.

95   "Let others write": Ibid., 280.

96   "Rebel Girl": Ibid., 279.

96   peaked: Renshaw, 58.

96   descendants of the Boston Associates: Foner, vol. 4, p. 321.

96   twelve textile mills: Dalzell, 73 and Foner, vol. 4, p. 308.

96   average wage, etc.: Foner, vol. 4, 312, p. 309.

96   "Better to starve": Ibid., p. 316.

96   "a revolution": Ibid., pp. 330–39.

96   Harvard students: Steve Early, "Save Our Unions," *Monthly Review* 65, no. 9 (Feb. 2014).

96   "signal victory": Adler, 189.

97   paled compared: Foner, vol 4, pp. 350, 147; and Philip S. Foner, *History of the Labor Movement in the United States*, vol. 5, *The AFL in the Progressive Era, 1910–1915* (New York: International Publishers, 1980), 3.

97   at a copper mine: Adler, 28.

97   "Tin-Jesus": Ibid., 271.

97   "Gentlemen": Ibid., 298.

97   "Well, it don't do": Ibid., 324.

97   "I have nothing to say": Ibid., 306.

97   "Good-by": Ibid., 325.

98   "substantial importance": Dylan, *Chronicles*, 54.

98   switching out: see Lori Elaine Taylor, "Joe Hill Incorporated: We Own Our Past," in *Songs About Work: Essays in Occupational Culture*, ed. Archie Green (Bloomington: Folklore Institution, Indiana University Press, 1993).

98   By mid-February: Phillip Buehler, *Woody Guthrie's Wardy Forty: Greystone Park State Hospital Revisited* (Mt. Kisco, NY: Woody Guthrie Publications, 2013), 123.

98   "full of energy": Dave Van Ronk with Elijah Wald, *The Mayor of MacDougal Street: A Memoir* (New York: Da Capo Press, 2005), 161.

98   At the concert: Todd Harvey, *The Formative Dylan: Transmission and Stylistic Influences, 1961–1963* (Lanham, MD: Scarecrow Press, 2001), 100.

98   "I like more": Dylan, interview by Cynthia Gooding, *Folksinger's Choice*, Mar. 11, 1962, WBAI-FM, http://expectingrain.com /dok/int/gooding.html.

99   "At the carnival": Ibid.

99   "traditional stuff": Dylan, *Chronicles*, 228.

99   "working class songs": David King Dunaway and Molly Beer, *Singing Out: An Oral History of America's Folk Music Revivals* (New York: Oxford University Press, 2011), 130.

100   pokes fun: Harvey, 88.

100   "subterranean world": "In the Wind," liner notes to Peter, Paul and Mary's *In the Wind* (Warner Brothers, 1963).

100   over two years: Ruhlmann.

101   "so goddamned real": Nat Hentoff quoting Harry Jackson in the notes to *The Freewheelin' Bob Dylan* (Columbia, 1963).

101   "The **Truth**": Ruhlmann.

101   "earnestly political": McPhee, "Joan Baez—Folk Singing: Sybil with Guitar," *Time*, Nov. 23, 1962, http://bobdylanroots.com /baez2.html.

101   "pervading feeling": The Port Huron Statement of the Students for a Democratic Society, http://coursesa.matrix.msu .edu/~hst306/documents/huron.html.

101   "occurred to me": Dylan, *Chronicles*, 71.

101   "Delta blues": Dylan, Ibid., 70.

102   some fifty originals: Clinton Heylin, *Revolution in the Air: The Songs of Bob Dylan, 1957–1973* (Chicago: Chicago Review Press, 2009), 63.

102   raised on Guthrie and Seeger: Suze Rotolo, *A Freewheelin' Time: A Memoir of Greenwich Village in the Sixties* (New York: Broadway Books, 2008), 75.

102   her sister was: Dylan, *Chronicles*, 264.

103   stylistic breakthrough: Van Ronk, 206.

103 had scared him: Dylan, interview by Studs Terkel, WFMT Chicago, Spring 1963, https://www.youtube.com /watch?feature=player_embedded&v=t4nA3QwGPBg.

103 "From folksongs, I learned": Bob Coltman, *Paul Clayton and the Folksong Revival*, American Folk Music and Musicians 10 (Lanham, MD: Scarecrow Press, 2008), 140.

104 "the code": MusicCares Person of the Year speech, 2015 Grammys, www.rollingstone.com/music/news/read-bob-dylans -complete-riveting-musicares-speech-20150209.

104 "We have waited": Dr. Martin Luther King Jr., "Letter from Birmingham Jail," Apr. 16, 1963, http://abacus.bates.edu/admin /offices/dos/mlk/letter.html.

105 *Broadside*: Broadside, Late May 1962, http://singout.org /downloads/broadside/b006.pdf.

105 "the most important": Scaduto, 172.

106 "wasn't a pop songwriter": MusicCares Person of the Year speech, 2015 Grammys.

107 "COMPLICATED CIRCLE": "For Dave Glover," Newport Folk Festival program, 1963, http://singout.org/downloads /broadside/b035.pdf.

108 "a historic center": Stephen Kinzer, "In Minnesota's Iron Range, a Rare Victory for Labor," *New York Times*, Aug. 6, 2004.

108 major strike: Sounes, 18.

108 225 locals: Marcus C. Robyns, Katelyn Weber, and Laura Lipp, "Reluctant Revolutionaries: Finnish Iron Miners and the Failure of Radical Labor and Socialism on the Marquette Iron Range, 1900–1914," in *Northern Border: Essays on Michigan's Upper Peninsula and Beyond*, ed. Robert Archibald (Marquette: Northern Michigan University Press, 2014), 214 and 227.

108 "thronged": Jensen, 247.

108 "all of the towns": Lamppa, 207–10.

109 THIS VILLAGE IS NOT: Foner, vol. 4, pp. 487 and 497.

109 "The I.W.W. is not": Ibid., 498.

109 patrolled: Lamppa, 213–14.

109 "All that summer": Michael G. Karni, "Elizabeth Gurley Flynn and the Mesabi Strike of 1916," *Range History* 5, no. 4 (Winter 1981), www.minnesotahumanities.org/Resources /ElizabethGurleyFlynnandthestrikeof1916.pdf.

109 officially ended: Foner, vol. 4, pp. 500 and 514.

109 "treasonable conspiracy": Adler, 343.

109 "effectively suppressed": Ibid., 341–42.

109 "extremely volatile": Dylan, *Chronicles*, 231.

109 "the town I grew up in": Dylan, "11 Outlined Epitaphs."

Chapter 7: To Handle Men

111 "substantial gift": Lankton, *Cradle*, 20.

111 $10,000: Dobbs, 103.

111 "large bequest": Tharp, 198.

111 begun to drop: Thomas Arthur Rickard, "The Copper Mines of Lake Superior," *Engineering and Mining Journal*, 1905, 46.

111 "increasingly skeptical": Van Pelt; and Agassiz, *Letters*, 66.

111 "in confusion": Van Pelt.

111 "huge open pits": Agassiz, *Letters*, 63.

112 "Even if the pits": Lankton, *Cradle*, 20.

112 "cold demeanor": Winsor, 204, 210.

112 "nearly unanimous": Van Pelt.

112 "The thing I drive": "The Founding of the Calumet and Hecla Mine: 1866–1916," no author, pamphlet published by Calumet and Hecla, July 5, 1916 [hereafter C and H pamphlet].

112 "served his notice": Agassiz, *Letters*, 83.

112 "I get fearfully blue": Ibid., 68.

112 "If Quin had ever known": Courter, 66; and Agassiz, *Letters*, 66.

113 "laughed at everything": Thurner, *Calumet Copper*.

113 "perfectly frantic": Agassiz, *Letters*, 74.

113 "I don't wonder": Gates, 41.

113 "dead standstill": Agassiz, *Letters*, 77.

113 "such a rage": Ibid., 78.

113 "tried the mill": Courter, 67.

114 "the best I could": Agassiz, *Letters*, 81–82.

114 "The watchman": Ibid., 84.

114 "the Irish": Anthony S. Wax, "Calumet and Hecla Copper Mines: An Episode in the Economic Development of Michigan," *Michigan History* 16 (1932).

114 "I should shoot": Ibid.

114 back up: Agassiz, *Letters*, 84.

114 185 tons: Ibid., 85.

115 "second to none": Lankton, *Cradle*, 44.

115 8 percent: Gates, 44.

115 "a last resort": Richie Ward, *Into the Ocean World: The Biology of the Sea* (New York: Knopf, 1974), 158, quoting G. R. Agassiz from *Letters*.

115 next fifteen years: see Frank William Taussig, *Some Aspects of the Tariff Question* (Cambridge: Harvard University Press, 1915).

115 corporate pool: Gates, 47–48.

116 only so much: Hyde, 59.

116 "increasingly important": Hyde, 66.

116 "substantial subsidy": Gates, 52.

116 "to its stockholders": Lankton, *Guide*, 100.

116 "As long as": Gates, 50.

116 $25 million: Ibid., 44.

116 "out of the Dividend": Tharp, 230.

116 "You will find Alex": Agassiz, *Letters*, 97.

116 "I want to go down": Ibid., 399.

116 several million dollars: see Dobbs.

117 "The University of": Upton Sinclair, *The Goose Step: A Study in American Education* (Self-published, 1923), 62.

117 "no incentive": Dobbs, 118.

117 "distract myself": Ibid., 123.

117 "permanently saddened": Agassiz, *Letters*, 124.

117 "accustomed": Ibid., 89–90.

117 "ten-power field glasses": Angus Murdoch, *Boom Copper: The*

Story of the First U.S. Mining Boom (Calumet, MI: Roy W. Drier and Louis G. Koppel, 1964 reprint), 148.

117 "apple pie order": Dobbs, 111.

117 "What Mr. Aggasiz accomplished": C and H pamphlet.

117 "an object lesson": Thurner, *Rebels*, 33–34.

118 "curious combination": Ibid., *Rebels*, 19.

118 "worker satisfaction": Ibid., *Rebels*, 19.

118 "Hell upon Earth": Fredrich Engels, *The Condition of the Working Class in England in 1844, (*London: Swan Sonnenschein, 1892), 45, 48–53.

118 "the great factory": *Manifesto of the Communist Party*, ch. 1, https://www.marxists.org/archive/marx/works/1848 /communist-manifesto/ch01.htm.

118 "improving landlord": Dalzell, 18.

118 "all alike": Lankton, *Guide*, 214.

118 a dollar a room . . . included: Gates, 100; and US House of Representatives Committee on Mines and Mining, *Conditions in the Copper Mines of Michigan*, 63rd Congress, 2nd Session (Washington, DC: US Government Printing Office, 1914) [hereafter *Conditions* Hearings], 1441.

118 a third: Bernard Cook "Hungarians in Michigan's Copper Country," in *Northern Border*, 75.

119 ten public schools: Lankton, *Cradle*, 170.

119 "self-inflicted wound": Ibid., 167–88.

119 "self-sufficient empire": C. Harry Benedict, *Red Metal: The Calumet and Hecla Story*, (Ann Arbor: University of Michigan Press, 1952), 214.

119 broom factory: *Strike in the Copper Mining District of Michigan: Letter from the Secretary of Labor*, (Washington, Committee of Education and Labor, 1914), 126 [hereafter Secretary *Letter*].

119 "No mining company": Lankton, 144.

119 "toilet": Gates, 112.

119 "more and more": Agassiz, *Letters*, 236.

120 "I am sick": Ibid.

120 "everybody drives all over": Ibid., 30.

120 never made public: Thurner, *Rebels*, 34; and Lankton, *Cradle*, 194.

120 ordered off: Lankton, *Cradle*, 154; and Secretary *Letter*, 139.

120 a thousand pounds of rock: Secretary *Letter*, 36.

121 two-thirds: Lankton, 152, 112.

121 "native white": Secretary *Letter*, 133.

121 "We got more criticism": Thurner, *Rebels*, 37.

121 "dividends rose": Hyde, 52 and 62.

121 "cheerful cooperation": Lankton, 204.

121 increased wages: Ibid.

121 "cannot be dictated to": Hyde, 64–65.

122 "a class of men": Gates, 113.

122 Great Uprising: Michael D. Yates, *Why Unions Matter* (New York: Monthly Review Press, 1998), 27.

122 "best paid wage-earner": Tom A. Hamm, *Mines and Mineral Statistics, State of Michigan* (Lansing, MI: Robert Smith, 1902–3).

122 "Arcadia": Thurner, *Rebels*, 26.

122 could advance: Hyde, 45.

122 "a well-ordered social pattern": Gates, 112.

123 "may be pardoned": Murdoch, *Boom Copper*, 156.

123 "the system verges": Lankton, 144.

123 one of the richest: Dobbs, 103.

Chapter 8: Till the World Is Level

125 "He never should have": Cray, 161.

126 a third living: Klehr, 161, 164.

126 "faker and forthcoming fascist": Ibid., 145.

126 "People's Front": Serge Guilbaut, *How New York Stole the Idea of Modern Art: Abstract Expressionism, Freedom, and the Cold War* (Chicago: University of Chicago Press, 1983), 17.

126 welcomed socialists: Klehr, 145–46.

126 "largest sustained surge": Denning, 6.

126 "golden sunsets": Adler, 122; and "The West Is Dead," Ralph

Chaplin, *Bars and Shadows: The Prison Poems of Ralph Chaplin* (London: Allen & Unwin, 1922), 31.

127 "the promise": Denning, 27.

127 "the womb": Klehr, 200.

127 "essential part": "Browder Asks United Political Action," *New London Day* [CT], May 28, 1938.

127 "Twentieth Century Americanism": Earl Browder, see *The Communist Election Platform 1936* (New York: Workers Library Publishers, 1936), https://ia801802.us.archive.org/35 /items/CommunistElectionPlatform1936/360800-cpusa -communistelectionplatform.pdf.

127 "It did not say": Denning, 61.

128 "culture of unity": Klehr, 194.

128 "Hitlerism is": Richard M. Fried, *Nightmare in Red: The McCarthy Era in Perspective* (New York, Oxford University Press, 1991), 50.

128 "some wars": PofP, 29.

128 "the world is level": Kaufman, 45.

128 "foreign affiliations": Fried, 52.

128 "of Karl Marx": Denning, 124.

129 on a bus: Cray, 162–63.

129 so popular: Richard K. Hayes, "God Bless America, Land That I Love," Kate Smith Commemorative Organization, katesmith .org/gba.html.

130 "a new hymn": John Shaw, *This Land That I Love: Irving Berlin, Woody Guthrie, and the Story of Two American Anthems* (New York: PublicAffairs, 2013), 134.

130 1940 conventions: Chuck Miller, "The History and Legacy of 'God Bless America,'" *Albany Times-Union*, July 3, 2010, http:// blog.timesunion.com/chuckmiller/the-history-and-legacy-of -god-bless-america/2315.

130 self-satisfied: Klein, 136.

131 Guthrie recorded: Ibid., 140, 447.

131 "a dictatorship": Maurice Isserman, *Which Side Were You On?*

The American Communist Party During the Second World War (Middletown, CT: Wesleyan University Press, 1982), 60.

132 "very quick": Heylin, 37.

132 "big truck": Szwed, 157–58.

132 "authentic music": Ibid., 143, 155.

132 burned it: Ibid., 9.

132 "the song heritage": Cantwell, 70.

133 "only true folk songs": Szwed, 11.

133 "true voice": Georgina Boyes, *The Imagined Village: Culture, Ideology and the English Folk Revival* (Manchester, UK: Manchester University Press, 1993), 7–9.

133 "lost England": Boyes, 71, quoting E. V. Lucas, *London Lavender* (London: Methuen, 1912).

133 "the negro": Cantwell, 71.

133 "Home on the Range": Ibid., 72.

133 "cold indifference": Szwed, 30.

134 "soaked": Ibid., 25.

134 "Communism": Ibid., 29.

134 "unless I go": Ibid., 33.

134 Calumet: Ibid., 127.

134 "summaries": Ibid., 38.

134 "to try and get": Ibid., 37.

134 mixed blues: Ibid., 71.

134 "my worst enemy": Ibid., 123.

134 "my big boss": March of Time newsreel, 1935, https://www.youtube.com/watch?v=QxykqBmUCwk.

135 "young admirer": Szed, 69.

135 "the wild land": Cantwell, 90; and Szwed, 154.

135 "stupid hill-billy show": Szwed, 118.

135 "broader and more interesting": Ibid., 143.

135 "just ambled out" Cantwell, 254.

136 "New York sure is": Klein, 150.

136 "that will fool": Cray, 168.

136 capture a history: Szwed, 69.

136 "I kept looking": LC.

137 "either an Indian": LC.

137 "hangknot": PofP, 37.

137 "The best way": *Woody Sez*, 135–36.

137 "rock bottom": Ibid.

137 "eight records": David King Dunaway, *How Can I Keep from Singing? Pete Seeger* (New York: McGraw-Hill, 1981), 93.

137 "poor farmers' songs": Cray, 182.

137 "Everybody knew": Ibid., 174.

137 "Karl Marx": Kaufman, 50.

137 Oklahoma's Communist: Cohen, *Rainbow Quest*, 27.

138 Guthrie's Joad: Thirty years later, Dylan would mix John Hardy with Tom Joad with Woody Guthrie to create a song about the fictional John Wesley Harding, "a friend to the poor / . . . always known to lend a helping hand."

138 "ain't about me": PofP, 41.

138 "ain't mine": PofP, 45.

138 "out of the hearts": Klein, 159.

139 "lost and hungry": PofP, 42.

139 "more radical": Klein, 159.

139 "not paid for": Dunaway, 69.

140 lost a professorship: Dunaway, 30.

140 Bolshevik model: see R. Serge Denisoff, *Great Day Coming: Folk Music and the American Left* (Urbana, IL.: University of Illinois Press, 1971).

140 "songs for the masses": Ann. M. Pescatello, *Charles Seeger: A Life in American Music* (Pittsburgh: University of Pittsburgh Press, 1992), 110.

140 "a badge of servitude": Cantwell, 92; and Kaufman, 35.

140 "Unquestionably": Cohen, *Rainbow Quest*, 22.

140 Young Communist League: Dunaway, 52.

140 "trying my best": Lead Belly, *Leadbelly Songbook*, ed. Moses Asch and Alan Lomax (New York: Oak Publications, 1962) 7.

140 "not authentic": Dunaway, 131.

140 Uncle Dave: Dunaway, 55.

140 Highlander: J Cynthia McDermott, "Horton, Highlander, and the Habituation of Democracy," www.academia.edu/364092 /horton_highlander_and_the_habituation_of_democracy.

141 "most valuable thing": Cray, 227.

141 "the *Daily Worker*": Cray, 189.

141 "a communist": PofP, 49.

141 a regular: Cray, 190.

141 a songfest: Szwed, 166.

142 Ray had joined: Szwed, 108; and Patrick McGilligan, *Nicholas Ray: The Glorious Failure of an American Director* (New York: HarperCollins, 2011), 28–29.

142 "act the fool": Szwed, 108.

142 "money so fast": Cray, 196.

142 "hungry folks": Ibid., 197.

143 boycott: Ibid., 195.

143 "got disgusted": PofP, 9.

143 "commonism": Klein, 179.

143 "depressed": Cray, 205.

143 "bloody revolution": notes to *Asch Recordings*, vol. 3, p. 8.

Chapter 9: We Are the Bosses Now

145 socialists: Steve Lehto, *Death's Door: The Truth Behind Michigan's Largest Mass Murder* (Troy, MI: Momentum Books, 2006), 15.

145 separate racial category: Gary Kaunonen and Aaron Goings, *Community in Conflict: A Working-Class History of the 1913–14 Michigan Copper Strike and the Italian Hall Tragedy* (East Lansing: Michigan State University Press, 2013), 50.

145 At nineteen: Wax, "Calumet and Hecla Copper Mines."

145 thirty-seven: Bob Carlton, "Brief History of the Miscowaubik Club," 1990, www.clintnmary.org/ClubHistory.htm.

146 Harvard geologist: Lankton, *Cradle*, 73.

146 "try and get out": *Conditions* Hearings, H. Res. 387, Part 4, March 2–4, 1914, p. 1476.

146 "I like him": Agassiz, *Letters*, 402.

146 the majority: Renshaw, 21.

146 70 percent: Ibid., 22.

146 1 percent: Jerry Stanley, *Big Annie of Calumet: A True Story of the Industrial Revolution,* (New York: Crown, 1996), 1.

147 signs of rebellion: Lankton, *Cradle*, 212–13.

147 a decade later: Ibid., 213.

147 "getting old": Gates, 92.

147 turned down: Ibid., 52.

147 kept rising: Ibid., 75.

147 80 percent: Hyde, 67.

147 20 percent: Gates, 59.

147 on average: Lankton, *Cradle*, 110–11.

147 Forty percent: Ibid., 111, 113.

148 complaint: Hyde, 69.

148 "be prepared": Thurner, *Rebels*, 36.

148 "coddled": Lankton, *Cradle*, 201, 217.

148 "prairie fire": Bloor, 54; and Renshaw, 32.

148 "dominant class": Thurner, *Rebels*, 30.

148 a foothold: Ibid., 28.

149 "You say you cannot": see Dale Featherling, *Mother Jones, the Miners' Angel,* (Carbondale: Southern Illinois Press, 1979); and Elliot J. Gorn, *Mother Jones: An American Life* (New York: Hill & Wang, 2015), 162.

149 "not to take": Lankton, *Cradle*, 209.

149 distracted: Jensen, 162.

149 fewer than thirty: Thurner, *Rebels*, 31, 35; and Lankton, *Cradle*, 219.

149 "unionism": Thurner, *Rebels*, 30.

149 A year later: Neil Betten, "Strike on the Mesabi—1907," *Minnesota History*, Fall 1967.

149 "no violence": Betten.

149 "linked": Thurner, *Rebels*, 31.

149 solidarity parade: Kaunonen, 45.

150 all-time high: see Gates.

150 highest wages: Lehto, 18; and Thurner, *Rebels*, 34.

150 left for Montana: Jensen, 276.

150 "heaviest individual taxpayer": Obituary: "Quincy A. Shaw Passes Away," *Boston Daily Globe*, June 13, 1908, http://rememberjamaicaplain.blogspot.com/2008/02/quincy-shaw-very-rich-guy.html#comment-form.

150 seventy-three: Dobbs, 247.

150 Rodolphe Agassiz: Secretary, *Letter*, 141.

150 "little kingdom": Jensen, 287.

151 "property rights": Foner, vol. 5, pp. 103, 115.

151 "monopoly of labor": Ibid., pp. 125–26.

151 one-man units: Lankton, *Cradle*, 105.

151 competitive: Secretary, *Letter*, 88.

151 "few would express": Thurner, *Rebels*, 38.

152 "years of speech-making": Thurner, *Rebels*, 39, quoting Angus Murdoch.

152 a thousand new: *Lankton,* Cradle, 220.

152 "We have slept": Kaunonen, 124.

152 "the gospel of discontent": *Conditions* Hearings, vol. 4–7, p. 1474.

152 twenty-two states: Secretary, *Letter*, 37; and Thurner, *Rebels*, 35.

152 "useful to": Jensen, 244.

152 "absolute necessity": Thurner, *Rebels*, 37.

152 "practically impossible": Kaunonen, 101.

152 "We hope you realize": Lehto, 25.

152 "Your failure": Ibid., 2, 21.

152 doubled again: Lankton, *Cradle*, 220; and Hyde, 71.

153 "Approve": Lankton, *Cradle*, 26–27.

153 Five days later: Lehto, 25; and Thurner, 46.

153 "precipitated the strike": *Commercial and Financial Chronicle*, Dec. 19, 1914, p. 1800.

153 "very quiet": Lehto, 28–29.

153 "A mob": Lehto, 30.

153 "We are the bosses": Thurner, *Rebels*, 6.

153 "very humiliating": Ibid., 6.

153 "red socialism": *Conditions* Hearings, 1382.

154 telegram: Lehto, 29–30.

154 "practically nothing": *Conditions* Hearings, 1487.

154 "No attempt": Secretary, *Letter*, 9.

154 "to avoid": Thurner, *Rebels*, 6.

154 "a foreign body": Lankton, *Cradle*, 225.

154 dispatched: Lehto, 32.

154 "We served": Thurner, *Rebels*, 49.

154 "private security": Lehto, 32–33.

155 "must be killed": Lankton, *Cradle*, 226.

155 "straight-backed": Lehto, 34, 35.

155 "feel convinced": Ibid., 34.

155 "The grass": Stanley, 29.

155 "too big for a cat": Lehto, 43.

155 their demands: Hyde, 71.

155 "If the Governor": Lehto, 42.

155 all the blame: *Conditions* Hearings, 1358.

156 "great majority": Kaunonen, 105.

156 "Industrious, loyal": Secretary, *Letter*, 58.

156 eighteen hundred: Lehto, 46; and Thurner, *Rebels*, 50–51.

156 "Where in the name": Thurner, *Rebels*, 52.

156 "wrong fundamentally": Jensen, 279.

156 "real grievances": MTU Archives, letter, Ferris to MacNaughton, Sept. 13, 1913.

156 pulling out: Thurner, *Rebels*, 60; and Jensen, 280.

156 "Nobody didn't have": Thurner, *Rebels*, 72–74.

156 thousands showed: Kaunonen, 154.

156 "Boston coppers": Thurner, *Rebels*, 74.

156 "very large": Lehto, 53.

157 three dollars a week: Secretary, *Letter*, 47–48.

157 "a nucleus": Kaunonen, 75.

157 "More picketing": Lehto, 60.

157 fourteen-thousand-man: Ibid., 63.

157 "Kill me!": Ibid., 62.

157 prohibiting all: Thurner, *Rebels*, 93.

157 "Don't be a scab": Secretary, *Letter*, 49.

158 three thousand: Lehto, 67.

158 throwing snowballs: Secretary, *Letter*, 72.

158 undercut: Staley, 63; and Lankton, *Cradle*, 234.

158 "imperative": *Conditions* Hearings, 1364.

158 "give us concern": Lehto, 78.

158 "a menace": Lehto, 77; and *Conditions* Hearings, 1536.

159 "little civil war": Thurner, *Rebels*, 125.

159 cut back: Ibid., 102.

159 "whipped": Lankton, *Cradle*, 234; and Thurner, *Rebels*, 125.

159 "iniquity": Thurner, *Rebels*, 101.

159 "chose to work": Ibid., 122.

159 FOREIGN AGITATORS: Lehto, 81.

159 "extermination": Ibid., 76–77.

160 more than two-thirds: Lankton, *Cradle*, 229.

160 *tsaari*: Kaunonen, 136.

160 "thousands of mothers": MTU Archives, letter, Ferris to MacNaughton, Dec. 15, 1913.

160 "alien agitators": MTU Archives, letter, MacNaughton to Ferris, Dec. 17, 1913.

160 "insured against": Lankton, *Guide*, 224.

160 "no right": Lehto, 81.

160 "absolutely and unqualifiedly": Lankton, *Cradle*, 236; and *Conditions* Hearings, 1471.

Chapter 10: The Truth Just Twists

162 750: Gary Younge, "1963: The Defining Year of the Civil Rights Movement," *Guardian*, May 7, 2013.

162 "a moral issue": John F. Kennedy, Civil Rights Address, June 11, 1963, www.americanrhetoric.com/speeches/jfkcivilrights.htm.

162 "They met us": "Marching for Freedom in Greenwood," Civil Rights Movement Veterans timeline, www.crmvet.org/tim /timhis63.htm#1963fdgreen.

163 "Bobby Dillon": "Northern Folk Singers Help Out at Negro Festival in Mississippi," *New York Times*, July 7, 1963, www .bobdylanroots.com/northern.html.

163 "first time": "Folk Artists, Local Citizens Attend SNCC Folk Festival in Mississippi Delta," SNCC News Release, July 8, 1963, http://content.wisconsinhistory.org/cdm/ref/collection /p15932coll2/id/4645.

163 "We all thought": Shelton, 149–50.

163 "his facility": Rotolo, 139.

163 Ladner: Joyce Ladner, "For a SNCC Member, Aug. 28, 1963, Was a Day of Joy, Anger and Hope." *Washington Post*, Aug. 27, 2013.

163 nonthreatening: James Forman, *The Making of Black Revolutionaries* (New York: Macmillan, 1972), 333.

164 "no truth": Dylan, "11 Outlined Epitaphs."

164 Brecht: Harvey, 64.

164 "Red Iron Ore": Ibid., 76.

166 "protest poet"; Rotolo, 350, quoting Richard Shelton's review, *New York Times*, Oct. 28, 1963.

166 "haywire": Scaduto, 187.

167 "an insider": Dylan, in *No Direction Home*.

167 "I wish sometimes": Transcript of Bob Dylan's Remarks at the Bill of Rights Dinner at the Americana Hotel, Dec. 13, 1963, "Bob Dylan and the NECLC," www.corliss-lamont.org/dylan .htm.

167 "I am sick": "A MESSAGE from Bob Dylan," www.corliss -lamont.org/dylan.htm.

167 "once this is straight": Ibid.

167 "I am with you": Letter from Bob Dylan to *Broadside* magazine, 1964, www.lettersofnote.com/2012/07/let-me-begin-by-not -beginnin.html.

168   "famous": Ibid.

168   "golden age": see *The Golden Age of Capitalism: Reinterpreting the Postwar Experience*, ed. Stephen A. Marglin and Juliet B. Schor (Oxford, UK: Clarendon Press, 1990).

168   tenfold: Hobsbawm, 258, 261.

168   America erected: Ibid., 263.

168   per capita output: Samule Bowles and Robert Boyer, "A Wage-Led Employment Regime: Income Distribution, Labor Discipline, and Aggregate Demand in Welfare Capitalism," in Marglin and Schor, 187.

168   Fordism: Hobsbawm, 261, 264–65.

168 $2 billion: Ibid., 328.

168   union wages: Melvyn Dubofsky and Foster Rhea Dulles, *Labor in America: A History* (Wheeling, IL: Halan Davidson, 2010), 362.

169   from a quarter: Hobsbawm, 270.

169   steelworkers: Dubofsky and Dulles, 355.

169   no idea: Scaduto, 193.

170   "jukebox / gumbo": notes to *Another Side of Bob Dylan* (Columbia, 1964).

171   "expectancy": Richard Fariña, "Baez and Dylan: A Generation Singing Out!" *Younger Than That Now: The Collected Interviews with Bob Dylan* (New York: Thunder's Mouth Press, 2004).

172   "Rock & roll": Dave Marsh, *The Beatles' Second Album* (New York: Rodale Books, 2007), 35.

172   "most brutal": Alan Hanson, "Did Sinatra Really Bad Mouth Elvis and His Music in '57?" elvis-history-blog.com/elvis-sinatra .html, quoting *Los Angeles Mirror News*, Oct. 28, 1957.

172   the only group: "The Beatles Occupy the Billboard Hot 100 Top Five," The Beatles Bible, www.beatlesbible.com/1964/04/04 /beatles-billboard-hot-100-top-five.

173   "America ought": Douglas R. Gilbert, *Forever Young: Photographs of Bob Dylan*, text by Dave Marsh (New York: Da Capo Press, 2005).

173   had collected: Dave Marsh, *The Heart of Rock and Soul* (New York: Plume, 1989), 64–65.

174 "politics": Bob Dylan, "My Back Pages."

174 "If white America": from "Walking with the Wind," by John Lewis, as quoted in "Mississippi Freedom Summer Events," www.crmvet.org/tim/tim64b.htm.

175 "Any songwriter": Irwin Silber, "An Open Letter to Bob Dylan," *Sing Out!* Nov., 1964.

176 "My whole concert": Heylin, 157.

177 "broker state": see Michael Lind, *Land of Promise: An Economic History of the United States* (New York: HarperCollins, 2012).

178 no-strike: Phillip Dray, *There Is Power in a Union: The Epic Story of Labor in America* (New York: Doubleday, 2010), 551.

178 "tame": Stephen Marglin, "Lessons of the Golden Age: An Overview," in Marglin and Schor, 6; and see Kevin Boyle, *The UAW and the Heyday of American Liberalism, 1945–1968* (Ithaca, NY: Cornell University Press, 1995).

178 fewer than 10 percent: Marglin and Schor, 44.

178 to fall: Dray, 513.

178 "going backward": Dubofsky, 345–46.

178 "reincarnation": Dray, 562.

178 now established role: Lichtenstein, 144.

178 "silent majority": Dray, 574.

178 refused to support: Lichtenstein, 187.

179 "few new ideas": Dubofksy, 363.

179 out of SNCC's: Robert Cohen, *Freedom's Orator: Mario Savio and the Radical Legacy of the 1960s* (New York: Oxford, 2009), 52.

179 six thousand: Cohen, 192.

179 "There's a time": Free Speech Movement, UC Berkeley—Online Audio Recordings, www.lib.berkeley.edu/MRC/FSM /fsmchronology1.html.

181 "all dead": liner notes to *Bringing It All Back Home* (Columbia, 1965).

182 feed the flames: see Malcolm X in Selma, Feb. 4, 1965, www .youtube.com/watch?v=mg5uQQw2leU.

182 over three hundred thousand: www.historycentral.com /Vietnam/rollingthunder.html.

182 Baez, Seeger: "The March to Montgomery," Mar. 7–24, Mississippi Freedom Summer Events, Civil Rights Movement Veterans timeline, www.crmvet.org/tim/timhis65 .htm#1965m2m.

182 "I felt": Shelton, 150.

183 "There's more to it": Dylan, interview by Paul J. Robbins, Santa Monica, CA, Mar. 1965, *Los Angeles Free Press*, Sept. 17 and 24, 1965, www.interferenza.com/bcs/interw/65-nov08.htm.

183 "the entire system": "Malcolm X Criticizes Civil Rights Bill," *NBC News*, June 24, 1964, NBC Learn, https://archives .nbclearn.com/portal/site/k-12/browse/?cuecard=1460.

183 "We shall eliminate": Martin Luther King Jr., foreword to *A Freedom Budget for all Americans* (New York: A. Philip Randolph Institute, Jan. 1967), 1.

183 "Let us march": Civil Rights Movement Veterans timeline, www.crmvet.org/tim/timhis65.htm.

183 change strategies: Clayborne Carson, *In Struggle: SNCC and the Black Awakening of the 1960s* (Cambridge, MA: Harvard University Press, 1981), 101–2, 142.

183 "to be effective": Carson, 151.

183 "to confront white America": Anne Braden, quoted in Carson, 208.

Chapter 11: Struggle

185 "common touch" Cray, 208.

185 "protect the system": FDR address at the Democratic State Convention, Sept. 1936.

186 "I have not sought": *Address at the Democratic State Convention, Syracuse, NY*, Sept. 29, 1936, www.presidency.ucsb.edu /ws/?pid=15142.

186 "only New Deal": Kaufman, 65.

186 "a purgative": Reisner, 165.

186 "economic democracy": *Roll On, Columbia: Woody Guthrie and* the *Bonneville Power Administration*, Michael Majdic and Denise Matthews, producers/directors (Eugene: University of Oregon, 2000) https://library.uoregon.edu/ec/wguthrie/brochure.pdf ; and Boyle, 25.

186 "several thousand": *Live Wire.*

186 impossible: *Roll On Columbia.*

187 "from just about every": liner notes, *Columbia River Collection*, (Rounder Records, 1987).

187 "He loved": *Roll On Columbia.*

187 "the pessimism": filmmaker Robert Grierson quoted in William Stott, *Documentary Expression and Thirties America* (Chicago: University of Chicago Press, 1973), 9.

187 "to show things": Lewis Hine, *Men at Work*, http://xroads .virginia.edu/~ma99/hall/documentary/coverpage.html.

187 to dignify the usual: Stott, 49.

187 "the fullest sense": John North quoted in Stott, 24.

187 "Art is a weapon": Hallie Flanagan, "A Theatre Is Born," *Theatre Arts Monthly* 15, no. 11 (Nov. 1931), 910.

188 "a-going to waste": Guthrie, *Live Wire.*

188 Over 90 percent: Reisner, 169.

188 "should tell": Stott, 29.

189 $266.66: Robert C. Carriker, "Ten Dollars a Song: Woody Guthrie Sells His Talent to the Bonneville Power Administration," *Columbia* 15, no. 1 (Spring 2001).

189 Almanacs were singing: Ronald Cohen and David Samuelson, *Songs for Political Action* (Bear Family Records, 1996), 17.

189 "stuck so full": PofP, 69.

189 "sad mismatch": Ibid., 69.

189 "the downtrodden": Cray, 213.

189 "live cooperatively": Hays, 85.

190 "chief helper": Doris Willens, *Lonesome Traveler: The Life of Lee Hays* (New York: Norton, 1988), 26.

190 "national movement": Willens, 81.

190 "we've got to do": PofP, "Dear Pete, Mill & Lee," 53–54.

191 American unions involved: Kaufman, 73.

191 "Our idea": PofP, 82.

191 San Francisco: Cray, 223.

191 "the most important thing": Robbin, 150.

192 Seeger remembered: Cray, 226–27.

192 Michigan's Upper Peninsula: Ibid., 227.

192 Flynn brought: Kaufman, 72.

192 "walked like somebody": Hays, 153.

192 "authentic thing": Cray, 229.

192 "pretended" and "never picked": Sis Cunningham, Gordon Friesen in Cray, 231.

193 "Woody represents": Hays, 150.

193 "You will see": Robbin, 154.

193 "on your mind": PofP, 78.

193 "confidential information": Memos dated June 9, 1941, and July 18, 1941, from FBI report on Woody Guthrie, obtained through the Freedom of Information Act.

193 "but greed": PofP, 104.

193 "great marching song": Koppleman, 90.

193 "a weapon": PofP, 91.

194 "doing good work": Letter to Lomax, Dec. 1941, Library of Congress, https://www.loc.gov/resource/afc1940004 .afc1940004_011/.

194 "exhilarating": Isserman, 127.

194 rally: Ibid., 158.

194 still tiny: Ibid., 3 and 149.

194 "weren't willing": Dunaway, 102.

195 Within weeks: Cray, 240.

195 "glad to be loose": BfG, 299.

195 "What is an outlaw?": PofP, 79–80.

196 "Dance is a weapon": Ellen Graff, *Stepping Left: Dance and Politics in New York City, 1928–1942* (Durham, NC: Duke University Press, 1997), 35.

196 *Folksay:* Graff, 142.

196   daughter of: PofP, 89.

196   *American Document:* Maureen Needham Costonis, "Martha Graham's American Document: A Minstrel Show in Modern Dance Dress," *American Music* 9, no. 3: 297–310.

196   "business of organization": PofP, 74.

196   "tromped": Ibid., 73.

196   "why socialism": Ibid., 74.

197   "lover and teacher": Klein, 326.

197   seventeen million: Guilbaut, 90.

197   nine million: Robert H. Ziegler, *American Workers, American Unions*, 1925–1985 (New York: McGraw-Hill, 1981), 97.

197   10 percent: Dubofksy, 92, 303–4.

197   thirty-four people: Isserman, 137.

197   40 percent: Marty Jezer, *The Dark Ages: Life in the United States 1945–1960* (Boston: South End Press, 1982), 25.

198   no-strike pledge: Isserman, 137.

198   "honor and the privilege": Holter and Deverell, 65.

199   many of his friends: Isserman, 181.

199   NMU: Robert Greenberg, "An Overview of the History of the National Maritime Union (NMU): 1935–1948," www .ciscohouston.com/essays/nmu.shtml.

199   "why we're fighting": PofP, 208.

199   "Talking Merchant Marine": Kaufman, 103.

199   highest percentage of dead: Cray, 270; and Greenberg.

199   read Marx: Cray, 271.

199   "men of all tongues": Woody Guthrie, "Ten Songs," *Woody Guthrie Songbook*, Apr. 3, 1945, www.woodyguthrie.de/songbook .html#east.

199   "to suspect": Cray, 271.

200   "When I seen": Klein, 271.

200   "some strange musician": Walt Whitman, "The Mystic Trumpeter," www.bartleby.com/142/249.html.

200   "born on that spot": Isserman, 157.

200   "permanent member": Ibid., 185 and 215.

200   1938 peak: Ibid., 205.

200   "I'm a communist": Cray, 276–77.

201   "hilltop and sunny mountain harmonies": Ibid., 277.

201   jump from: see *Woody at 100* for list of recordings, 140–41.

201   hundred fifty songs: *Woody at 100*.

202   "give a damn": *Asch Recordings*, vol. 2.

202   "twisted and hurt": Cray, 280.

202   "pro-Russian": FBI, Feb. 1944.

202   "thank my God": Cray, 283.

203   "I hate a song": Woody Guthrie, "I Hate a Song," www
       .woodyguthrie.org/biography/woodysez.htm.

204   "Every band": Cray, 286.

204   "musical newspaper": Ibid., 287.

204   "dramatic documentary": Ibid., 195.

204   "word for word": Kaufman, 118.

205   "Buffalo Skinners": Jurgen Kloss, "On the Trail of 'The Buffalo
       Skinners,'" 2010–2012, http://justanothertune.com/html
       /buffaloskinners.html.

206   "Worker's Life": Letter to Asch from Brooklyn 1945, *Woody at
       100*, 48.

206   Foster was: William Z. Foster, *Pages from a Worker's Life* (New
       York: International Publishers, 1939; 1978), 40.

206   "notorious revision": Isserman, 217–18.

207   elected: Ibid., 229.

207   "one organization": Kaufman, 112.

207   basic training: Cray, 289.

207   "pet album": Ibid., 287.

207   "disillusioned": *Woody at 100*.

208   "a human being is": *American Folksongs*, 45–46.

208   "best sounding": PofP, 157, 160.

208   "bubbly": Ibid., 176.

209   "inevitable result": Stalin, Speech at Meeting of Voters of Stalin
       Electoral District, Moscow, Feb. 9, 1946, www.marx2mao.com
       /Stalin/SS46.html.

209 "[p]olice governments": *Winston Churchill's Iron Curtain Speech,* http://history1900s.about.com/od/churchillwinston/a/Iron-Curtain.htm.

209 Two million workers: Dubofsky, 323; and Jezer, 78.

209 conservative Republican: Lichtenstein, 112.

209 "don't like my": PofP, 173.

209 "empty spot": Cray, 311.

209 "Just dizzy": Klein, 304.

210 Guthrie's turn: PofP, 157.

Chapter 12: Take a Trip with Me in 1913

211 "mittens": Bloor, 122.

211 first body: Ibid., 123.

212 most of the donors: Ibid., 124.

212 "I love my children": Ibid., 125.

212 Moments after: Ibid., 125, 126.

212 "a red flag": Ibid., 126.

212 not very successful: Ibid., 129.

212 "granted": Ibid., 131.

213 4,200: Secretary, *Letter,* 133.

213 divided in two: Stanley, 69.

213 twenty-three steps: Benedict, 229.

213 "foreigners": Lankton, *Cradle,* 230.

213 Mother Goose: Stanley, 67.

213 "Well, Peter": *Condition* Hearings, 2074.

214 began to shove: Lehto, 88–92.

214 "on my knees": Kaunonen, 184.

214 "going out so fast": Ibid., 184.

214 "all filled up": Ibid., 186.

214 "one solid mass": Thurner, *Rebels,* 146.

214 less than three: Stanley, 71.

214 photographs taken: See J. W. Nara photographs, in MTU Archives, http://nara.lib.mtu.edu.

214 "Disaster": Lehto, 95.

215 fifty of those: Stanley, 70.

215 "full up": Thurner, *Rebels*, 150.

215 Almost fifty: Lankton, *Cradle,* 237; and Lehto, 148.

215 a photograph: see Nara photograph in MTU Archives.

215 more than double: Lankton, *Cradle*, 237.

215 "My information": Thurner, *Rebels*, 153.

215 "to capitalize": Lehto, 102–3; and Thurner, *Rebels*, 158.

215 "notorious": Lehto, 108.

216 "put up job": Ibid., 105.

216 "to incite": Ibid., 110.

216 $25,000: Lankton, *Cradle,* 237.

216 "revolver": *Conditions* Hearings, 2258.

216 "If you ever": Ibid., 2259.

216 later denied: Lehto, 120; Thurner, *Rebels*, 163.

216 small coffins: See Nara photos in MTU Archives.

217 kidnapped: Lehto, 123.

217 "not charity": Ibid.

217 "the stampede": Ibid., 143.

217 no indictments: Ibid., 143, 152.

217 inconclusive: Bloor, 126–27.

217 two thousand: Thurner, *Rebels*, 178.

217 "is just": Ibid., 162.

217 "too many Socialists": Ibid., 178.

218 "I am going to say": Ibid., 179.

218 "jackals": Ibid., 241–42.

218 "if the men": Ibid., 218.

218 $800,000: Lankton, *Guide*, 235.

218 "we still believe": Thurner, *Rebels*, 227.

218 Nine months after: Thurner, *Rebels*, 229.

218 never again: Lankton, *Cradle*, 239–40.

219 20 percent: Ibid., 246.

219 C&H cut: Ibid., 242.

219 eight thousand: Ibid., 244.

219 halve: Ibid., 245.

219 scavenged: Lankton, *Guide*, 266.

219 finally got a union: Lankton, *Cradle*, 258. Around this time, a folk song collector in the region discovered that Finns—now mostly farmers and loggers—still observed the anniversary of Joe Hill's execution each November 19. See James P. Leary and Richard March, "Farm, Forest and Factory: Songs of Midwestern Labor," in *Songs About Work: Essays in Occupational Culture for Richard A. Reuss*, ed. Archie Green (Bloomington: Folklore Institute, Indiana University Press, 1993), 242.

222 "conspiratorial deputies": Thurner, *Rebels,* 151–53.

223 "lousy, miserable song": Lehto, 184.

223 "post-war repression": Bloor, 111, 139.

223 doubling: Jeremy Brecher, *Strike!* (San Francisco: Straight Arrow Books, 1972), 103, 111, 117.

223 hundreds of Wobblies: Bloor, 144.

223 to Russia: Yates, 64–65.

223 "The land and all": Bloor, 141.

223 cofounding: Ibid., 160.

223 "real folk history": PofP, 197.

225 Blacklisting: see Richard M. Fried.

225 "1913 Massacre": *Struggle* was reissued with some additional songs in 1976, as Moe Asch's idea of an alternative bicentennial celebration.

226 early girlfriend: Heylin, 33.

226 "just now": PofP, 172–73.

226 look at blueprints: see Lehto, 175–78; and *1913 Massacre*, documentary film, Ken Ross and Louis V. Galdieri, producers /directors (Dreamland Pictures, 2011), http://1913massacre.com.

227 even at: Lehto, 88.

227 mostly found: Ibid., 177.

228 "nothing in the world": PofP, 104.

Chapter 13: How Does It Feel?

229 "part of the American tradition": Helen C. Camp, *Iron in her Soul: Elizabeth Gurly Flynn and the American Left* (Pullman: Washington State University Press, 1995), 213.

229 "The real issue": Cedric Belfrage, *The American Inquisition 1945–1960: A Profile of the "McCarthy Era"* (New York: Thunder's Mouth Press, 1989), 33–34.

230 "thirty-five years": Jezer, 96.

230 "witch hunt": John C. Culver and John Hyde, *American Dreamer: A Life of Henry Wallace* (New York: Norton, 2001), 445.

230 "musical desk": Cray, 327.

230 "The road is rocky": "The Road Is Rocky," Association for Cultural Equity archives, http://research.culturalequity.org/get -audio-detailed-recording.do?recordingId=12995.

230 "being used": Culver and Hyde, 459–67.

231 "nigger lover": Ibid., 493.

231 "the hopes and dreams": Willens, 106.

231 "following Communist": FBI report; and Cray, 322.

231 continuing to appear: Guthrie, "My Constitution and Me."

231 local papers: Martin Duberman, *Paul Robeson* (New York: The New Press, 1995), 369.

231 "Our objective": Steve Courtney, "Peekskill's Days of Infamy: The Robeson Riots of 1949," *Peekskill Reporter Dispatch*, Sept. 5, 1982, www.bencourtney.com/peekskillriots.

231 "back to Russia": Courtney.

232 "seen a lot": Willens, 114.

232 WAKE UP: Courtney.

232 "infiltrate every phase": *Red Channels: The Report of Communist Influence in Radio and Television* (New York: Counterattack, June 1950), 5.

232 "beat the blacklist" Willens, 134.

233 "such a box": Cantwell, 179.

233 a "great synthesis": Willens, 111.

233 "unreliable performer": Seeger interview by Tim Robbins, Pacifica Radio, 2006, https://www.youtube.com /watch?v=RX3aP1DAH-c.

233 "The Peekskill Story": Fred Hellerman biography, www .allmusic.com/artist/fred-hellerman-mn0000797811/biography.

233 "We felt": Willens, 111.

234 "the opposite": Ibid., 133.

234 "congratulating myself": Ibid., 120–21.

234 "self-censoring": Ibid., 152.

234 "didn't approve": Ronald D. Cohen, *Woody Guthrie: Writing America's Songs* (New York: Routledge, 2012), 38.

234 "so wrapped up": Willens, 134.

234 might make reference: *The Weavers at Carnegie Hall* (Vanguard Records, 1957).

234 Travers heard: Dunaway, 131.

234 advance check: Cray, 338.

234 offer him: Ibid., 344.

234 soundtrack: Kaufman, 120.

234 "only question": Willens, 126.

235 "ultimate purpose": FBI report, June 2, 1950.

235 "Allan Lomack": FBI report, Aug. 4, 1950.

235 financed by royalties: Szwed, 66, 293. The Lomaxes ended up with copyright on a number of Lead Belly's numbers.

235 Communist Index Card: per Pete Seeger in *Seeing Red*, documentary film (Heartland Productions, 1983).

235 "I love America": "Will Geer," Evan Finch, Indiana Historical Society, www.indianahistory.org/our-collections/reference /notable-hoosiers/will-geer#.UsAYzyyA1Mw.

235 not to attend: Ronald Cohen, 77.

235 Six months: Cray, 353.

235 "ranting": Klein, 379.

235 Detcom and Comsab: FBI report, Oct. 1953.

235 "beat up": FBI report, Aug. 15, 1954.

236 "fairly well advanced": FBI report, May 18 and June 3, 1955.

236 "only people": Cray, 372.

236 "halfways knocked out": Ibid., 372.

236 cited the Fifth Amendment: Willens, 162–63.

236 "sung in hobo jungles": HUAC transcript, Aug. 18, 1955, historymatters.gmu.edu/d/6457.

236 the American inquisition: see Belfrage.

236 "Our own field": Dunaway, 99.

236 "make fools of us": Lichtenstein, 148.

237 twenty thousand: Camp, 271.

237 military spending: Jezer, 119.

237 $350 billion: Ziegler, 183.

237 45 percent: Ibid., 193.

237 almost tripled: Jezer, 135.

237 a smaller share: Ibid., 201–3.

237 "people felt": Thomas Piketty, *Capital in the Twenty-First Century* (Cambridge, MA: Belknap Press, Harvard University, 2013), 350.

237 "the silent generation thing": Dunaway, 114.

238 Dave Guard: Ibid., 110.

238 "folk wisdom": Allen Ginsberg, interview Aug. 11, 1996, http:// nsarchive.gwu.edu/coldwar/interviews/episode-13/ginsberg3 .html.

238 moved to Hollywood: McGilligan, 98.

238 Kazan gave HUAC: Ibid., 210 and 109.

238 "When Brando": Elia Kazan, *A Life* (New York: Knopf, 1988), 500.

238 "my share of films": McGilligan, 263.

238 "insidious social conformity": Ibid., 269.

239 "the Hillbilly field": Peter Guralnick, *Last Train to Memphis: The Rise of Elvis Presley* (Boston: Little, Brown, 1994), 184.

239 covered their songs: see Richard Boussiron, *Elvis: A Musical Inventory 1939–55* (York, UK: Music Mentor Books, 2004).

240 "no reference point": Guralnick, 170–73.

240 a clenched fist: Cray, 375.

240 "canonization": Klein, 411.

240 "last free place": Cray, 378.

241 "John Hammond came": Dylan, interview by Laurie Henshaw, May 12, 1965, for *Disc Weekly*, www.interferenza.com/bcs /interw/65-may12.htm.

241 "gonna clap on": Dylan, San Francisco press conference, KQED-TV, Dec. 3, 1965, transcript, *Rolling Stone*, Dec. 14, 1967, www.rollingstone.com/music/news/bob-dylan-gives-press -conference-in-san-francisco-19671214.

241 "I'd literally quit": Greil Marcus, *Like a Rolling Stone: Bob Dylan at the Crossroads* (New York: PublicAffairs, 2006), 70.

241 Harvard graduate: Marcus, 104; and www.producertomwilson .com/discography.

242 "real old blues": Nick Lerman and Alex Wernquest, *The Michael Bloomfield Story*, video documentary, https://www.youtube.com /watch?v=YJa8KIF1A24.

242 "he wanted blues": Marcus, *Like a Rolling Stone*, 110.

242 "No one knew": Ibid.

243 "My will is easy": Joe Hill, "Last Will," Nov, 18, 1915, folkarchive.de/lastwill.html.

245 "lights, sound, and anger": Elijah Wald, *Dylan Goes Electric* (New York: HarperCollins/Dey Street Books, 2015), 285.

245 number two: David Hajdu, *Positively 4th Street: The Lives and Times of Joan Baez, Bob Dylan, Mimi Baez Fariña, and Richard Fariña* (New York: MacMillan/Picador, 2011), 259.

245 "definitely the thing": Marcus, *Like a Rolling Stone*, 70.

245 "time-wise": see outtakes of "Like a Rolling Stone," http:// gaslightrecords.com/articles/bob-dylan-writing-like-a-rolling -stone.

246 "a whole way": Dunaway, 153.

248 "Every song tails off": San Francisco press conference, KQED-TV.

249 $30 million: Quincy Mining Company Collection, MS 001, Archives, Jan. 3, 1914.

250 seven thousand feet: Robb Gillespie, William B. Harrison III, and G. Michael Grammer, *Geology of Michigan and the Great Lakes*, Michigan Geological Repository for Research and Education, Western Michigan University, 2008, http:// custom.cengage.com/regional_geology/data/Geo_Michigan_ Watermarked.pdf.

250 Half: see Michigan Tech's website, www.mtu.edu.

250 "on his return": MTU Archives, Agassiz to Shaw, May 10, 1867.

250 "Moyer is trying": MTU, MacNaughton to Quin Shaw Jr., Dec. 26, 1913.

251 safety hazard: Gross and Galdieri, "1913 Massacre."

252 Eliina and Wesley: Houghton Keweenaw County Genealogical Society, *Families Left Behind: The Italian Hall Tragedy 1913* (Houghton, MI: Houghton Keweenaw County Genealogical Society, 2013) [henceforth *Families*], no page numbers.

253 "fish tumors": Region Five Superfund, United States Environmental Protection Agency, State of Michigan, Michigan Department of Natural Resources, Surface Water Quality Division. 1990. "Fish Growth Anomalies in Torch and Portage Lakes 1974–1988 Houghton County," Michigan. MI/DNR /SWQ-90/029; and "Torch Lake," U.S. Environmental Protection Agency website, https://archive.epa.gov/epawaste /nonhaz/industrial/special/web/pdf/copper1b.pdf.

254 dropped by half: Arthur W. Thurner, *Strangers and Sojourners: A History of Michigan's Keweenaw Peninsula* (Detroit: Wayne State University Press, 1994), 257.

254 final shutdown: Ibid., 282, 285–86.

255 peak of union: Gar Alperowitz, *America beyond Capitalism: Reclaiming Our Wealth, Our Liberty, and Our Democracy* (New York: John Wiley, 2005), 14.

255 overseas: Richard Wolff, *Democracy at Work: A Cure for Capitalism* (Boston: Haymarket Books, 2012), 46–47.

255 Real hourly income: Wolff, 40; and Alperowitz, 18.

255 Less than a quarter: Dubofsky, 365; and Yates, 134.

255 19 percent: Roger J. Vaughn, "A Framework for Economic Development in Michigan's Upper Peninsula," U.P. Plan Steering Committee, Michigan Department of Commerce, Dec. 1989, https://www.nmu.edu/sites/Drupalceee/files/UserFiles/Files/Pre-Drupal/SiteSections/UPResearch/Framework.pdf.

255 Grant School: *Thirty-Third Annual Report of the Department of Labor of the State of Michigan* (Lansing, MI: Wynkoop, Hallenbeck, Crawford, 1916).

255 Klaric: *Families.*

255 decline: Fred Magdoff and John Bellamy Foster, "The Plight of the U.S. Working Class," *Monthly Review* 65, no. 8, Jan. 2014.

255 controlled 12 percent: John Bellamy Foster and Robert W. McChesney, "Monopoly-Finance Capital and the Paradox of Accumulation," *Monthly Review* 61, no. 5 (Oct. 2009).

255 from 15 percent of: Yates, 134; and Alperowitz, 14.

256 last sustained: Wolff. 40.

256 real growth rate: Foster and McChesney, "Monopoly-Finance Capital."

256 hardest to climb: Dubofsky, 370.

256 couldn't both pay: Hobsbawm, 250.

256 dissolved: Ibid., 486.

256 Cvetkovich: *Families.*

256 began lobbying: "Keweenaw National Historical Park: Volunteer Management Plan," National Park Service, 2006, https://www.nps.gov/kewe/learn/management/upload/Volunteer%20Manual%20for%20Keweenaw%20National%20Historical%20Park.pdf.

257 historic landmark: "Keweenaw National Historical Park: Volunteer Management Plan."

257 "heritage sites": "Keweenaw National Historical Park Advisory

Commission Goals and Objectives," www.nps.gov/kewe
/parkmgmt/commission-strategic-plan.htm.

257 "historic synergism": Public Law 102–543, Oct. 27, 1992, to
establish the Keweenaw National Historical Park, www.nps.gov
/kewe/parkmgmt/lawsandpolicies.htm.

257 "Come live": Laurium Manor Inn, www.laurium.info.

257 approached 25 percent: Robert W. McChesney, "This Isn't What
Democracy Looks Like," *Monthly Review* 64, no. 6 (Nov. 2012).

257 three times: Foster and McChesney, "Monopoly-Finance Capital
and the Paradox of Accumulation."

257 One quarter of all: Michael Yates, "The Great Inequality,"
Monthly Review 63, no. 10 (Mar. 2012).

257 "needs bubbles": Paul Krugman, "Secular Stagnation, Coalmines,
Bubbles, and Larry Summers," *New York Times*, Nov. 16, 2013.

258 Burcars: *Families.*

258 in 1983: 1940 U.S. Census.

258 nearly 15 percent: Fred Magdoff and John Bellamy Foster, "Class
War and Labor's Declining Share," *Monthly Review* 64., no. 10
(Mar. 2013); and Fred Magdoff and John Bellamy Foster, "The
Plight of the U.S. Working Class," *Monthly Review* 65, no. 8.

258 five and a half million: Fred Magdoff, "The Jobs Disaster in the
United States," *Monthly Review* 63, no. 2 (June 2011).

258 $33,000: Joseph E. Stiglitz, "Inequality Is Holding Back the
Recovery," *New York Times*, Jan. 20, 2013.

258 lived below: Magdoff and Foster, "Class War and Labor's
Declining Share."

258 Nearly 40 percent: Paul Krugman, "Liberty, Equality,
Efficiency," *New York Times*, Mar. 10, 2014.

258 the worst: Magdoff, "Jobs Disaster."

259 lost half: from the Senate Budget Update as quoted in "Oakland
University Leadership Briefing," Nov. 18, 2008, www
.powershow.com/view/3c3ae4-YmEzN/Leadership_Briefing
_powerpoint_ppt_presentation.

259 highest unemployment rate: Katharine Q. Seelye, "Michigan's

Economic Woes," *New York Times*, Oct. 9, 2007; and Greg Gardner, "After Firestorm, Michigan Right-to-Work Law Has Had Little Spark," *Detroit Free Press*, Sept. 1, 2013.

259 "birthplace": Robert P. Hunter, "The Prevalence of Unions in Michigan," Mackinac Center for Public Policy, Aug. 24, 1999.

259 dropped to 11 percent: Magdoff and Foster, "Class War and Labor's Declining Share."

259 lowest level: Magdoff and Foster, "The Plight of the U.S. Working Class."

SELECTED BIBLIOGRAPHY

BOOKS

Adams, Henry. *The Education of Henry Adams: An Autobiography*. Boston: Houghton Mifflin, 1918.

Adler, William M. *The Man Who Never Died: The Life, Times, and Legacy of Joe Hill, American Labor Icon*. New York: Bloomsbury, 2011.

Agassiz, Alexander. *Letters and Recollections of Alexander Agassiz*, ed. G. R. Agassiz. Boston: Houghton Mifflin, 1913.

Agassiz, Louis, and J. Elliot Cabot. *Lake Superior: Its Physical Character, Vegetation and Animals, Compared with Those of Other Similar Regions*. Boston: Gould, Kendall and Lincoln, 1850.

Alperowitz, Gar. *America beyond Capitalism: Reclaiming Our Wealth, Our Liberty, and Our Democracy*. New York: Wiley, 2005.

Archibald, Robert, ed. *Northern Border: Essays on Michigan's Upper Peninsula and Beyond*. Marquette, MI: Northern Michigan University Press, 2014.

Avery, Thomas. *Copper Country—God's Country*. Au Train, MI: Avery Color Studios, 1973.

Baird, W. David, and Danney Goble. *Oklahoma: A History*. Norman, OK: University of Oklahoma Press, 2008.

Bart, Phillip, ed. *Highlight of a Fighting History: 60 Years of the Communist Party USA*. New York: International Publishers, 1979.

Belfrage, Cedric. *The American Inquisition 1945–1960: A Profile of the "McCarthy Era"*. New York: Thunder's Mouth, 1989.

Benedict, C. Harry. *Red Metal: The Calumet and Hecla Story*. Ann Arbor: University of Michigan Press, 1952.

Bloor, Ella Reeve. *We Are Many*. New York: International Publishers, 1940.

Bogart, Ernest Ludlow. *Economic History of the American People.* New York: Longmans, Green, 1937.

Boussiron, Richard. *Elvis: A Musical Inventory 1939–55.* York, UK: Music Mentor Books, 2004.

Boyle, Georgina. *The Imagined Village: Culture, Ideology, and the English Folk Revival.* Manchester, UK: Manchester University Press, 1993.

Boyle, Kevin. *The UAW and the Heyday of American Liberalism, 1945–1968.* Ithaca, NY: Cornell University Press, 1995.

Brecher, Jeremy. *Strike!* San Francisco: Straight Arrow Books, 1972.

Buehler, Phillip. *Woody Guthrie's Wardy Forty: Greystone Park State Hospital Revisited.* Mt. Kisco, NY: Woody Guthrie Publications, 2013.

Cantwell, Robert. *When We Were Good: The Folk Revival.* Cambridge, MA: Harvard University Press, 1996.

Carson, Clayborne. *In Struggle: SNCC and the Black Awakening of the 1960s.* Cambridge, MA: Harvard University Press, 1981.

Chaplin, Ralph. *Bars and Shadows: The Prison Poems of Ralph Chaplin.* London: Allen & Unwin, 1922.

Cohen, Robert. *Freedom's Orator: Mario Savio and the Radical Legacy of the 1960s.* New York: Oxford University Press, 2009.

Cohen, Ronald D. *Rainbow Quest: The Folk Music Revival and American Society, 1940–1970.* Amherst: University of Massachusetts Press, 2002.

———. *Woody Guthrie: Writing America's Songs.* New York: Routledge, 2012.

Coltman, Bob. *Paul Clayton and the Folksong Revival,* American Folk Music and Musicians 10. Lanham, MD: Scarecrow Press, 2008.

Cray, Ed. *Ramblin' Man: The Life and Times of Woody Guthrie.* New York: Norton, 2004.

Culver, John C., and John Hyde. *American Dreamer: A Life of Henry Wallace.* New York: Norton, 2001).

Dalton, Daniel. *James Dean: The Mutant King.* San Francisco: Straight Arrow Books, 1974.

Dalzell Jr., Robert F. *Enterprising Elite: the Boston Associates and the World They Made.* New York: Norton, 1987.

Denisoff, R. Serge. *Great Day Coming: Folk Music and the American Left.* Urbana: University of Illinois Press, 1971.

Denning, Michael. *The Cultural Front: The Laboring of American Culture in the Twentieth Century.* New York: Verso, 1997.

Dobbs, David. *Reef Madness: Charles Darwin, Alexander Agassiz, and the Meaning of Coral.* New York: Pantheon, 2005.

Dray, Phillip. *There Is Power in a Union: The Epic Story of Labor in America.* New York: Doubleday, 2010.

Duberman, Martin. *Paul Robeson.* New York: The New Press, 1995.

Dubofsky, Melvyn, and Foster Rhea Dulles. *Labor in America: A History.* Wheeling, IL: Halan Davidson, 2010.

Dunaway, David King. *How Can I Keep from Singing? Pete Seeger.* New York: McGraw-Hill, 1981.

Dunaway, David King, and Molly Beer. *Singing Out: An Oral History of America's Folk Music Revivals.* New York: Oxford University Press, 2011.

Dylan, Bob. *Chronicles, Volume One.* New York: Simon & Schuster, 2005.

———. *Tarantula.* New York: Scribner, 1966.

Eckstein, Stephen D. *History of the Churches of Christ in Texas.* Lubbock, TX: Bible Publications, 1992.

Featherling, Dale. *Mother Jones, the Miners' Angel: A Portrait.* Carbondale: Southern Illinois University Press, 1979.

Foner, Philp S. *History of the Labor Movement in the United States,* vol. 4, *The Industrial Workers of the World, 1905–1917,* and vol. 5, *The AFL in the Progressive Era, 1910–1915.* New York: International Publishers, 1965 and 1980.

Forman, James. *The Making of Black Revolutionaries.* New York: Macmillan, 1972.

Fried, Richard M. *Nightmare in Red: The McCarthy Era in Perspective.* New York: Oxford University Press, 1991.

Gates Jr., William B. *Michigan Copper and Boston Dollars: An Economic History of the Michigan Copper Industry.* Cambridge, MA: Harvard University Press, 1951.

George-Warren, Holly. *Public Cowboy #1: The Life and Times of Gene Autry.* New York: Oxford University Press, 2007.

Gilbert, Douglas R. *Forever Young: Photographs of Bob Dylan*, text by Dave Marsh. New York: Da Capo Press, 2005.

Gorn, Elliot J. *Mother Jones: An American Life*. New York: Hill & Wang, 2015.

Gould, Stephen Jay. *The Panda's Thumb: More Reflections on Natural History*. New York: Norton, 1980.

Graff, Ellen. *Stepping Left: Dance and Politics in New York City, 1928–1942*. Durham, NC: Duke University Press, 1997.

Green, Archie, ed. *Songs About Work: Essays in Occupational Culture*. Bloomington: Folklore Institution, Indiana University Press, 1993.

Guilbaut, Serge. *How New York Stole the Idea of Modern Art: Abstract Expressionism, Freedom, and the Cold War*. Chicago: University of Chicago Press, 1983.

Guralnick, Peter. *Last Train to Memphis: The Rise of Elvis Presley*. Boston: Little, Brown, 1994.

Guthrie, Woody. *Alonzo Zilch's Own Collection of Original Songs and Ballads*. Pampa, TX: self-published, 1935.

———. *American Folksong*, ed. Moses Asch. New York: DISC Company of America, 1947.

———. *Born to Win*, ed. Robert Shelton. New York: Collier Books, 1965.

———. *Bound for Glory*. New York: Dutton/Signet, 1943.

———. *Pastures of Plenty: A Self-Portrait*, ed. Dave Marsh and Harold Leventhal. New York: HarperCollins, 1990.

———. *Woody Sez*. New York: Grosset & Dunlap, 1975.

Hajdu, David. *Positively 4th Street: The Lives and Times of Joan Baez, Bob Dylan, Mimi Baez Fariña, and Richard Fariña*. New York: MacMillan/Picador, 2011.

Hamm, Tom A. *Mines and Mineral Statistics, State of Michigan*. Lansing, MI: Robert Smith, 1902–3.

Harvey, Todd. *The Formative Dylan: Transmission and Stylistic Influences, 1961–1963*. Lanham, MD: Scarecrow Press, 2001.

Hays, Lee. *"Sing Out, Warning! Sing Out, Love!": The Writings of Lee Hays*, ed. Robert S. Koppleman. Amherst: University of Massachusetts Press, 2003.

Heylin, Clinton. *Revolution in the Air: The Songs of Bob Dylan, 1957–1973.* Chicago: Chicago Review Press, 2009.

Hobsbawm, Eric. *The Age of Extremes: A History of the World, 1914–1991.* New York: Vintage, 1994.

Holter, Darryl, and William Deverell. *Woody Guthrie: L.A. 1937 to 1941.* Santa Monica, CA: Angel City Press, 2015.

Houghton Keweenaw County Genealogical Society, *Families Left Behind: The Italian Hall Tragedy 1913.* Houghton, MI: Houghton Keweenaw County Genealogical Society, 2013.

Hyde, Charles K. *Copper for America: The United States Copper Industry from Colonial Times to the 1990s.* Tucson: University of Arizona Press, 1998.

Irmscher, Christoph. *Louis Agassiz: Creator of American Science.* Boston: Houghton Mifflin, 2013.

Isserman, Maurice. *Which Side Were You On? The American Communist Party During the Second World War.* Middletown, CT: Wesleyan University Press, 1982.

Jensen, Vernon H. *Heritage of Conflict: Labor Relations in the Nonferrous Metals Industry up to 1930.* New York: Greenwood Press, 1950.

Jezer, Marty. *The Dark Ages: Life in the United States 1945–1960.* Boston: South End Press, 1982.

Kaufman, Will. *Woody Guthrie: American Radical.* Champaign: University of Illinois Press, 2011.

Kaunonen, Gary, and Aaron Goings. *Community in Conflict: A Working-Class History of the 1913–14 Michigan Copper Strike and the Italian Hall Tragedy.* East Lansing: Michigan State University Press, 2013.

Klehr, Harvey. *The Heyday of American Communism: The Depression Decade.* New York: Basic Books, 1984.

Klein, Joe. *Woody Guthrie: A Life.* New York: Knopf, 1980.

La Chapelle, Peter. *Proud to Be an Okie: Cultural Politics, Country Music, and Migrations to Southern California.* Oakland: University of California Press, 2007.

Lamppa, Marvin G. *Minnesota Iron Country: Rich Ore, Rich Lives.* Duluth, MN: Lake Superior Port Cities, 2004.

Lankton, Larry. *Cradle to Grave: Life, Work and Death at the Lake Superior Copper Mines.* New York: Oxford University Press, 1991.

Lead Belly. *The Leadbelly Songbook,* ed. Moses Asch and Alan Lomax. New York: Oak Publications, 1962.

Lehto, Steve. *Death's Door: The Truth Behind Michigan's Largest Mass Murder.* Troy, MI: Momentum Books, 2006.

Lichtenstein, Nelson. *State of the Union: A Century of American Labor.* Princeton, NJ: Princeton University Press, 2002.

Lind, Michael. *Land of Promise: An Economic History of the United States.* New York: HarperCollins, 2012.

Loftis, Anne. *Witnesses to the Struggle: Imaging the 1930s California Labor Movement.* Reno: University of Nevada Press, 1998.

Lukas, J. Anthony. *Big Trouble: A Murder in a Small Western Town Sets Off a Struggle for the Soul of America.* New York: Simon & Schuster, 1997.

Malone, Bill C., and Jocelyn R. Neal. *Country Music U.S.A.: A Fifty-Year History.* Austin: University of Texas Press, 1968.

Marcus, Greil. *Like a Rolling Stone: Bob Dylan at the Crossroads.* New York: PublicAffairs, 2006.

———. *The Old, Weird America: The World of Bob Dylan's Basement Tapes.* New York: MacMillan/Picador, 2011.

Marglin Stephen A., and Juliet B. Schor, eds. *The Golden Age of Capitalism: Reinterpreting the Postwar Experience.* Oxford, UK: Clarendon Press, 1990.

Marsh, Dave. *The Beatles' Second Album.* New York: Rodale Books, 2007.

———. *The Heart of Rock and Soul.* New York: Plume, 1989.

McGilligan, Patrick. *Nicholas Ray: The Glorious Failure of an American Director.* New York: HarperCollins, 2011.

McNamara, Francis J., Vincent Hartnett, Alfred Kohlberg, et al. *Red Channels: The Report of Communist Influence in Radio and Television.* New York: Counterattack, June 1950.

McWilliams, Carey. *Factories in the Field: The Story of Migratory Farm Labor in California.* Santa Barbara, CA: Peregrine Publishers, 1935, 1971.

Murdoch, Angus. *Boom Copper: The Story of the First U.S. Mining Boom.* Calumet, MI: Roy W. Drier and Louis G. Koppel, 1964 reprint.

Parkman, Samuel. *Lives of American Merchants*, vol. 2. (New York: Freeman Hunt, Derry and Jackson, 1858.

Pescatello, Ann M. *Charles Seeger: A Life in American Music*. Pittsburgh: University of Pittsburgh Press, 1992.

Piketty, Thomas. *Capital in the Twenty-First Century*. Cambridge, MA: Belknap Press/Harvard University Press, 2013.

Reisner, Marc. *Cadillac Desert: The American West and Its Disappearing Water*. New York: Penguin, 1993.

Renshaw, Patrick. *The Wobblies: The Story of Syndicalism in the United States*. New York: Anchor, 1967.

Robbin, Edward. *Woody Guthrie and Me*. Berkeley, CA: Lancaster–Miller, 1979.

Rotolo, Suze. *A Freewheelin' Time: A Memoir of Greenwich Village in the Sixties*. New York: Broadway Books, 2008.

Salvatore, Nick. *Eugene V. Debs: Citizen and Socialist*. Urbana: University of Illinois Press, 1982.

Scaduto, Anthony. *Bob Dylan*. New York: Signet, 1973.

Seale, Bobby. *Seize the Day: The Story of the Black Panther Party and Huey P. Newton*. Baltimore: Black Classic Press, 1991.

Sellars, Nigel Anthony. *Oil, Wheat and Wobblies: The Industrial Workers of the World in Oklahoma*. Norman: University of Oklahoma Press, 2012.

Shaw, John. *This Land That I Love: Irving Berlin, Woody Guthrie, and the Story of Two American Anthems*. New York: PublicAffairs, 2013.

Shelton, Robert. *No Direction Home: The Life and Music of Bob Dylan*. New York: Da Capo Press, 1997.

Sinclair, Upton. *The Goose Step: A Study in American Education*. Self-published, 1923.

Sounes, Howard. *Down the Highway: The Life of Bob Dylan*. New York: Grove Press, 2001.

Stanley, Jerry. *Big Annie of Calumet: A True Story of the Industrial Revolution*. New York: Crown, 1996.

Steinbeck, John. *The Grapes of Wrath*. New York: Viking, 1939.

———. *In Dubious Battle*. New York: Viking, 1938.

Stott, William. *Documentary Expression and Thirties America*. Chicago: University of Chicago Press, 1973.

Suggs Jr., George G. *Colorado's War on Militant Unionism*. Detroit: Wayne State University Press, 1972.

Szwed, John. *Alan Lomax: The Man Who Recorded the World*. New York: Penguin, 2010.

Taussig, Frank William. *Some Aspects of the Tariff Question*. Cambridge, MA: Harvard University Press, 1915.

Tharp, Louise Hall. *Adventurous Alliance: The Story of the Agassiz Family of Boston*. Boston: Little, Brown, 1959.

Thomas, Hugh. *The Slave Trade: The Story of the American Slave Trade, 1440–1870*. New York: Simon & Schuster, 1997.

Thompson, Toby. *Positively Main Street: Bob Dylan's Minnesota*. Minneapolis: University of Minnesota Press, 2008.

Thomson, Elizabeth, and David Gutman, eds. *The Dylan Companion*. New York: Dell, 1991.

Thurner, Arthur W. *Calumet Copper and People: History of a Michigan Mining Community, 1864–1970*. Privately printed, 1974.

———. *Rebels on the Range: The Michigan Copper Miners' Strike of 1913–1914*. Lake Linden, MI: John H. Forster Press, 1984.

———. *Strangers and Sojourners: A History of Michigan's Keweenaw Peninsula*. Detroit: Wayne State University Press, 1994.

Tunis, Edwin. *Colonial Living*. Baltimore: Johns Hopkins University Press, 1999.

Van Ronk, Dave, with Elijah Wald. *The Mayor of MacDougal Street: A Memoir*. New York: Da Capo Press, 2005.

Wald, Elijah. *Dylan Goes Electric*. New York: HarperCollins/Dey Street Books, 2015.

Ward, Richie. *Into the Ocean World: The Biology of the Sea*. New York: Knopf, 1974.

Wein, George. *Myself Among Others: A Life in Music*. New York: Da Capo Press, 2004.

Willens, Doris. *Lonesome Traveler: The Life of Lee Hays*. New York: Norton, 1988.

Winsor, Mary P. *Reading the Shape of Nature: Comparative Zoology at the Agassiz Museum.* Chicago: University of Chicago Press, 1991.

Wolff, Richard. *Democracy at Work: A Cure for Capitalism.* Boston: Haymarket Books, 2012.

Yagoda, Ben. *Will Rogers: A Biography.* Norman: University of Oklahoma Press, 2003.

Yates, Michael D. *Why Unions Matter.* New York: Monthly Review Press, 1998.

Ziegler, Robert H. *American Workers, American Unions, 1920–1985.* New York: McGraw-Hill, 1981.

Mark Zwonitzer with Charles Hirshberg, *Will You Miss Me When I'm Gone? The Carter Family and Their Legacy in American Music.* New York: Simon & Schuster, 2004.

ARTICLES, etc.

Abbott, Lynn, and Doug Seroff. "America's Blues Yodel." *Musical Traditions* 11 (1993).

Berger, John. "The Nature of Mass Demonstrations." *New Society* 11 (1968).

Calumet and Hecla. *The Founding of the Calumet and Hecla Mine: 1866–1916*, pamphlet. Calumet and Hecla, July 5, 1916.

Carlton, Bob. "Brief History of the Miscowaubik Club," 1990, www.clintnmary.org/ClubHistory.htm.

Carriker, Robert C. "Ten Dollars a Song: Woody Guthrie Sells His Talent to the Bonneville Power Administration." *Columbia* 15, no. 1 (Spring 2001).

Costonis, Maureen Needham. "Martha Graham's American Document: A Minstrel Show in Modern Dance Dress." *American Music* 9, no. 3: 297–310.

Courter, Ellis W. *Michigan's Copper Country*, Michigan Geology, Department of Environmental Quality, 1992, www.michigan.gov/documents/deq/CMG92_301731_7.pdf.

Courtney, Steve. "Peekskill's Days of Infamy: The Robeson Riots of 1949," *Peekskill Reporter Dispatch*, Sept. 5, 1982, www.bencourtney.com/peekskillriots.

Dylan, Bob. "11 Outlined Epitaphs," sleeve note to *The Times They Are a-Changin'*, 1963, https://beatpatrol.wordpress.com/2010/04/05/bob -dylan-11-outlined-epitaphs-1963.

———. "For Dave Glover," Newport Folk Festival program, 1963, http:// singout.org/downloads/broadside/b035.pdf.

———. Interview by Cynthia Gooding. *Folksinger's Choice*, WBAI-FM, Mar. 11, 1962, http://expectingrain.com/dok/int/gooding.html.

———. Interview by Nat Hentoff. *Playboy*, Feb. 1966.

———. Interview by Kurt Loder, *Rolling Stone*, June 21, 1984, www .rollingstone.com/music/features/the-rolling-stone-interview-bob -dylan-19840621.

———. Interview by Paul J. Robbins, Santa Monica, CA, Mar. 1965. *Los Angeles Free Press*, Sept. 17 and 24, 1965, www.interferenza.com/bcs /interw/65-nov08.htm.

———. Interview by Studs Terkel. *The Studs Terkel Program*, WFMT, Chi-cago, Spring 1963, https://www.youtube.com/watch?feature=player _embedded&v=t4nA3QwGPBg.

———. "Last Thoughts on Woody Guthrie," read at Town Hall, New York, Apr. 12, 1963, www.woodyguthrie.de/lastth.html.

———. Letter to the Emergency Civil Liberties Committee, "Bob Dylan and the NECLC," www.corliss-lamont.org/dylan.htm.

———. Liner notes to *Bringing It All Back Home*. Columbia Records, 1965.

———. Liner notes to Peter, Paul and Mary's *In the Wind*. Warner Broth ers, 1963.

———. "A Message from Bob Dylan," www.corliss-lamont.org/dylan.htm.

———. MusicCares Person of the Year speech, 2015 Grammys, www .rollingstone.com/music/news/read-bob-dylans-complete-riveting -musicares-speech-20150209.

———. "My Life in a Stolen Moment," in concert notes, New York Town Hall, Apr. 12, 1963, https://beatpatrol.wordpress.com/2010/03/05 /bob-dylan-my-life-in-a-stolen-moment-1962.

———. Press conference, KQED, San Francisco, Dec. 3, 1965, www .rollingstone.com/music/news/bob-dylan-gives-press-conference-in -san-francisco-19671214.

———. Remarks at the Bill of Rights Dinner at the Americana Hotel, Dec. 13, 1963, "Bob Dylan and the NECLC," http://www.corliss -lamont.org/dylan.htm.

Early, Steve. "Save Our Unions," *Monthly Review Press*, Vol 65, #9, February 2014.

Eldot, Walter. "My Son the Folknik." *Duluth News Tribune*, Oct. 20, 1963.

Fariña, Richard. "Prologue: Baez and Dylan: A Generation Singing Out!" in *Younger Than That Now: The Collected Interviews with Bob Dylan*. New York: Thunder's Mouth Press, 2004.

Flanagan, Hallie. "A Theatre Is Born." *Theatre Arts Monthly* 15, no. 11 (Nov. 1931).

Foster, John Bellamy, and Robert W. McChesney. "Monopoly-Finance Capital and the Paradox of Accumulation," *Monthly Review* 61, no. 5 (Oct. 2009).

Gardner, Greg. "After Firestorm, Michigan Right-to-Work Law Has Had Little Spark," *Detroit Free Press*, Sept. 1, 2013.

Gerstle, Gary. "Race and Nation in the Thought and Politics of Woodrow Wilson," in John Milton Cooper Jr., ed., *Reconsidering Woodrow Wilson: Progressivism, Internationalism, War, and Peace*. Princeton/Baltimore: Woodrow Wilson Center Press/Johns Hopkins University Press, 2008.

Gillespie, Robb. William B. Harrison III, and G. Michael Grammer. *Geology of Michigan and the Great Lakes*. Michigan Geological Repository for Research and Education, Western Michigan University, 2008.

Greenberg, Robert. "An Overview of the History of the National Maritime Union (NMU): 1935–1948," Cisco Houston, www.ciscohouston .com/essays/nmu.shtml.

Guthrie, Woody. *California to the New York Island*. New York: Oak Publications, 1958.

———. "I Hate a Song," www.woodyguthrie.org/biography/woodysez.htm.

———. "My Constitution and Me." *Daily Worker*, June 19, 1949, as cited in FBI report, see http://web.ncf.ca/fl512/woody_guthrie /april_10_1951.html.

———. "Ten Songs," *Woody Guthrie Songbook*, Apr. 3, 1945, www .woodyguthrie.de/songbook.html#east.

Hentoff, Nat. Liner notes to *The Freewheelin' Bob Dylan*. Columbia Records, 1963.

Hillburn, Robert. "Rock's Enigmatic Poet Opens a Long-Private Door," *Los Angeles Times*, Apr. 4, 2004, http://articles.latimes.com/2004 /apr/04/entertainment/ca-dylan04.

Hunter, Robert P. *The Prevalence of Unions in Michigan*. Mackinac Center for Public Policy, Aug. 24, 1999.

Hyde, Charles K. *An Economic and Business History of the Quincy Mining Company*. Historic American Engineering Record, National Park Service, Library of Congress, 1978.

Karni, Michael G. "Elizabeth Gurley Flynn and the Mesabi Strike of 1916." *Range History* 5, no. 4 (Winter 1981), www.minnesotahuman ities.org/Resources/ElizabethGurleyFlynnandthestrikeof1916.pdf.

Katz, Michael B., and Mark J. Stern. "Poverty in Twentieth Century America." America at the Millenium Project, Working Paper 7, Nov. 2001.

Keweenaw National Historical Park Advisory Commission. "Goals and Objectives," www.nps.gov/kewe/parkmgmt/commission-strategic -plan.htm.

Keweenaw National Historical Park, *Volunteer Management Plan*, National Park Service, 2006, https://www.nps.gov/kewe/learn/management /upload/Volunteer%20Manual%20for%20Keweenaw%20Na- tional%20Historical%20Park.pdf.

King Jr., Martin Luther. "Letter from Birmingham Jail," Apr. 16, 1963, http://abacus.bates.edu/admin/offices/dos/mlk/letter.html.

Kinzer, Stephen. "In Minnesota's Iron Range, a Rare Victory for Labor." *New York Times*, Oct. 6, 2004.

Kloss, Jurgen. "On the Trail of 'The Buffalo Skinners,'" 2010–2012, http://justanothertune.com/html/buffaloskinners.html.

Krugman, Paul. "Liberty, Equality, Efficiency." *New York Times*, Mar. 10, 2014.

———. "Secular Stagnation, Coalmines, Bubbles, and Larry Summers." *New York Times*, Nov. 16, 2013.

Ladner, Joyce. "For a SNCC Member, Aug. 28, 1963, Was a Day of Joy, Anger and Hope." *Washington Post*, Aug. 27, 2013.

Lankton, Larry. *Keweenaw National Historical Park: Historic Resource Guide.* National Park Service, US Department of the Interior, 2005.

Lead Belly. March of Time newsreel, 1935, https://www.youtube.com/watch?v=QxykqBmUCwk.

Lerman, Nick, and Alex Wernquest. *The Michael Bloomfield Story,* video documentary, https://www.youtube.com/watch?v=YJa8KIF1A24.

Magdoff, Fred. "The Jobs Disaster in the United States." *Monthly Review* 63, no. 2 (June 2011).

Magdoff, Fred, and John Bellamy Foster. "Class War and Labor's Declining Share." *Monthly Review* 64, no. 10 (Mar. 2013).

———. "The Plight of the U.S. Working Class." *Monthly Review* 65, no. 8 (Jan. 2014).

Majdic, Michael, and Denise Matthews, producers/directors. *Roll on Columbia: Woody Guthrie and the Bonneville Power Administration,* documentary film. Eugene: University of Oregon, 2000.

Malcolm X. Speech in Selma, Feb. 4, 1965, www.youtube.com/watch?v=mg5uQQw2leU.

McChesney, Robert W. "This Isn't What Democracy Looks Like." *Monthly Review* 64, no. 6 (Nov. 2012).

McDermott, J. Cynthia. "Horton, Highlander, and the Habituation of Democracy," www.academia.edu/364092/horton_highlander_and_the_habituation_of_democracy.

McPhee, John. "Joan Baez—Folk Singing: Sybil with Guitar," *Time,* Nov. 23, 1962, excerpt at http://bobdylanroots.com/baez2.html.

Menand, Louis. "Morton, Agassiz, and the Origins of Scientific Racism in the United States." *Journal of Blacks in Higher Education,* no. 34 (Winter 2001–2).

Michigan Technological University Archives, MS-002 Calumet and Hecla Mining Companies Collection.

Miller, Chuck. "The History and Legacy of 'God Bless America.'" *Albany Times Union,* July 3, 2010, http://blog.timesunion.com/chuckmiller/the-history-and-legacy-of-god-bless-america/2315.

Miller, Scott. "Inside 'The Cradle Will Rock,'" www.newlinetheatre.com/cradle.htm.

Nara, J. W. Photographs, in Archives, http://nara.lib.mtu.edu.

Rickard, Thomas Arthur. "The Copper Mines of Lake Superior." *Engineering and Mining Journal*, 1905.

Rosenbaum, Ron. "Interview," *Playboy*, March 1978. www.interferenza .com/bcs/interw/play78.htm.

Ross, Ken, and Louis V. Galdieri, producers/directors. *1913 Massacre*, documentary film. Dreamland Pictures, 2011.

Ruhlmann, William. "Peter, Paul and Mary: A Song to Sing All Over This Land." *Goldmine*, Apr. 12, 1996, www.peterpaulandmary.com /history/f-ruhlmann1.htm.

Scorsese, Martin, director. *No Direction Home: Bob Dylan*. Paramount Pictures, 2005.

Seeger, Pete. HUAC transcript, Aug. 18, 1955, http://historymatters.gmu .edu/d/6457/.

———. Interview by Tim Robbins. Pacifica Radio, 2006, https://www .youtube.com/watch?v=RX3aP1DAH-c.

Seelye, Katharine Q. "Michigan's Economic Woes." *New York Times*, Oct. 9, 2007.

Silber, Irwin. "An Open Letter to Bob Dylan." *Sing Out!* Nov. 1964.

Sinclair, Upton. "End Poverty in California: The EPIC Movement." *Literary Digest*, Oct. 13, 1934, www.sfmuseum.org/hist1/sinclair.html.

Spiroff, Kiril. "Geological History of Michigan." Paper presented at 20th Annual Field Trip Convention, Midwest Federation of Mineralogical and Geological Societies, July 1–4, 1964, www.michigan.gov/docu ments/deq/GIMDL-GGGHM_302331_7.pdf.

Steinbeck, John. "The Harvest Gypsies." *San Francisco News*, Oct. 5–12, 1936.

Stevens, Horace J. *The Copper Handbook: A Manual of the Copper Industry of the United States and Foreign Countries*. Houghton, MI: Stevens, 1902.

Stiglitz, Joseph E. "Inequality Is Holding Back the Recovery," *New York Times*, Jan. 20, 2013.

Students for a Democratic Society. *The Port Huron Statement*, 1962, http:// coursesa.matrix.msu.edu/~hst306/documents/huron.html.

Sweezy, Paul M. "Why Stagnation?" *Monthly Review*, June 1982.

US Department of Labor. *Strike in the Copper Mining District of Michigan: Letter from the Secretary of Labor* per Senate Res. Jan. 29, 1914, re: strike in Michigan Copper District that began July 23, 1913. Washington, DC: Committee of Education and Labor, 1914; repr. Forgotten Books, 2016.

US House of Representatives Committee on Mines and Mining. *Conditions in the Copper Mines of Michigan: Hearings Before a Subcommittee of the Committee on Mines and Mining*, vol. 4–7, House of Representatives, 63rd Congress, 2nd Session. Washington, DC: US Government Printing Office, 1914.

Van Pelt, J. R. "Boston and Keweenaw—an Etching in Copper," in Robert W. Kelley, ed., *Our Rock Riches: A Selected Collection of Reprinted Articles on Michigan's Mineral Resources by Various Authors*, Geological Survey, Bulletin 1. Lansing, MI: 1964.

Vaughn, Roger J. *A Framework for Economic Development in Michigan's Upper Peninsula*. Prepared for the UP Plan Steering Committee, Michigan Department of Commerce, Dec. 1989, https://www.nmu.edu/sites/Drupalceee/files/UserFiles/Files/Pre-Drupal/SiteSections/UPResearch/Framework.pdf.

Wax, Anthony S. "Calumet and Hecla Copper Mines: An Episode in the Economic Development of Michigan." *Michigan History* 16 (1932).

Yates, Michael. "The Great Inequality." *Monthly Review* 63, no. 10 (Mar. 2012).

Younge, Gary. "1963: The Defining Year of the Civil Rights Movement." *Guardian*, May 7, 2013.

economic decline of 1970s, 256–57. *See
also* income inequality
Ed Sullivan Show, The (TV show), 171
"Eight Days a Week," 5
Eisenhower, Dwight D., 241
elections
(1912), 39, 51, 150–51
(1934), 75–76
(1936), 186
(1938), 78
(1944), 202
(1946), 209
(1948), 230–31
electrification, 2, 186
Elliott, Ramblin' Jack, 27, 106, 225
Emerson, Ralph Waldo, 63
Emory University, 170
employment sharks, 95
End Poverty in California, 75–76
Engels, Friedrich, 50, 118
English and Scottish ballads, 49, 103,
132–33
English immigrants, 146
Environmental Protection Agency
(EPA), 253
Evans, Walker, 44
"Eve of Destruction," 7
Everly Brothers, 171
Evers, Medgar, 162–63

Factories in the Field (McWilliams),
80, 86
"Farewell to Sicily," 161
"Farewell to the Creeks," 161
Farmer Labor Party, 109
farmworkers strike (1933), 79–82, 85,
226

fascism, 82, 87, 126, 128, 187, 188,
193–94, 196–97, 201, 208, 225, 228
Federal Bureau of Investigation (FBI),
193, 202, 230–31, 235–36
Federal Theatre Project, 86, 142
Ferris, Woodbridge, 154–56
Fifth Amendment, 236
Filipino immigrants, 79, 81–82
Finnish American Center (Hancock),
257
Finnish immigrants, 2, 35, 59, 109,
120, 134, 145–47, 149, 151–52, 155,
160, 211, 252
Finnish Socialist Federation, 108
First Amendment, 236
Five Tribes, 34
Florida, 34
Flo (spiritualist), 27
Flynn, Elizabeth Gurley, 95–96, 109,
192, 229
folk music, 22–27, 99, 105–6, 192,
233–35, 237–38, 241. See also
specific artists; songs; and types
authenticity and, 100–101
Autry and, 71
British Invasion and, 173
collectors and, 100
defining, 23–24
Dylan and, 22–27, 98–101, 107, 133,
142, 175
Guthrie and, 24, 75, 87, 101, 241
Lomaxes and, 132–35, 142
Sandburg and, 169
folk rock, 173, 175
Folksay (Maslow), 196
Folk Song U.S.A. (Lomax), 23
food stamps, 127, 178, 258

DANIEL WOLFF is the author of *The Fight for Home*; *How Lincoln Learned to Read*; *4th of July/Asbury Park*; and *You Send Me: The Life and Times of Sam Cooke*, which won the Ralph J. Gleason Music Book Award. He's been nominated for a Grammy, published three collections of poetry, and collaborated with, among others, songwriters, documentary filmmakers, photographers, and choreographer Marta Renzi, his wife.